Contextualizing Compliance in the Public Sector

Studying compliance to uncover whether compliance is occurring, and what motivates it, is central to the broader study of governance. *Contextualizing Compliance in the Public Sector: Individual Motivations, Social Processes, and Institutional Design* develops an interdisciplinary approach for answering a classic and essential question in any rule-governed context: What factors influence the decision of an individual or organization to comply (or not) with governing rules?

Analyzing compliance from an interdisciplinary and multi-level perspective, this book examines the question of what motivates compliance in the context of salient policy issues, such as energy policy, water governance, police profiling, and drug policy, among others. The book brings together an interdisciplinary group of experts who explore the psychological, social, and institutional factors that shape compliance with formal rules embodied in laws and regulations and/or informal rules embodied in social norms. In doing so, they offer a platform for assessing individual compliance, compliance by or in the context of groups, and compliance on a systemic or societal level.

Contextualizing Compliance in the Public Sector: Individual Motivations, Social Processes, and Institutional Design is an excellent resource for researchers and scholars of public administration and public policy conducting research on compliance, rules, behavior, and policy outcomes.

Saba Siddiki is Assistant Professor in the Maxwell School of Citizenship and Public Affairs at Syracuse University. Her research expertise is in policy design, collaborative policymaking, and sustainability related technology and behavior adoption. She has studied the design and associated outcomes of public policies used in food systems and environmental governance. Within these domains, she has also studied the role of multi-stakeholder collaboration in policy design and implementation.

Salvador Espinosa is Associate Professor of Public Affairs at San Diego State University. He specializes in public financial administration, public policy analysis, and institutional analysis. Dr. Espinosa's current research agenda applies theories and methods from the cognitive and behavioral sciences to improve the effectiveness of regulations and public policy outcomes.

Tanya Heikkila is Professor and Associate Dean for Faculty Affairs at the University of Colorado Denver. Her research expertise is in comparative institutional analysis and the management of collaboration and conflict around common pool resources. She has studied institutions for coordinating groundwater and surface water in the western United States, interstate water conflicts and cooperation, the organization of collaborative ecosystem restoration programs, as well as the political landscape of hydraulic fracturing in the United States.

Routledge Research in Public Administration and Public Policy

Environmental Justice through Research-Based Decision-Making
William M. Bowen

The Politics of Foster Care Administration in the United States
Rebecca H. Padot

Advancing Collaboration Theory
Models, Typologies, and Evidence
Edited by John C. Morris and Katrina Miller-Stevens

Anticipatory Policymaking
When Government Acts to Prevent Problems and Why It Is So Difficult
Rob A. DeLeo

Administrative Ethics and Executive Decisions
Channeling and Containing Administrative Discretion
Chad B. Newswander

Citizen Participation in the Age of Contracting
When Service Delivery Trumps Democracy
Anna A. Amirkhanyan and Kristina T. Lambright

Community Development and Public Administration Theory
Promoting Democratic Principles to Improve Communities
Edited by Ashley E. Nickels and Jason D. Rivera

Contextualizing Compliance in the Public Sector
Individual Motivations, Social Processes, and Institutional Design
Edited by Saba Siddiki, Salvador Espinosa, and Tanya Heikkila

For a full list of titles in this series, please visit www.routledge.com

Contextualizing Compliance in the Public Sector

Individual Motivations, Social Processes, and Institutional Design

Edited by Saba Siddiki, Salvador Espinosa, and Tanya Heikkila

Routledge
Taylor & Francis Group
LONDON AND NEW YORK

First published 2019
by Routledge

2 Park Square, Milton Park, Abingdon, Oxfordshire OX14 4RN
52 Vanderbilt Avenue, New York, NY 10017

Routledge is an imprint of the Taylor & Francis Group, an informa business

First issued in paperback 2020

Library of Congress Cataloging-in-Publication Data
A catalog record for this book has been requested

ISBN: 978-1-138-55237-1 (hbk)
ISBN: 978-0-367-66605-7 (pbk)

Typeset in Times New Roman
by Apex CoVantage, LLC

To our mentors, who have paved the way for understanding compliance—and the institutions, behaviors, and contexts that shape compliance—from an interdisciplinary perspective.

To our readers, for their willingness to advance new ways of assessing and motivating compliance.

Contents

Figures

Tables

Contributors

Cindy Brooks Dollar is Assistant Professor in the Department of Sociology at the University of North Carolina at Greensboro. Her research focuses on crime and deviance, power inequalities, and (in)formal social control.

Joshua Chanin is Associate Professor in the School of Public Affairs at San Diego State University. His research interests include police behavior and accountability, organizational reform, and transparency in public organizations.

Cali Curley is Assistant Professor in the School of Public and Environmental Affairs at Indiana University–Purdue University Indianapolis. Her research interests include sustainability, energy policy, institutions, local government, and service delivery mechanisms such as co-production.

Daniel A. DeCaro is Assistant Professor at the University of Louisville in the Department of Urban and Public Affairs and the Department of Psychological and Brain Sciences. His research focuses on public participation, regulations, incentive systems, and the interdisciplinary psychology of motivation and decision making as they pertain to compliance and cooperation in governance systems.

Salvador Espinosa is Associate Professor at San Diego State University in the School of Public Affairs. His research interests include the use of cognitive and behavioral sciences to address questions in public finance, public policy and regulatory design, as well as debt management and capital market development in subnational governments.

Tanya Heikkila is Professor and Associate Dean for Faculty Affairs at the School of Public Affairs, University of Colorado Denver. Her research focuses on institutional analysis and the management of collaboration and conflict around common pool resources.

Stuart Henry is Professor at San Diego State University in the School of Public Affairs. His research interests include criminological theory, deviant behavior, law and society, school violence, and occupational crime.

Dana Nurge is an Associate Professor in Criminal Justice in the School of Public Affairs at San Diego State University. Her research interests include delinquency/gang prevention and intervention, and juvenile justice policy.

Bradley Ray is Assistant Professor in the School of Public and Environmental Affairs at IUPUI and Director of the Center for Criminal Justice Research at the Indiana University Public Policy Institute. His research focuses on individuals struggling with substance use disorder or mental health issues, particularly where these populations intersect with criminal justice, public safety, and treatment systems.

Edella Schlager is Professor at the University of Arizona in the School of Government and Public Policy. Her research focuses on comparative institutional analyses of water laws, policies, property rights, and compacts in the western United States.

Saba Siddiki is Assistant Professor in the Maxwell School of Citizenship and Public Affairs at Syracuse University. Her research focuses on policy design and implementation, regulatory compliance, collaborative governance, and sustainability.

William L. Swann is Assistant Professor at the University of Colorado in the School of Public Affairs. His research interests include local government, public management, collaborative governance, urban sustainability, and environmental policy.

Megan Welsh is Assistant Professor in the School of Public Affairs at San Diego State University. Her research focuses on prisoner reentry, policing, and homelessness.

1 Building a Framework for Contextualizing Compliance

Saba Siddiki, Tanya Heikkila, and Salvador Espinosa

The Importance of Compliance

It is difficult to imagine a situation not governed by norms, rules, or laws. As children, authority figures teach us what we are forbidden, required, and allowed to do at certain times, situations, and places. As we grow older and expand the scope of our activities, we are subject to various cultural norms and rules of the groups and organizations where we are members (e.g., school, workplaces, clubs), and to the laws of the jurisdictions where we live or travel. On one level, learning rules of behavior at a young age can ensure that we can effectively socialize with those in our surrounding contexts. At another level, learning rules and norms from a particular culture or subculture can bring us into conflict with those of another culture or subculture.

These various types of cultural, subcultural, organizational, and governmental norms and rules are referred to broadly here as behavioral directives. People design these directives to shape the behavior of individuals and groups toward some desired outcome or set of outcomes. Behavioral directives serve many broad functions. From a functionalist perspective, behavioral directives are mechanisms that identify the behaviors that promote stable societies or social control (Parsons, 1951, 1962; Treviño, 2008). They can establish rights, help distribute income and wealth, and encourage consistency and predictability of social behavior. Behavioral directives perform an educational function and socialization role by reinforcing what is desirable and acceptable (Podgórecki, 1974). By reflecting what their designers perceive to be acceptable, even ideal behavior for realizing desired social outcomes, behavioral directives also play a normative role. Because behavioral directives represent underlying norms and values, they can be ideological and require coercion, depending on who exercises the power and influence over their creation, application, and enforcement. As a result, they can also create conflict and promote resistance (Turk, 1969, 1982).

Ultimately, behavioral directives are only effective at achieving the intended results of their creators if those they govern follow them. A critical question in contexts governed by rules and norms, which this book addresses, is thus: What factors influence the decision of an individual or organization to comply (or not) with a rule or norm? Practically, compliance can be thought of as merely following directives. On a deeper level, compliance can suggest that those governed by directives acknowledge their legitimacy and accept that they are consistent with their values or beliefs, or that they are committed to the social goals that compliance can achieve—such as safety, equity, order, and social welfare. Alternatively, compliance may suggest that followers fear the consequences of noncompliance. Fearful compliance may indicate that followers oppose the directives and only follow them to the extent that they are enforced. In some cases, compliant individuals may only follow directives superficially as a cover to allow their informal practice of deviant noncompliance. Superficial compliance indicates that directives provide a protective framework within which individuals can exploit loopholes, gaps, fissures, and contradictions, and can replace those directives with alternative norms. Indeed, a host of factors can complicate and even compromise compliance, including competing norms and rules, differences in interpretation, changing environments, and resistance. Thus, studying compliance to uncover whether it is occurring, as well as what motivates it and neutralizes its authority, is central to the broader study of governance.

The following examples illustrate some of the situations where compliance is critical to successful governance:

Safety and quality of food systems: On a daily basis, we expect that the food we consume will be safe and that food producers will follow rules and regulations. Aquaculture—or farmed seafood—is an example of a growing food industry governed under a complex regulatory system, but we know little about how and under what conditions aquaculture producers are likely to comply. Farmers' compliance may be motivated by their agreement with new regulations, social pressure from other farmers, as well as farmers' own commitment to produce high quality products. Understanding compliance in relatively newly regulated industries, like aquaculture, is critical for developing successful regulatory programs.

Drug policy: A growing number of countries and American states have chosen to legalize or decriminalize the use of marijuana. This, however, does not mean that their governments should not persuade users to limit their consumption patterns given the potential public health consequences of high levels of marijuana consumption. Think, for example, about a college student who smokes marijuana regularly as a way to cope with stress. The student is not aware of the potential long-term health effects, but might change his habit if presented with compelling evidence about the negative effects. What factors should government officials consider when designing programs to discourage this type of drug use?

Motivating voluntary compliance: Not all activities or behaviors are driven by mandates. In fact, organizations and governments often create programs that require voluntary compliance to produce some intended social or group benefits. For example, getting people to voluntarily reduce their energy consumption in their homes or offices can save money and reduce pollution. How can we design such programs to foster voluntary compliance?

Alternative methods of justice procurement: The approach to sentencing for many types of convicted offenders often fails to address underlying problems (e.g., drug use, mental health conditions, and access to resources). Alternative systems for processing such offenders are emerging across the United States to help deal with some of these underlying challenges and reduce criminal behaviors. How can we design these processes to ensure that they incentivize compliance with the law, while giving people opportunities to overcome the underlying challenges that often inhibit compliance?

Sharing water resources across state lines: Most major river basins in the United States cross multiple state lines. River basins provide critical resources for agricultural production, urban water supplies, recreation, and industrial productivity. Because of the dependence that downstream states have on upstream states to ensure that sufficient water supplies are available to meet these needs, many states have entered into interstate agreements or compacts to allocate supplies. However, when new demands emerge or when the volume of stream flows diminish (i.e., due to droughts), what ensures that states will comply with the agreements they enter into?

Police behavior: In the wake of Michael Brown's death at the hands of Ferguson, Missouri, police officer Darren Wilson, the U.S. Department of Justice (DOJ) initiated an investigation of the Ferguson police department under the authority of Section 14141 of the 1994 Crime Act (see U.S. Department of Justice, 2015). In such cases, when the DOJ finds police have misused force or engaged in discriminatory policing, the DOJ has authority to sue to bring the department into compliance with federal law. Ferguson avoided litigation by agreeing to implement a series of reforms such as enhanced officer training and internal and external accountability systems. Understanding the factors that shape local police compliance with these agreements can shed light on the conditions that will support lawful police behavior.

These examples underscore not only the importance of compliance or noncompliance in society, but also the potential complex array of factors that can affect compliance and noncompliance and fundamental questions about what compliance even means. Learning about the factors animating compliance has been the focus of thought-provoking discussions in academia and the world of policymaking. Numerous empirical studies, theories, and analytical lenses have improved our knowledge of this topic. While this research spans multiple fields and contributes complementary insights, there has been surprisingly little cross-fertilization across these fields. This is where the contribution of this book resides.

Contextualizing Compliance in the Public Sector adopts an interdisciplinary approach to the study of compliance by bringing together the reflections and empirical analyses of a group of scholars interested in the connections among alternative governance settings; the potential behavioral responses of individuals, groups, and organizations; and the ways that such connections may inform policymaking. The exchange of ideas started with a two-day workshop at San Diego State University with colleagues from across the United States who are trained in social psychology, criminology, public policy, and public administration. Integrating the diverse perspectives of the participants led to a framework that put us closer to a more unified lens for studying compliance. The remainder of this introductory chapter focuses on describing this analytical framework.

The chapters that follow illustrate how the different factors identified in the framework play out in various compliance contexts at different levels of analysis (i.e., individual, or micro level; group, or meso level; systems, or macro level). They thus help identify better ways to measure and assess compliance. Additionally, this work can provide insights into the design of rules and directives that may foster compliance, or potentially minimize noncompliance, deviance, and resistance. Ultimately, through these analyses, the authors aim to stimulate a conversation among scholars, students, and future practitioners) in public administration and policy, criminal justice, sociology, political science, and other fields. This conversation is enabled by the unveiling of connections among governance directives, compliance behavior, and policy outcomes.

What Is Compliance?

We define compliance as a behavioral state in a specific time, situation, and place that conforms (completely or partially) to behavioral directives, such as those embodied in laws, social norms, and organizational policies. Logically, then, we define *noncompliance* as a behavioral state that does not conform to behavioral directives. In the following section, we elaborate on key components of these definitions.

The first part of this definition identifies compliance as manifested in individual or collective behavior, where individual behavior refers to the conduct of a person and collective behavior refers to the conduct of a group of people. We distinguish the act of compliance as being different from the ability to comply, attitudes about compliance, and intentions and motivations of compliance. Though we limit our definition of compliance behaviorally, it is still broad enough to account for relevant behavioral complexities. For example, behavior is not static. Sometimes individuals act in conformance with behavioral directives, while other times not, based on a variety of subjective factors (Tyler, 2006). Further, behavior can be partially in conformance with behavioral directives. Individuals may only conduct a portion of the full array of activities to be deemed compliant. In other words, we recognize the range of behavioral activity falling within the opposing conceptual poles of compliance and noncompliance.

The second part of our definition of compliance acknowledges that a precondition of compliance is the existence of explicit or understood directives. These directives usually convey expectations about specific behaviors under some mix of spatial and temporal conditions. Just as our definition of compliance accommodates some of the complexities associated with conformance to behavioral directives, it also accommodates complexities associated with the behavioral directives themselves. It acknowledges, for example, that different types of directives can complement or contradict each other in substance or interpretation.

We delineate behavioral directives in two ways. First, we categorize directives in terms of their coerciveness, or prescriptive force, and enforceability through sanctioning. This first categorization leads to a distinction of directives as being strategies, norms, and rules (Crawford & Ostrom, 1995). We borrow this distinction from Crawford and Ostrom (1995), who define behavioral directives as written, verbal, or understood expectations about the opportunities and constraints of action in a given situation. According to Crawford and Ostrom, rules are those directives that explicitly identify whether a specific behavior is allowed, required, or forbidden and identify sanctions for noncompliance. Norms are directives that identify what is allowed, required, or forbidden but do not explicitly identify sanctions for noncompliance. Finally, strategies specify activities for certain conditions but lack a mandate (e.g., may, must, must not) and clear sanctions.

The second way we delineate behavioral directives is in terms of "in-form" directives and "in-use" directives (Ostrom, 2005). This categorization is akin to the long-standing socio-legal concepts of formal law (i.e., written, or "law in the books") and legal realism (i.e., law in practice "what the courts do") (Holmes, 1881; Llewellyn, 1962). In-form and in-use directives may be viewed as equally legitimate and salient to those governed by them, but differ in terms of their codification in written form by an authorized entity. Examples of in-form directives include government laws and regulations or organizational policies and bylaws. In-use directives are often unwritten and generally accepted and, like in-form directives, specify how individuals should behave. In-use directives are established once a relatively large group of individuals recognizes them over a significant period of time. Both in-form and in-use directives are enforceable, although the enforcing entity often differs. Governmental or organizational mechanisms often enforce in-form directives, while community-based social control mechanisms typically enforce in-use directives.

In-form and in-use directives relating to a specific behavior at a given time or place may or may not be consistent. For example, a formal regulation may require enforcement personnel to administer a financial penalty for every observed incidence of noncompliance with regulatory directives. In reality, the agency charged with administering the regulation may have informally adopted a culture of allowing noncompliers the opportunity to correct their behavior before administering a penalty. An analogous example is an understanding among police officers that drivers are allowed to drive five or more miles per hour over the official speed limit before a speeding ticket is issued. Over time, the in-use directives are perceived and accepted by those implementing them as well as by those governed by them. The speeding enforcement also points to a situational variant that affects compliance. Some drivers will conform to the normative practice of driving no more than five miles over the speed limit in situations where they perceive high risk of enforcement, as indicated by the visible signs of police or advanced notice from a radar detector. However, in situations of a lower perceived risk, they may be noncompliant with both in-form and in-use directives. This would be an illustration of selectively situational compliant behavior and the crucial importance of the context of compliance.

Our definition of compliance recognizes different combinations of compliance and noncompliance that may arise in situations where in-form and in-use directives are inconsistent. That is, our definition of compliance is not limited to a particular type of directive. One can be in compliance or partial compliance at any given time with in-form directives, in-use directives, both, or neither on a regular basis. Table 1.1 introduces some of the combinations of compliance that may result in a social setting governed by in-form directives and in-use directives. Different combinations of compliance are illustrated with an example of a nonprofit organization board that is required by its bylaws to conduct board votes according to Robert's Rules of Order, a protocol for decision making in collective action settings. Robert's Rules of Order require a majoritarian voting system.

The key lessons from the preceding examples are that (1) situations are governed by sets of in-form and in-use directives that may or may not be consistent; and (2) depending on the extent to which they overlap, individuals may be in compliance with none, both, or one or the other, constantly or situationally. When there is discrepancy between in-form and in-use directives that regulate the same behavior, individuals will tend to comply with the type of directive that appeals to their personal beliefs, morals, values, or broader normative framework. In the public realm, for example, individuals may conform to social norms from a group or community, but not necessarily follow rules imposed by public entities if the latter are out of alignment with individuals' normative frameworks. Similarly, reflecting the phenomenon of partial compliance, individuals may follow directives selectively, omitting those conflicting with their normative commitments. Also, enforcers of directives may exhibit the same compliance tendencies. For example, they may develop and adopt in-use directives that differ from in-form directives relating to enforcement because the former better align with their cultural contexts or personal beliefs and values.

Table 1.1 Compliance Scenarios

Compliance Scenario	*Baseline Scenario*	*Compliance Example*
Compliance with in-form directives and in-use directives	The board of a nonprofit organization must vote on official matters using Robert's Rules of Order according to organizational bylaws. Board members agree that Robert's Rules provide the best way to make decisions.	The board always conducts voting based on Robert's Rules.
Non-compliance with in-form directives and compliance with in-use directives	The board of a nonprofit organization must vote on official matters using Robert's Rules of Order according to organizational bylaws. Board members have informally agreed to make decisions on official matters using a consensus-based decision-making approach.	Consensus-based decision making is the common practice.
Compliance with in-form directives and non-compliance with in-use directives	The board of a nonprofit organization must vote on official matters using Robert's Rules of Order according to organizational bylaws. Board members have informally agreed to make decisions on official matters using consensus-based decision making.	A new board president is elected and decides one meeting to conduct a vote based on Robert's Rules of Order rather than using a consensus-based approach to arrive at a decision.
Non-compliance with in-form and in-use directives	The board of a nonprofit organization must vote on official matters using Robert's Rules of Order according to organizational bylaws. Board members have informally agreed to make decisions on official matters using consensus-based decision making.	A new board president is elected and decides voting rights will be restricted to the president, vice-president, and treasurer of the board.[i]
Partial or situational compliance with in-form and in-use directives	The board of a nonprofit organization must vote on official matters using Robert's Rules of Order according to organizational bylaws. Board members have informally agreed to make decisions on official matters using consensus-based decision making, but to invoke Robert's Rules of Order if consensus cannot be reached.	A new board president is elected and decides to use Robert's Rules of Order as a background structure to run meetings, but is open to the board members conducting business in an informal dialogical exchange, unless proceedings stall, then Robert's Rules are invoked.

[i] This example is not meant to imply that the change from the baseline to the compliance scenario is spurred by a change in participants or participants occupying a particular role. The same participant or set of participants may alter their behavioral expectations.

Why Study Compliance?

The complexity of the examples just described illustrates the importance of studying compliance. Research on compliance helps to identify when it is or is not occurring, whether or not we are achieving the objectives of behavioral directives, and what factors affect compliance behavior. It can allow us to understand how individuals identify with and validate directives emerging from different sources. Compliance with one type of directive and noncompliance with the other can signal discord between community values and those articulated in policy outputs or implementation, a dominance of individual or social over legal pressure, or lacking, ineffective, or differential enforcement mechanisms. At the very least, one can look at different combinations of compliance trends as signals of compatibility between in-form and in-use directives.

Persistent and widespread non-compliance may be damaging or destructive to social cohesion and the capacity to solve important social problems (e.g., from reducing air pollution to ensuring productive learning environments to maintaining reliable traffic patterns). However, as Durkheim (1895) pointed out, noncompliance can also help illuminate when directives might be ineffective, or where two different types of directives that address the same issue are in conflict. It affords the opportunity for a society to clarify moral boundaries that promote social unity and highlights where rules may be dissonant with cultural norms and values. In doing so, noncompliance can lead to changes to rules, norms, and strategies, a reinforcement or challenging of social values, and other types of minor or major social transformations.

Compliance is also important because it can reflect cooperation or negotiation between those promulgating directives and those following them. From this perspective, the social outcomes expected to result from compliance can be thought of as co-produced; that is, both implementers and followers of directives cooperatively participate in producing the desired social outcome. In some cases, that co-production is explicit if followers of directives actively work with enforcers and other community members to encourage compliance (Tyler & Fagan, 2008). In other cases, the co-production of compliance is more passive. Either way, cooperation as discussed here is distinct from compliance, though both concepts in practice are mutually reinforcing. Importantly, when enforcers of directives collaborate to co-produce a negotiated practice of compliance, the situational and contextual criteria may supersede in-form directives with in-use directives (Henry, 1983).

How to Study Compliance

We can analyze compliance descriptively, diagnostically, and/or normatively. Each type of analysis offers practical and theoretical value. Descriptive assessments of compliance identify whether and how compliance or noncompliance is occurring, under what situational conditions, and by whom. This type of information is critical, for example, for public safety personnel engaged in monitoring and enforcement, and for policymakers who need to determine the appropriateness and effectiveness of policies and practices. Descriptive assessments are also foundational to any study of compliance because they help clarify the conceptual bounds of compliance. Describing the contexts and conditions under which compliance occurs can further help build hypotheses that eventually can contribute to explanatory theories of compliance.

Diagnostic studies of compliance focus on relating physical and non-physical factors associated with compliance to different kinds of directives and different patterns of enforcement practice. In other words, they can explore and test explanations of why people engage in compliant or non-compliant behaviors. Examples of physical factors that relate to compliance include the presence and frequency of policing or enforcement to penalize compliance/noncompliance (Burby & Paterson, 1993; Gray & Scholz, 1993; Helland, 1998; May, 2005). Examples of non-physical factors include attitudes about compliance or rule internalization (Ryan & Deci, 2000); belief congruency between rule enforcers and rule followers regarding the way a domain should be managed (Bardach & Kagan, 1982); technical competence of the enforcing authorities perceived by rule followers (Bardach & Kagan, 1982); and perceptions of trust and legitimacy between rule enforcers and rule followers (Scholz & Lubell, 1998; Tyler, 2006). Diagnostic studies offer useful insight for policy designers who must consider how to structure policy incentives and enforcement mechanisms to encourage compliance. Diagnostic studies of compliance also can test specific hypothesis about the relative influence of different factors in shaping behavior and are thus critical for theory building.

Normatively oriented studies of compliance probe into the tangible and intangible implications of compliance/noncompliance, at the individual, group, or societal level.[1] These studies question, for example, whether systemic compliance/noncompliance leads to more ideal, legitimate, or appropriate outcomes. They build practically and theoretically on descriptive and diagnostic studies of compliance.

Ultimately, professional, disciplinary, and methodological values will inform the study of compliance. Indeed, the topic of compliance has been studied extensively by scholars across the social sciences, including by policy analysts, philosophers, sociologists, criminologists, anthropologists, political scientists, social psychologists, and health and behavioral scientists. Studies from these disciplines shed light on factors that influence compliance in different contexts. To understand compliance more holistically, however, one needs to draw insights from across these diverse fields. In part this is because complex social problems, such as compliance, need a comprehensive analysis that addresses multiple levels of societal structure (Henry, 2009; Henry & Bracy, 2012; Henry, 2017). For instance, one can observe individual students in a classroom choosing to follow classroom behavior directives designated on a syllabus. We can also observe a company complying with laws to protect worker safety. Or, we can observe state or countries following (or not) an international agreement to reduce the production of greenhouse gas emissions. As we discuss later, all of these levels of behavior can be influenced by individual-level and contextual factors. The framework we developed can help organize and systematize how we approach these factors.

A Framework for the Study of Compliance

As the concept of compliance is inherently interdisciplinary, a framework is helpful for providing a shared language and road map to facilitate analysis and understanding. A framework is a conceptual map that guides analysis of a given phenomenon (Ostrom, 2005).[2] According to Schlager (1999), well-developed frameworks include several features.

First, they need to be flexible enough to accommodate multiple theories and models related to the phenomenon of interest, as well as tackle different research questions. Frameworks also should pay explicit attention to categories of variables that relate to, influence, and interact with the key phenomenon of interest. Additionally, frameworks should identify levels of analysis at which to study the phenomenon of interest and logical relationships between them over time (e.g., see Bronfenbrenner, 1979). Like a geographic map, frameworks, may provide multiple layers of conceptual detail that allow analysts to scale up or down to different levels of analysis.

Rarely do scholars test an entire framework. Instead, they use theories and models relating to specific categories of variables in the framework for testing and empirical analysis. That is, researchers can use frameworks to zoom into specific categories of variables and examine relationships among them. The benefit of a framework is that it can allow for clarity on how models and theories from different disciplines can be applied to examine a common set of variables and how these models and theories fit together.

The framework we develop (shown in Figure 1.1), was inspired by several theories of compliance, as well as the analytical architecture of the Institutional Analysis and Development Framework (Ostrom, 2005) and Bronfenbrenner's (1979) systemic ecological model. As we discuss in detail in the next section, the framework identifies three distinct levels of analysis for studying compliance decisions or actions. The framework also includes the general categories of factors or variables that are important in studying compliance across all three levels. Given the complexities of the nature of compliance, the framework does not offer an exhaustive list of all factors that are relevant in the literature on compliance. Rather, it introduces the categories of factors that shape compliance generally, leaving the more nuanced discussions of specific factors or variables to the individual chapters that follow.

Decision Context: Three Levels of Compliance Behavior

Compliance behaviors emerge at different levels of analysis. The three levels of analysis that we consider important in studying compliance are micro level

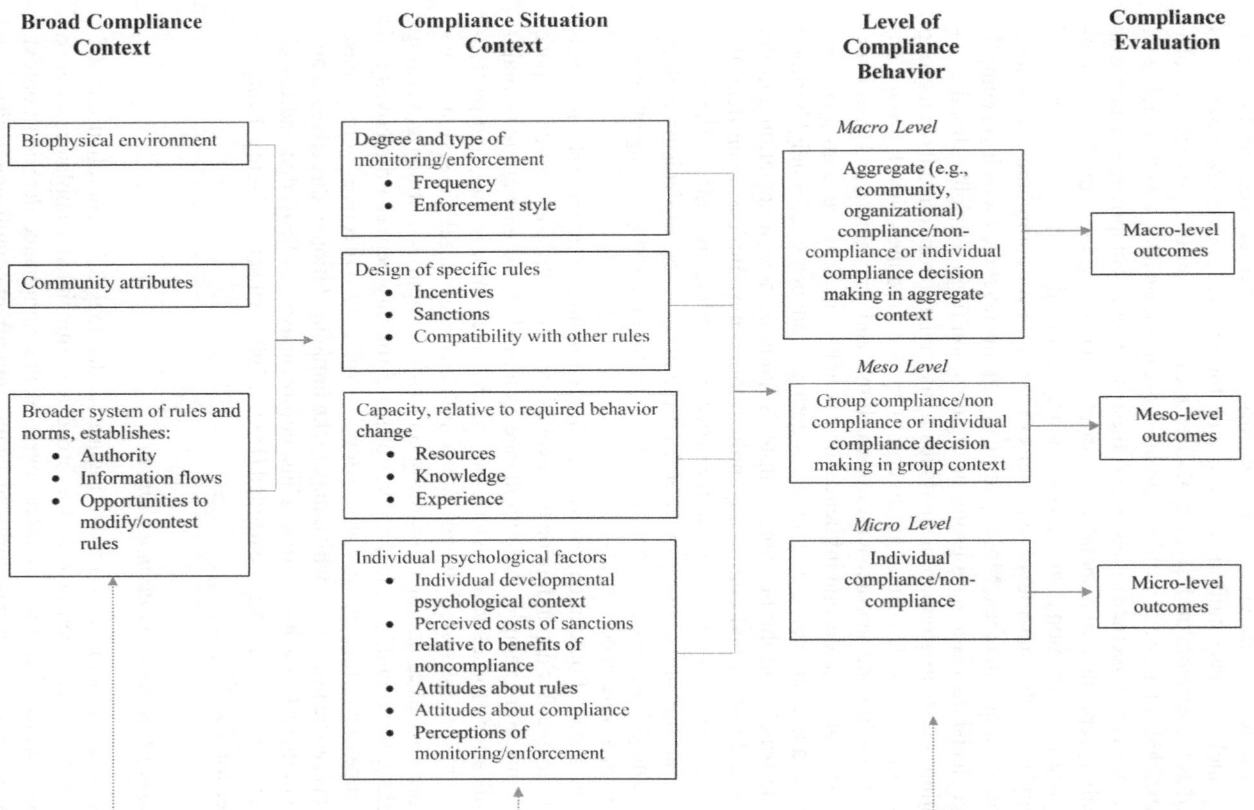

Figure 1.1 Compliance Framework

(individual), meso level (group/organization), and macro level (social system). The micro level of analysis focuses on compliance (or non-compliance) behaviors by individuals. Relevant individuals may include anyone who is responsible for following a set of in-form or in-use directives, but they also may include those individuals who monitor, enforce, or regulate others, as well as the creators or designers of directives. These individuals are typically embedded, or nested, within a broader organizational or institutional (i.e., rule or norm governed) context, so their individual compliance behavior is rarely independent of a social and institutional context. Individual level compliance is foundational to the compliance actions that occur at all levels of analysis. At the meso level, we focus on group-level compliance behaviors, processes, or outcomes. More specifically, at this level the focus is on compliance decisions made by a group or organization (e.g., a neighborhood association, self-help group, or a sports team) as well as by individuals in a group that collectively determine group compliance. At the meso level, groups are nested within and interact with organizations and communities. These interactions frame, guide, and influence their actions. For instance, a group of tenants in a housing complex may act together to advocate for a neighborhood crime watch, but the housing complex's home owners' association and the local ordinances and community police policy may limit or even deny the desires of these residents to become proactive in crime prevention. The macro level can operate across groups or multiple meso levels of decision making (e.g., neighborhoods in a community, cities in a metropolitan region, water users in a watershed, etc.).[3]

The types of outcomes resulting from compliance or noncompliance decisions may differ depending on the level of analysis at different points in space and time. For example, noncompliance by an individual may not have major implications for a social system, but when scaled up to group, and particularly at societal system levels, noncompliance may highlight serious flaws in the directives and/or monitoring and enforcement conditions governing society. Important, too, is the level of synchronicity between directives and practices operating at the various levels over time. Directives across these levels can be in conflict, which may make implementation of directives at any one of these levels ineffective. Thus, comprehensive policies that address all levels in the system may be needed (Henry, 2009; Muschert, Henry, Bracy, & Peguero, 2014).

Parsing Out the Compliance Context

The types of factors identified in Figure 1.1 that may drive compliance at different levels are identified in the broad and situational compliance context boxes, which feed into all three levels of the compliance decision context. We expect that these categories of factors will affect compliance decisions at any of the three levels in the framework. However, they may have differential effects at each level due to group or collective dynamics. Again, as this is not a theory with specific hypotheses. We do not clarify the conditions under which particular factors may influence compliant behavior more than others, or the conditions under which certain types of compliance result in particular outcomes. These types of inquires will emerge in the chapters that follow. Drawing from a diversity of compliance scholarship, we describe the key categories of variables we recognize as important in shaping compliance.

Compliance Situation Context

Several individual-level biological and cognitive factors may motivate compliance (or noncompliance). For example, these include individuals' perceptions of the costs and benefits or payoffs of following a given rule. The perceptions of costs could be contingent upon external sanctions or the likelihood of getting caught with specified negative consequences. They may also be based on whether following or breaking rules is compatible or not with individual values or norms around rule-following behavior (the "right thing to do"), the appropriateness of rule enforcement, or the legitimacy of the rule itself. For instance, I may choose not to comply with a rule because I believe it discriminates against certain individuals or because the parties charged with enforcing the rules are taking bribes.

Individuals may not always base their decision calculus on a conscious assessment of costs or normative values. Some behavioral decisions might result from unconscious decisions—such as heuristics that people employ, or even social pressures. For instance, they tend to follow the flow of traffic when other drivers are on the road and therefore may choose to violate speeding laws because everyone is speeding. Alternatively, biological predispositions to act impulsively, without rational calculation (i.e., as a result of fight or flight response mechanisms) can lead to actions not based on conventional rational choice.

Further, factors relating to individuals' developmental psychological context, or their individual biographies over the life-course influence compliance. The extent to which decisions about compliance are affected by patterns of childhood development, or past experiences of rewards and/or pain and trauma, can trigger subsequent compliance decisions. Indeed, a pattern of compliance or noncompliance may reflect this developmental context that can affect families and can be transmitted inter-generationally to the point where some people become noncompliant-persistent (meaning they fail to follow directives over the life course). They may also become noncompliant-limited, or exhibit noncompliant behavior during young adulthood but because of life course events, triggers, and changes, such as marriage, family, and career, they desist and begin to follow rules or norms of convention resulting in compliance. This is a familiar pattern with juvenile delinquents (Moffitt, 1993; Sampson & Laub, 1993). Yet others may fall between these positions and become compliant-limited in that they follow rules to a point but modify, reinterpret, and otherwise fail to comply systematically over time.

The capacity of actors to comply with directives, relative to the behavioral change needed for compliance, also shapes compliance behavior. The capacity to comply includes the resources that the actor (individual or group) needs to follow directives, the knowledge or information an actor possesses about them, and their level of experience with situations where directives apply. Capacity, however, is relative. Some behavior change needed for compliance is much more extensive than others. Extensive behavioral change, or highly complex changes (e.g., new regulations on car manufacturers requiring increased fuel efficiency that would involve a major redesign of conventional automobile engines) are likely to require more capacity than behavior that is less complex in terms of the number of actors or institutional rules. However, individual-level complexity can also emerge if compliance decisions or behaviors involve multiple steps. Capacity can also have an interactive effect with an individual's cognitive characteristics, whereby capacity may shape, for instance, perceptions of the costs of compliance.

Behaviors related to compliance are shaped by the design of specific directives and the degree of monitoring and enforcement capacity associated with them. One characteristic of directive design that may be important is the degree to which a directive incentivizes (or rewards) compliance, versus the degree to which it imposes penalties on non-compliers. Another design consideration is whether the directive is compatible with others or with societal norms, or even subcultural norms of a specific population. For example, many administrative processes of departments within a university are governed by university-level rules that are commonly applied across all departments. If the design of university-level rules does not appropriately fit the culture of a department, the department may choose to adopt another set of norms that deviate from university rules or informally adapt university rules when they are applied. The creation of department-specific norms or the adaptation of university-level rules would both be characterized as noncompliance in response to perceived inappropriateness of university rules, or in response to perceived situational exceptions.

The decision to deviate from a directive may also depend on the process by which it was designed (i.e., in forums that are perceived to be more or less legitimate) or the ambiguity or flexibility of interpretation provided by the directive. Indeed, the very language used to frame directives, their appropriateness, or their legitimacy can be mediated by subcultural values and norms that have immediate situational or even historical relevance. Without taking these factors into account, general directives are unlikely to be effective in bringing about compliance (Mars, 1982).

In addition to the design of directives, the extent to which monitoring and enforcement relating to them is required and undertaken will directly influence compliance behavior, as will the extent to which enforcers are open to negotiation about which directives are to be applied in specific situations, to specific populations. The outcome of such interactive redesign are norms-in-use (or even rules-in-disuse).

Broad Compliance Context

Features of the broader context in which compliance decision making is occurring may directly affect the institutional or individual factors that drive compliance behavior or interact with those characteristics. In some cases, however, they may shape compliance behavior more directly. Some of the factors we include under the broader contextual setting are described next with examples of the more specific variables that fall under these factors. This is not an exhaustive list. Rather it is illustrative of some examples of why these factors are important for a compliance framework.

1. *Biophysical environmental characteristics* of a compliance context can matter in several ways. For instance, this context may make the nature of compliance behavior required more or less complex due to the spatial extent and diversity of the context. This can then influence the degree to which the behavioral response is feasible with a given set of capacity features, or the extent to which monitoring and enforcement is feasible. For instance, trying to monitor fishing regulations in the ocean is much more difficult than monitoring fishing regulations on a small lake. If the biophysical setting involves a context where the effects of noncompliance may be more visible or immediate, the incentive structure for compliance may be different or the norms that an individual possesses around that compliance decision may differ.
2. *Community characteristics* may vary substantially across compliance contexts. These might include factors such as the extent and number of individuals involved in a community where compliance behaviors take place or the degree to which a community's norms promote compliance. Likewise, whether or not community norms shape compliance behavior will depend on whether the norms and values of the individuals who are supposed to be following directives see these directives as compatible with those norms. Community characteristics may also include the power structure in a community, which can affect individual perceived legitimacy of directives, as well as enforcement capacity (Tyler, 2006).
3. *The overarching system of directives*, under which compliance decisions about a specific rule or norm are made, is related to the design of directives. For example, for any given rule, other rules exist that may structure who has authority to make or revise rules, how information about the rules is shared or provided to regulated entities, and how monitoring and enforcement occur (Hart, 1961). The overarching system of directives also establishes the venues or opportunities for people to contest those that they may not perceive as legitimate or appropriate for the compliance context. It is also important to consider the overarching system of directives as it relates to different levels of analysis; specifically, the extent of compatibility between directives and practices operating at the various levels and how these play out over time.

Compliance Evaluation

Shown on the far right side of Figure 1.1 are the outcomes that can result from compliance behaviors. At one level, compliance behaviors or choices that express compliance or noncompliance (or some variant in between), in and of themselves, can be seen as the first-order outcomes of our framework (as shown in the levels of compliance behaviors). Here, however, our interest is in describing the effects of those different behaviors on individuals, groups, and social systems. Some compliance behaviors may result in individual or collective benefits or costs (i.e., a good feeling for compliance, or a guilty feeling for non-compliance, or financial or resource costs).

Depending on the type of behavior and the degree of enforcement, those costs and benefits may be minimal, or they could be seriously detrimental to the individual, or group, or society. Micro-level compliance decisions that are driven largely by emotional or symbolic cognitive processes may lead to rule avoidance.

At the meso, or group, level, compliance behaviors may result in ongoing social acceptance of a group, or noncompliance could lead to the identification of social pariahs. Alternatively, depending upon the group, compliant actors may not be trusted and may be seen as deviant from the norm of rule noncompliance, depending upon who are seen as the rule creators. At the meso level, neighborhood, community, or organizational forces may impose compliance through formal social control mechanisms, with the outcome being relatively high conformity.

Moving up to macro-system levels, compliance outcomes may be more complex. For instance, compliance or noncompliance at the system level may result in the reinforcement or erosion of social norms, or awareness of conflicts among socially agreed upon or informally accepted rules or norms. As reflected in the framework, any of these outcomes can also have feedback effects on individual norms, community norms, or decisions by communities to change the systems of directives governing behavior.

Applying the Framework

The value of the framework is to help expose possible pathways to compliance/non-compliance and alternative research questions that may then require more tailored theories or models to answer them. For instance, when considering the different levels of analysis, different disciplines may be needed to explain compliance. Theories from psychology may help examine questions around how or why individuals do or do not comply with particular directives (i.e., why an individual would obey speed limits or pay their taxes). Theories from public administration or sociology might be more relevant for understanding meso-level questions related to how or why regulated industries comply with regulations, or why a lack of compliance with rules or norms is more prevalent in some industries than others. Most theories of group-level compliance either explicitly or implicitly draw on individual level theories. For instance, theories of regulatory compliance among firms commonly employ deterrence theories that rely on a rational choice model of human behavior (e.g., see Gunningham, Thornton, & Kagan, 2005), which are also used in criminology theories to explain some individual behavior (Cornish & Clarke, 1986; Piquero & Tibbetts, 2002).

Deterrence theories generally assume that punishment of actors who violate rules will discourage those same actors (specific deterrence) and others (general deterrence) from violating those rules in the future. Similarly, theories of firm-level regulatory compliance, like theories of individual crime, recognize the role of the perceived legitimacy of directives in shaping the compliance decisions of actors. While these theorized drivers of compliance may be similar across these levels, the ways in which they influence individuals versus a group of actors in organizations, and what other factors may interact with these drivers, can differ. Moreover, cost-benefit analysis that underlies the deterrence model does not apply when other cognitive, emotional, and expressive processes are at play, or where there is a lack of self-control, a desire for immediate gratification or the thrill of risk-taking, or the satisfaction of "beating the system" regardless of the risk. Indeed, noncompliance can be the outcome of such non-rational actions. Alternatively, if one is interested more in the ways in which the design of directives matters for explaining compliance outcomes (at any level) versus the ways in which the social context matters, there are obviously different theoretical foci or traditions of inquiry that will be appropriate for delving into those factors of the framework.

Overview of Chapter Contents

Scholars from diverse academic backgrounds and areas of expertise have contributed to this book. This adds great richness to the discussion of compliance at different levels of analysis. An overview of this book's chapters follows.

Chapter 2: This chapter, written by Saba Siddiki, showcases a micro-level analysis of compliance in the context of U.S. aquaculture. In this chapter, Siddiki explores motivations of regulatory compliance among aquaculture producers and regulatory authorities charged with implementing aquaculture regulations in two American states, Virginia and Florida. In this research, Siddiki focuses on assessing the relative influence of various individual and social factors in shaping regulatory compliance, including the perceived competence of regulatory authorities as well as farmers' reputational concerns, feelings of guilt or shame, and fear of monetary incentives. Siddiki also examines factors that temper the effect of these compliance motivations in the reported research.

Chapter 3: This chapter explores the links that may exist between rule perceptions among marijuana users and their willingness to comply with rules aimed at discouraging drug use. Salvador Espinosa starts his chapter by claiming that while the decision to consume drugs corresponds to consumers themselves, governments may try to prevent or discourage actions that are considered harmful to an individual's well-being or that raise public health concerns. A variety or rules, norms, and policy designs can help accomplish this. How can we be sure that such rules, norms, and policy designs will attain their intended outcomes? This chapter argues that success will depend upon our ability to understand the connections among behavioral directives and the attitudes of the individuals that one is trying to persuade.

Chapter 4: The fourth chapter, by Cali Curley and William L. Swann, explores compliance as cooperation at the individual (micro) and organizational (meso) levels in the context of voluntary energy conservation programs. When considering compliance, one often thinks about decisions made in response to rules and regulations with which there is a mandate to comply. However, there are instances where individuals and firms comply voluntarily. Consider an example where hotels may have earned a "green" designation for voluntarily adopting a number of energy efficiency programs. Similarly, individuals may use governmental monies via rebates and loans by purchasing high energy efficiency equipment for their homes. However, to receive the benefits of making these higher energy efficiency choices, the individual must be compliant both in the purchase process and the equipment use after installation. Drawing on economic and sociological institutional theory, Curley and Swann examine the decision process and success of two scenarios in which compliance requires voluntarily adopting some agreed upon standards of participation.

Chapter 5: The fifth chapter offers a micro- and meso-level investigation of compliance. In this chapter, Bradley Ray and Cindy Brooks Dollar look at compliance in the context of problem-solving courts (PSCs), which offer an alternative approach to sentencing by linking offenders with community-based treatments or services that address the underlying causes of criminal behavior. This chapter uses the theory of procedural justice to examine PSC outcomes. The theory suggests that if a person perceives that the process is fair and that they are treated with respect, they will be more likely to accept the decision and will be motivated towards self-regulation and compliance with the law. Ray and Brooks Dollar investigate how the unique organization of the PSC is more conducive towards procedural justice principles and use survey data from multiple PSCs to examine whether perceptions of procedural justice vary across courts, by court actors, and over time, but also whether these perceptions are associated with increased compliance.

Chapter 6: Tanya Heikkila and Edella Schlager present a macro-level assessment of compliance in this chapter. It draws upon original research that examines compliance and noncompliance actions occurring across western interstate river compacts over the course of the 20th century. First, it examines the settings under which compliance problems arise in interstate river compacts. This chapter also examines the interplay between the compliance context and compliance outcomes as states and interstate commissions that govern compacts work toward addressing problems associated with noncompliance. It explores the strategies used in a cross-scale institutional setting to motivate not only states but also individual water users to maintain compliance with interstate agreements. These strategies, which emerge from compliance outcomes, include investing in capacity building, monitoring and enforcement, and rule compatibility, and then result in modifications to the compliance context.

Chapter 7: This chapter offers a multi-level analysis of compliance. In this chapter, Stuart Henry, Joshua Chanin, Megan Welsh, and Dana Nurge explore compliance in the context of police subculture and profiling. Their chapter looks at the processes involved in decisions police make to enforce the law, and how in the process they decide to violate procedures and processes. It examines various pressures toward noncompliance. These include local police subculture; neighborhood cultural practices and patterns of criminal activity in the community; police internal investigation processes at a departmental level or even inter-departmental reviews; and political trends, including technology (cameras) that records police actions in stop and search, auto-stop, and arrest situations. This chapter demonstrates that compliance with behavioral directives is a complex, interactive process. Police compliance with the terms of pattern or practice reform agreements is affected by a range of nested contexts or semi-autonomous social orders that combine with individual, situational officer experiences and cognitive processes to produce, at best, a patchwork of compliance and noncompliance.

Chapter 8: Daniel DeCaro draws examples from each of the empirical chapters in this book to examine at a deeper level the foundations of human motivation and decision making that underlie cooperation and compliance. DeCaro's chapter synthesizes lessons learned about compliance decision making from an interdisciplinary, social decision-making standpoint, to identify major conceptual and empirical shortcomings in current behavioral theory. Further, this review helps in the development of a more robust and descriptive behavioral theory, which may be better able to account for known limitations and clarify some particularly persistent puzzles about compliance that cut across the cases and issues discussed in this book.

Chapter 9: Salvador Espinosa, Tanya Heikkila, and Saba Siddiki conclude the with a synthesis of the empirical findings reported in the preceding chapters and explain how they fit within the analytical framework presented in this introduction. This chapter also offers conclusions about the book's key insights.

Notes

1 We differentiate normative studies from normative compliance motivations or normative perspectives on why people comply with rules. Compliance scholars (see Tyler, 2006, p. 3) contrast normative and instrumental perspectives on compliance. According to the instrumental perspective, individuals are primarily motivated in their compliance decision making by tangible, immediate incentives. From the normative perspective, one views compliance decision making as influenced by individuals' perceptions about what is just, moral, and legitimate.

2 Frameworks differ from theories and models (Schlager, 1999; Ostrom, 2005). Whereas a framework is a broad conceptual map that lays out the landscape of

factors that analysts should consider when exploring a given phenomenon, theories focus more on the expected nature of relationships among variables in explaining the phenomenon in a given context. Frameworks may incorporate multiple theories. Models are more precise tools for examining hypothesized relationships among variables. While some scholars adhere to the framework, theory, model distinction, others see the terms as interchangeable. This notion of framework has parallels with . Kuhn and Ritzer's concept of paradigm, which can contain multiple theories, a distinctive set of methods, and a community of academic researchers that work within the paradigm (Kuhn, 1962; Ritzer, 1975).

3 The micro, meso, macro distinction draws heavily from Bronfenbrenner's (1979) systemic ecological model originally developed to explain childhood socialization. His model further conceptualizes relationships that occur between different levels of analysis (labeled the "exo" level) and how these play out over time (labeled the "chrono" level).

References

Bardach, E., & Kagan, R. A. (1982). *Going by the book: The problem of regulatory unreasonableness*. London: Transaction Publishers.

Bronfenbrenner, U. (1979). *The ecology of human development*. Cambridge, MA: Harvard University Press.

Burby, R. J., & Paterson, R. G. (1993). Improving compliance with state environmental regulations. *Journal of Policy Analysis and Management, 12*, 753–772.Cornish, D. B., & Clarke, R. V. (Eds.). (1986). *The reasoning criminal: Rational choice perspectives on offending*. New York, NY: Springer-Verlag.

Crawford, Sue E. S., & Ostrom, E. (1995). A grammar of institutions. *American Political Science Review, 89*(3), 582–600.

Durkheim, E. (1895). *The rules of sociological method*. New York, NY: Free Press.

Gray, W. B., & Scholz, J. (1993). Does regulatory enforcement work? A panel analysis and OSHA enforcement. *Law & Society Review, 27*, 177–213.

Gunningham, N. A., Thornton, D., & Kagan, R. A. (2005). Motivating management: Corporate compliance in environmental protection. *Law & Policy, 27*(2), 289–316.

Hart, H. L. A. (1961). *The concept of law*. Oxford: Clarendon Press.

Helland, E. (1998). The enforcement of pollution control laws: Inspections, violations, and self-reporting. *Review of Economics and Statistics, 80*, 141–153.

Henry, S. (1983). *Private justice: Towards integrated theorizing in the sociology of law*. London: Routledge & Kegan Paul.

Henry, S. (2009). School violence beyond columbine: A complex problem in need of an interdisciplinary analysis. *American Behavioral Scientist, 52*, 1246–1265.

Henry, S. (2017). Interdisciplinarity in the fields of law, justice and criminology. In R. Frodeman, J. T. Klein, & C. D. Santos Pacheco (Eds.), *The Oxford handbook of interdisciplinary studies* (pp. 397–411). New York, NY: Oxford University Press.

Henry, S., & Bracy, N. L. (2012). Integrative theory in criminology applied to the complex social problem of school violence. In A. Repko, W. H. Newell, & R. Szostak (Eds.), *Case studies in interdisciplinary research* (pp. 259–282). Thousand Oaks, CA: Sage Publications.

Holmes, O. W. (1881). *The common law* (M. Howe, Ed.). Boston, MA: Little, Brown and Company.

Kuhn, T. S. (1962). *The structure of scientific revolutions*. Chicago, IL: University of Chicago Press.

Llewellyn, K. (1962). *Jurisprudence: Realism in theory and practice*. Chicago, IL: University of Chicago Press.
Mars, G. (1982). *Cheats at work*. Winchester, MA: Allen and Unwin.
May, P. J. (2005). Compliance motivations: Perspectives of farmers, homebuilders, and marine facilities. *Law & Policy*, *27*(2), 317–347.
Moffitt, T. E. (1993). Adolescent-limited and life-course-persistent antisocial behavior: A developmental taxonomy. *Psychological Review*, *100*, 674–701.
Muschert, G., Henry, S., Bracy, N. L., & Peguero, A. (Eds.). (2014). *Responding to school violence: Confronting the Columbine effect*. Boulder, CO: Lynne Rienner Publishers.
Ostrom, E. (2005). *Understanding institutional diversity*. Princeton, NJ: Princeton University Press.
Parsons, T. (1951). *The social system*. London: Routledge & Kegan Paul.
Parsons, T. (1962). The law and social control. In W. M. Evan (Eds.), *Law and sociology: Exploratory essays* (pp. 56–72). Glencoe, IL: The Free Press of Glencoe.
Piquero, A. R., & Tibbetts, S. G. (Eds.). (2002). *Rational choice and criminal behavior: Recent research and future challenges*. New York, NY: Routledge.
Podgórecki, A. (1974). *Law and society*. London: Routledge and Kegan Paul.
Ritzer, G. (1975). *Sociology: A multiparadigm science*. Boston, MA: Allyn & Bacon.
Ryan, R. M., & Deci, E. L. (2000). Self-determination theory and the facilitation of intrinsic motivation, social development, and well-being. *American Psychologist*, *55*, 68.
Sampson, R. J., & Laub, J. H. (1993). *Crime in the making: Pathways and turning points through life*. Cambridge: Cambridge University Press.
Schlager, E. (1999). A comparison of frameworks, theories, and models of policy processes. In P. Sabatier (Ed.), *Theories of the policy process* (pp. 233–260). Boulder, CO: Westview Press.
Scholz, J. T., & Lubell, M. (1998). Trust and taxpaying: Testing the Heuristic approach to collective action. *American Journal of Political Science*, *42*, 398–417.
Treviño, A. J. (2008). *The sociology of law: Classical and contemporary perspectives*. New York, NY: Routledge.
Turk, A. (1969). *Criminality and legal order*. Chicago, IL: Rand McNally.
Turk, A. (1982). *Political criminality: The defiance and defense of authority*. Beverly Hills, CA: Sage Publications.
Tyler, T. R. (2006). *Why people obey the law*. Princeton, NJ: Princeton University Press.
Tyler, T. R., & Fagan, J. (2008). Legitimacy and cooperation: Why do people help the police fight crime in their communities. *Ohio State Journal of Criminology and Law*, *6*, 231.
U.S. Department of Justice. (2015, March 4). *Investigation of the Ferguson police department*. DOJ/Civil Rights Division.

2 Policy Compliance

Personal, Social, and Institutional Motivations

Saba Siddiki

Introduction

The topic of this chapter is policy compliance motivations. This topic has been explored extensively by scholars across disciplines given its criticality for effective governance. Previous research confirms that policy compliance is motivated by myriad factors emerging from the structural, institutional, social, and physical environments in which policy directives are being applied and acted upon by individuals. A promising next step for research in this area is to discern how different types of motivational factors interact to influence decisions to comply with institutional directives, such as those constituting public policies. Institutional directives are defined as statements designed to structure the behavior of certain policy targets within specified temporal and spatial conditions by establishing behavioral opportunities and constraints (Crawford & Ostrom, 1995).

In line with the aforementioned recommendation for advancing the study of policy compliance, the research reported in this chapter offers an exploratory and inductive assessment regarding how individuals weight feelings of guilt or shame, fear of social disapproval, and fear of monetary sanctions against each other when making compliance decisions and factors on which the expression of these different motivations are linked. The reported research is informed by previous scholarship on policy compliance as well as behavioral and institutional assumptions presented within the institutional analysis and development (IAD) framework. Within these bodies of scholarship it is recognized that institutional directives can exert explicit, as well as, implicit pressures on individuals to behave in certain ways. Indeed, institutional directives embodying public policies are often specifically designed with the specific intent of compelling behavior. These institutionally oriented pressures interact with a host of individual psychological factors (e.g., perceived emotional and material costs of sanctions) to inform individual decision making regarding compliance.

The study context is U.S. aquaculture. Aquaculture is a salient natural resource–based industry in the United States that few scholars have examined from a social science perspective (Amberg & Hall, 2010; Mazur & Curtis, 2006). Aquaculture is defined as "the propagation and rearing of aquatic species in controlled or selected environments" (NOAA, 1980). Among the reasons that U.S. aquaculture is an appropriate setting in which to explore compliance motivations from an institutional perspective is that it is a relatively newly regulated industry. Aquaculture production, however, has occurred in some states for several decades, allowing for the development of community norms and industry-level best management practices that may or may not be reflected in current state level policies. Coupled with individual characteristics and circumstances, such community norms exert behavioral pressures on individuals, ultimately affecting their decisions to comply, or not, with state-level policies (Ostrom, 2005). Environmental pressures, such as depleting wild fish stocks, have also encouraged a heavier reliance on the aquaculture industry in many coastal states. To facilitate the growth of the industry, many states have urged new industry entrants, affecting the composition of aquaculture producers in terms of backgrounds, aquaculture-specific expertise, and, potentially, industry-related motivations.

Compliance as it relates to this study is characterized as individuals' (e.g., aquaculture producers and regulators) conformance with institutional directives embodying state-level aquaculture policies. State level aquaculture policies govern a wide range of issues pertaining to aquaculture production, such as, the transportation of aquatic organisms, aquaculture siting, the discharge of aquaculture-related waste, and the design of infrastructure used to support aquaculture production. Key objectives of aquaculture policies are to protect human and environmental health. Various provisions are included within policies that are designed to prevent contamination of aquaculture products and protect the natural resource environments surrounding aquaculture facilities. Aquaculture policies specify civil penalties for noncompliance with regulatory directives. Many policies also pose the revocation of aquaculture licenses as a sanction for noncompliance. Beyond just the monetary costs to producers, noteworthy are the potentially serious human health–related consequences that can result from regulatory noncompliance. Like policymakers, aquaculture producers are highly attuned to this potentiality.

At several points throughout the chapter, the reported research is connected to the compliance framework presented in the introduction of the book. Initially, the research study is situated within the compliance framework. In addition, the chapter identifies the analytical leverage that can be gained from applying the framework in relation to the focus of this study, and also generally. Also discussed is how the study, and findings yielding therefrom, may be used as a platform for future research applying the compliance framework. This discussion focuses on ways to develop more precise assumptions about how variables in the "compliance situation context" and "levels of compliance behavior" elements of the framework relate to the other variables in these same and different framework elements. Finally, the chapter concludes with insights drawn from the compliance framework for practitioners involved in the design, implementation, and monitoring and enforcement of policies and a note about the generalizability of the compliance framework across different institutionally governed contexts.

The following section provides a brief overview of the scholarship that informs the reported research.

Brief Overview of Scholarship Guiding Research Study

To frame the study reported in this chapter, the author drew from multiple, related bodies of scholarship. Drawing from these, and the compliance framework presented in this book, the compliance situation or decision context is assumed to be informed by (1) institutional directives, including those codified in formal documents, such as laws or regulations, as well as those reflected in social norms; (2) attributes of the broader social context, or community, in which decision making is occurring; and (3) attributes of the physical or material environment in which decision making is occurring (Ostrom, 2005). Each of these general factors establishes parameters of decision making by essentially conveying a set of behavioral opportunities and constraints. Physical or material attributes and community attributes can also affect the design of institutions that govern decision making. These factors can also influence how individuals interpret and respond to behavioral directives.

Also influencing decision making are individuals' personal characteristics, or what are referred to in the compliance framework as various individual psychological factors that interact with cognitive biases. Central to the latter is that individuals are considered boundedly rational. That is, they are goal oriented and cognitively limited in their ability to internalize and process information and other sources of external stimuli (Ostrom, Schroeder, & Wynne, 1993), for example, information and pressures emerging from institutional directives. They also vary in terms of the value they assign to different behavioral motivations. Where some individuals assign utmost consideration to avoiding financial penalties, others are primarily motivated by their desire to maintain social norms of reciprocity (Crawford & Ostrom, 1995; McCay, 2002; Shepsle, 2006, pp. 24–25). As a result, individuals' responses to institutional directives relate to their personal motivations in different situations.

The discussion of compliance motivations in this chapter is centered on their ability to explain the behavior exhibited by individuals on a daily basis in response to institutional directives. Three types of compliance motivations are the primary focus in this chapter: the personal shame or guilt that individuals experience from not complying with institutional directives, fear of social disapproval, and fear of incurring monetary sanctioning resulting from noncompliance. Numerous scholars have demonstrated the significance of these motivations, as well as other types of factors, in shaping compliance decision making. Scholarship from sociology and social psychology (Elster, 1989; Coleman, 1990; Ajzen, 1988) shows that a variety of factors contribute to regulatees' cost-benefit estimations regarding when to comply with regulatory directives (Hatcher, Jaffry, Thebaud, & Bennett, 2000), including social sanctions and influence, or social disapproval (Sutinen & Kuperan, 1999; Braithwaite & Makkai, 1991), and feelings of personal shame or guilt (Grasmick & Bursik, 1990). Hatcher et al. (2000), for example, found that social pressures served as an effective deterrent to noncompliance relating to catch quotas, or individual fishing quotas, in the United Kingdom. Similarly, Kuperan and Sutinen (1995) have explored the relationship between compliance and feelings of moral obligation among regulatees regarding fishery zoning regulations in Malaysia.

Regulatory scholars have also studied a number of political and regulatory variables in seeking to understand factors that influence compliance, including enforcement practices, specifically, frequency of inspections (Burby & Paterson, 1993; Gray & Scholz, 1993; Helland, 1998; May, 2005), belief congruency between regulators and regulatees regarding the way an industry should be managed (May, 2005), the perceived technical capacity of regulatory personnel (Bardach & Kagan, 1982), and the presence of trust between regulators and regulatees (Scholz & Lubell, 1998). The "compliance situation context" element of the compliance framework encapsulates many of these factors; positing their probable influence on individuals' compliance choices.

While the factors just listed have been widely studied, few scholars have assessed their relative influence in specific compliance decision contexts. Even fewer have sought to understand how different types of factors interact to shape compliance decision making. This research responds to both of these limitations. The following section describes the methods through which regulatory compliance motivations among aquaculture producers were assessed.

Methods

Case Selection

The study under consideration was based on a most similar case study design involving two U.S. states—Virginia and Florida. For the study, the objective was to analyze compliance within the contexts of two states that have similar political, social, community, and industry characteristics; bio-physical attributes; and overall levels of policy compliance but differ with respect to the level of stringency of state aquaculture policies.

In addition to comparability on theoretical variables, Virginia and Florida are comparable in the types of aquaculture produced, the presence of both marine and inland aquaculture, and the relative establishment of the aquaculture industry. Virginia and Florida also have common biophysical characteristics.

Shellfish aquaculture in both states is supported by ample water resources. The Chesapeake Bay as well as numerous estuaries along the Atlantic coast in Virginia and the coastal environments of Florida offer plentiful sites for shellfish production.

The governments of both states support the aquaculture industry on the grounds that shellfish production offers both economic and environmental benefits. Among the environmental benefits of shellfish production are improved water quality, local ecosystem diversity, and the preservation of wild fish stocks (Virginia Marine Resources Commission, 2011). Both states have encouraged newcomers to the industry as well as aquaculture training programs for commercial fisherman interested in transitioning trades. Both of these latter efforts have increased heterogeneity among farmers engaged in aquaculture.

Government efforts to stimulate the growth of the aquaculture industry have been successful. The industry has grown in terms of sales and number of farmers. This growth has captured the attention of policymakers and the public, as well as increased the extent of positive and negative impacts associated with aquaculture development. To respond to these developments, a variety of state level policies have been established to manage the industry. In Virginia, the Virginia Marine Resources Commission is the primary regulating agency charged with implementing and enforcing state level aquaculture policies. In Florida, the Division of Aquaculture was established in 1999 within the Department of Agriculture and Consumer Services for this purpose. A combination of new policies and industry entrants with diverse professional backgrounds has significantly impacted the landscapes of the aquaculture industries in both states. Such changes exert diverse regulatory and social pressures on the respective state industries.

The rationale for the case study design used in this study was that it allowed the author to examine the potential influence of a set of intervening factors (i.e., compliance motivations) alongside policy stringency on compliance, while holding other contextual variables relatively constant. Consistency in compliance levels and contextual characteristics across cases, despite variation policy stringency, suggests other factors are driving compliance decision making; for example, personal and/or peer-based motivations.

Data Collection and Analysis

Data for this study was obtained in two steps. First, the researcher coded all state level aquaculture policies in Virginia and Florida, and second, the researcher conducted interviews with 15 members of the aquaculture communities in each state, for a total of 30 interviews. The interviews consisted of two parts. In the first part, the researcher conducted a semi-structured interview using a set of predesigned questions. Interview questions were designed to capture perceptions regarding aquaculture policies as well as compliance motivations. The second part of the interview consisted of a Q-Sort exercise specifically designed to capture interviewees' level and perceptions of compliance with state aquaculture policies.

Coding

To gain a comprehensive understanding of the policies governing aquaculture in the two study states, and to serve as a basis for questions posed in the interviews and design of the Q-sort exercise, all of the state-level aquaculture policies from Virginia and Florida were first comprehensively coded. Coding of the policies focused on identifying the main elements of the institutional directives comprising the policies. First, the policies were parsed into individual directives. These institutional directives identify, at least, an action; a policy target relating to this action; what is being acted upon by the policy target; and the temporal, procedural, and/or spatial conditions in which the action occurs. For example, "aquaculture producers submit a facility report annually." In this case, "aquaculture producers" are the policy target, "submit" is the action, "a facility report" is what is being acted upon, and "annually" is the temporal condition of the action. Some institutional directives also specify whether policy targets are allowed, required, or forbidden to perform the action they are connected to in an institutional directive. For example, "aquaculture producers must submit a facility report annually." The additional inclusion of "must" in this directive makes the action of submitting a facility report annually mandatory. Some directives, in addition to all of this information—action, policy target, action conditions, prescriptiveness of policy action, receiver of policy action—also stipulate rewards or sanctions associated with compliance/noncompliance with institutional directives. For example, "aquaculture producers must submit a facility report annually or have their aquaculture licenses revoked." "License revocation" is the sanction imposed for aquaculture producers' failure to annually submit a facility report.

Once policies were broken into institutional directives, each was coded for the relevant action, policy target, action conditions, prescriptiveness of policy action (if specified), and rewards or sanctions for policy compliance (if specified). For the prescriptiveness of policy action, it was noted whether a policy target must, must not, may, or may not perform a policy action.

The full population of aquaculture policies enacted as of the time of this research, in both states, was coded. In total, eight policy documents were coded for Virginia (n = the number of institutional directives per document): Virginia State Code Ch. 28 relating to aquaculture (n = 82), Virginia State Code Ch. 150 relating to shellfish sanitation (n = 13), Aquaculture Structures Rule (n = 10), Harvest Reporting Rules (n = 32), Enclosures Rule (n = 63), Striped Bass Rule (n = 55), Cobia Rule (n = 16), and the Shellfish Restrictions Rule (n = 32). Four regulatory documents were coded for Florida: Florida Statute Ch. 597 relating to aquaculture (n = 281), Florida BMPs Rules (n = 544), Florida Submerged Lands Statute relating to aquaculture (n = 14), and the Florida Submerged Lands Rule (n = 172).

Interviews

Thirty two-part interviews were conducted for this study; 22 in person and eight by phone. A purposive, snow-ball sampling technique was used to select interview participants in Florida. A regulatory official provided a list of 50 names to the researcher to contact for participation in the study, from which 11 potential interviewees were randomly selected. Those aquaculture producers contacted for an interview expressed varying degrees of familiarity with the state regulators. For Virginia, the researcher randomly selected participants from a directory of Virginia aquaculture producers. The final sample of interview participants across the two states consisted of 18 shellfish producers, seven regulatory officials, two ornamental fish producers, two aquaculture processors/handlers and ornamental fish producers, and one shellfish and finfish producer.

Questions posed to interviewees in the first part of the interview related to the perceived appropriateness of state aquaculture policies and interviewees' personal motivations for compliance. To link interview responses with the coding exercise, interviewees were asked questions relating to different elements of institutional directives. The following questions were asked of interviewees:

- [Policy Target] You are one of the people most often referred to in this legislation. Does this accurately reflect your level of involvement in the aquaculture industry?
- [Receiver of Policy Action] You are/are not listed is relation to many "items." [Interviewee provided examples; "facility report" in institutional directive example listed in this section.] How do you think this reflects the scope of activities that you are involved in on a daily basis?
- [Prescriptiveness of Policy Action] Some of the prescribed activities that are assigned to you in the legislation include [X]. How do you interpret different prescriptive operators in relation to these? [may, may not, must, must not]
- [Action Conditions] How do prescribed conditions influence how you interpret prescriptive operators? [for example must, must not, may, may not]
- [Rewards or Sanctions for Policy Compliance] I noticed there [are/are not] a lot of sanctions described in the legislation for instances in which compliance is not achieved. Why do you think this is the case? How do you feel about the current level of stringency of state aquaculture policies?

Asking interviewees what tempered their interpretation of the prescriptive force of different directives sheds light on their compliance motivations. For further insight on such, interviewees were also asked to answer the following questions: Who holds you accountable [people, organizations, etc.] for performing duties as prescribed in this regulation? Along with this question, interviewees were asked to comment on whether fear of monetary sanctions, personal feelings of guilt or shame, or fear of social disapproval were most influential in shaping their decisions to comply with regulatory directives.

A second facet of compliance motivations explored using this set of questions was to identify linked compliance factors; i.e., factors associated with feelings of guilt or shame, fear of social disapproval, or fear of monetary sanctions. In many cases, interviewees provided elaborations on their weighting of compliance motivations (i.e., fear of monetary sanctions, personal feelings of guilt or shame, and fear of social disapproval). Thus, in order to assess linked compliance factors, the researcher examined, first, how interviewees weighted the motivations provided by the researcher, and, second, interviewees' elaborations as to why these motivations were influential to them. For example, one aquaculture producer stated that social disapproval is his primary compliance motivation, and then further elaborated that this stems from a desire to maintain a positive image of his family business, which has operated in the community for a long time and has a good reputation among members of the industry. In analyzing a response such as this one, social disapproval would be identified as a compliance motivation, and the desire to maintain a positive business image would be characterized as a linked compliance factor.

In the second part of the formal interviews, study participants were asked to participate in a Q-Sort exercise to assess individual interviewee compliance with regulatory directives. The Q-Sort is a methodological technique that allows study participants to subjectively sort a pre-selected set of statements into a set of categories designated by the researcher (McKeown & Thomas, 1988). Sample statements can be chosen following an unstructured or structured approach. In the latter approach, the researcher chooses the statements that will be sorted based upon prior collected information, such as through preliminary interviews or from the examination of existing documents.

A modified, structured Q-Sort was used in the discussed study in which each participant was given a set of 20 cards containing directives that describe activities that relate to her/his position in relation to aquaculture as prescribed in regulatory documents but without the prescribed prescriptive operator. The participant was asked if she/he "must," "must not," "may," or "may not" perform the activity described on the card based on what she/he actually does, not what she/he knows or thinks the regulation says. Once the sorting exercise was completed, the researcher asked the participant to explain the placement of directives.

To analyze the Q-Sort data, a percent agreement rate was calculated to reflect how much an interviewee's activities align with what is prescribed in policy directives. This was done by comparing the prescriptive operator (i.e., must, must not, may, may not) that interviewees assigned to different directives versus the prescriptive operators really assigned to the directives in the policies. Lack of agreement between prescriptive operators would be characterized as a discrepancy between prescribed and actual behavior, or a case of non-compliance. As both Virginia and Florida had multiple policies from which Q-Sort directives were drawn, the number of directives chosen in the Q-Sort sample from each document was proportionate to the number of directives in a particular document relative to the total number of directives across all policy documents for a particular policy target.

Results

Measuring Compliance Using the Q-Sort Exercise

Table 2.1 summarizes the results from the Q-Sort showing average percent agreement on prescriptive operators for institutional directives used as part of the Q-Sort exercise, in and between Virginia and Florida. Table 2.1 also presents the issues on which the most discrepancy was observed between prescribed and actual behavior. The findings from the Q-Sort exercise show that discrepancies between prescribed and actual activities are lowest for "must" directives (average agreement = 79%) and highest for "may" (average agreement = 40%) and "may not" directives (average agreement = 38%). Virginia and Florida differed in levels of discrepancy relating to "must not" directives, with much higher discrepancies being observed in Virginia.

In Virginia, the most discrepancy between prescribed and actual behavior was observed on issues pertaining to the use of hydraulic dredges (must not), infrastructure design (must not), placement of temporary protective enclosures (must not and may), and navigation (may not). In Florida, most discrepancy

Table 2.1 Summary of Q-Sort Results: Agreement Between Prescribed and Actual Behavior

	Virginia	*Florida*	*Total*	*Issues With Most Discrepancy With Policies (VA)*	*Issues With Most Discrepancy With Policies (FL)*
Must	80%	77%	79%	Few issues with high disagreement	Treatment and retaining of effluent
Must Not	34%	69%	50%	Use of hydraulic dredge, extending structures higher than 12 inches, placement of temporary protective enclosures	Discharge of effluent into wetlands
May	39%	41%	40%	Placement of temporary enclosures	Treatment and discharge of effluent
May Not	25%	52%	38%	Effects on navigation from aquaculture activities	Discharge of effluent, sale and transfer of Atlantic sturgeon, medication use for extra-label purposes

was observed, across all four deontic categories, regarding treatment and discharge of effluent. In the may not category, the sale and transfer of Atlantic sturgeon and use of medications for extra label purposes were also issues on which high discrepancy was noted. Interviewees expressed perceptions that directives pertaining to these different topics were either unclear or inappropriately matched to the industry contexts.

Compliance Motivations

A central focus of this study relating to compliance motivations was understanding the relative influence of fear of monetary fines, fear of social disapproval, and feelings of guilt and/or shame in shaping individuals' decisions to comply. While many interviewees indicated that all three factors were influential in their decisions about complying with aquaculture policies, only 16% of individuals cited fear of monetary sanctioning as their primary compliance motivation. Forty-four percent of producers cited fear of social disapproval as their primary compliance motivation. Forty percent of individuals cited feelings of guilt or shame as being their primary compliance motivation. Further, while not asked about this factor directly, 24% of producers cited producing a quality product as their primary compliance motivation.

A second objective of this research was to identify factors linked to the expression of the aforementioned compliance motivations. Table 2.2 provides a list of factors cited most often by interviewees in connection with the compliance motivations they were specifically asked to comment on. These factors were explicitly linked to the compliance motivations by interviewees, often coming through in interviewee's rationales regarding why the different motivations were relevant in their compliance decision making. Following Table 2.2 are quotations from interviewees in which they link such factors

Table 2.2 Contingent Compliance Motivations

Probed Motivations	*Linked Compliance Factors*
Fear of Monetary Sanctioning	• Concern over an inability to pay fines
Fear of Social Disapproval	• Maintaining reputation of family or business • An interest in maintaining the long-term sustainability of the state aquaculture industry
Feelings of Guilt or Shame	• A moral commitment to conduct aquaculture appropriately • A regard for the rules • A desire to have a prosperous business • A desire to protect the natural environment • An adherence to religious values to abide by the law • A desire to prevent consumer illness associated with eating a contaminated aquaculture product

with compliance motivations. It is important to note that no directionality of influence among different types of compliance motivations can be surmised from these data. That is, one cannot posit based on these data which factors are moderating others.

Interviewees linked monetary penalties with the viability of their operations or job security. Interviewee 29, for example, voiced concern that monetary penalties could mean one's operation shutting down. Interviewee 15 commented that no one wants to risk losing a job as a result of incurring penalties for noncompliance. Reflecting factors linked with fears of social disapproval, interviewee 29 also said, "producers put pressure on each other to do things right because the whole industry could be negatively impacted." Interviewee 20 responded when asked whether a fear of monetary sanctions, fear of social disapproval, or feelings of guilt/shame most directly inform compliance decisions: "Peer pressure—[farmer] works for family business that has been around for forty years. The business has maintained a good reputation for that whole time and wants to keep it that way into the future."

Factors linked to feelings of guilt or shame include concerns regarding environmental degradation, religious obligations, and underlying value systems. The following statements provide examples of ways in which these factors were expressed in interviewees' responses. Interviewee 12 said, "Don't want to be responsible for any environmental degradation because [I] failed to administer environmental regulations properly." Interviewee 19 commented, "Want to do what is right—avoid sin." Interviewee 24 said, "Just worry about what is right and wrong in my mind."

Discussion

With the broad objective of seeking to understand what motivates policy compliance, the reported study responds to the following questions based on data obtained through an exploratory, qualitative, comparative case study. First, what motivating factors are most influential to individual decision makers regarding compliance with state level aquaculture policies: fear of monetary sanctioning, fear of social disapproval, or feelings of personal guilt or shame, and second, what types of factors are linked to these compliance motivations?

With regard to compliance, one clear finding that emerged from the interviews was that compliance is linked to particular issues. Further, that noncompliance, as measured through the Q-Sort exercise, has often to do with perceived ambiguity or appropriateness of institutional directives. The Q-Sort results also indicate that, generally, aquaculturists tend to know what exactly they must do in their operations, and are less informed or exhibit varying degrees of conformity (by either over complying or under complying) with directives that specify allowed activities.

With respect to compliance motivations, the results indicate that a fear of monetary sanctions is the least influential motivator to comply with policies. Rather, the most influential motivator was found to be fear of social disapproval, followed by feelings of guilt or shame. In addition to these motivations, which were specifically probed by the researcher, the desire to maintain a quality product was also cited by several interviewees as an influential factor shaping compliance decisions. The results from the interviews also indicated that the expression of these primary compliance motivations is linked to a variety of other factors, such as a desire to protect the natural environment, to prevent consumers from becoming sick as a result of consuming a contaminated product, and to prevent conflict with neighbors and other resource users.

This research offers insights on the social aspects of aquaculture production. Much of the research that has been conducted on aquaculture to date has focused on the physiological or infrastructural aspects of the industry. However, social considerations abound in this growing industry from resistance from the general public (Amberg & Hall, 2010; Mazur & Curtis, 2006) to the role of collaborative decision making in aquaculture policy development (Leach, Weible, Vince, Siddiki, & Calanni, 2013). Understanding the social aspects of the industry is critical for informing its long-term sustainability. Evident in the findings from this study is that aquaculture producers have a strong internal ethic to produce a good quality product that will not pose threats to the industry at large or to aquaculture consumers. This industry level consciousness is also reflected in the finding that fear of social disapproval is the primary motivator driving producers' compliance decisions. The extent to which the findings from this study are generalizable may be ascertained by exploring similar variables within different natural resource–based industry contexts.

The findings from this research provide a platform for developing the compliance framework presented in this book, and/or guiding future applications thereof, for the study of institutional compliance. Included next are recommendations relating to the following framework elements: "compliance situation context" and "levels of compliance behavior."

With respect to the compliance situation context, further research could inform how exactly factors relating to "degree and type of monitoring/enforcement," "design of specific rules," "capacity," and "individual psychological factors" interact to affect individual compliance decision making. This research seeks to uncover, through an inductive, qualitative assessment of compliance motivations, the relationship between factors belonging to these different categories. These same relationships, or rather interactions, could be assessed by applying statistical techniques to larger sets of quantitative data points. This research could then be used as a basis for offering more precise propositions relating to the "compliance situation context" component of the framework.

Relating to the "level of compliance behavior" element of the framework, future research applications could assess the affect of what are deemed as linked compliance motivations in this study when individuals are engaging in decision making in group settings; that is, in contexts in which private compliance decisions are immediately made known to others within groups in which they are participating. Of analytical importance here would be determining how decision making within groups moderates the expression or influence of different compliance motivations. Substantial research on cooperative theory (Ostrom, 1990) could be used to inform expectations about how individuals might behave.

Finally, there are insights that can be drawn from this research for practitioners charged with designing, implementing, or monitoring and enforcing policy directives. Foremost, the factors that inform compliance decision making are multifarious and interacting. Aquaculture producers are driven by commitments to their peers, as well as an awareness of the implications of their practices for consumers of their products and the industry at large. They also tend to be highly competent in their trade and thus have strong views about how aquaculture should be practiced. Policy targets in different cases, as a result of differences in their personal characteristics or attributes in the context in which they operate, may be influenced by different constellations of motivations. It is thus important for policymakers, implementers, and monitors and enforcers to have a keen understanding of the environments in which they are operating. The compliance framework posited in this book offers a useful guide as to what contextual factors to consider as well as the various motivations that may affect decision making. Also valuable about the framework offered in this book is that it is agnostic to any particular structure of governance. It can easily be applied in different jurisdictional (local, state, national) contexts.

References

Ajzen, I. (1988). *Attitudes, personality, and behavior*. Buckingham, Great Britain: Open University Press.

Amberg, S., & Hall, T. E. (2010). Precision and rhetoric in media reporting about contamination in Farmed Salmon. *Science Communication, 32*(4), 489–513.

Bardach, E., & Kagan, R. A. (1982). *Going by the book: The problem of regulatory unreasonableness*. London: Transaction Publishers.

Braithwaite, J., & Makkai, T. (1991). Testing an expected utility model if corporate deterrence. *Law & Society Review, 25*(1), 7–40.

Burby, R. J., & Paterson, R. G. (1993). Improving compliance with state environmental regulations. *Journal of Policy Analysis and Management, 12*, 753–772.

Coleman, J. S. (1990). *Foundations of social theory*. Chicago, IL: Belknap Press.

Crawford, Sue E. S., & Ostrom, E. (1995). A grammar of institutions. *American Political Science Review, 89*(3), 582–600.

Elster, J. (1989). *The cement of society: A study of social order*. Cambridge: Cambridge University Press.

Grasmick, H. G., & Bursik, Jr. R. J. (1990). Conscience, significant others, and rational choice: Extending the deterrence model. *Law & Society Review, 24*(3), 837–861.

Gray, W. B., & Scholz, J. (1993). Does regulatory enforcement work? A panel analysis and OSHA enforcement. *Law & Society Review, 27*, 177–213.

Hatcher, A., Jaffry, S., Thebaud, O., & Bennett, E. (2000). Normative and social influences affecting compliance with fishery regulations. *Land Economics, 76*(3), 448–461.

Helland, E. (1998). The enforcement of pollution control laws: Inspections, violations, and self-reporting. *Review of Economics and Statistics, 80*, 141–153.

Kuperan, K., & Sutinen, J. G. (1995). Compliance with zoning regulations in Malaysian fisheries. In D.S. Liao (Eds.), *International Cooperation for Fisheries and Aquaculture Development: Proceedings of the VIIth Conference of the International Institute of Fisheries Economics and Trade, Vol. I.* Keelung. Taiwan: National Taiwan Ocean University.

Leach, W. D., Weible, C. M., Vince, S. R., Siddiki, S. N., & Calanni, J. C. (2013). Fostering learning through collaboration: Knowledge acquisition and belief change in marine aquaculture partnerships. *Journal of Public Administration Research and Theory, 24*(3), 591–622.

May, P. J. (2005). Regulations and compliance motivations: Examining different approaches. *Public Administration Review, 65*(1), 31–44.

Mazur, N., & Curtis, A. L. (2006). Risk perceptions, aquaculture, and issues of trust: Lessons from Australia. *Society and Natural Resources, 19*, 791–808.

National Oceanic and Atmospheric Administration. National Aquaculture Act. Public Law 96-362, 94 Stat. 1198, 16 U.S.C. 2801, et seq. 1980. http://www.nmfs.noaa.gov/sfa/sfweb/aqua_act.htm

McCay, B. J. (2002). Emergence of institutions for the commons. In E. Ostrom, T. Dietz, N. Dolsak, P. C. Stern, S. Stonich, & E. U. Weber (Eds.), *The drama of the commons* (pp. 361–402). Washington, DC: National Academy Press.

Ostrom, E. (1990). *Governing the commons: The evolution of institutions for collective action.* New York, NY: Cambridge University Press.

Ostrom, E. (2005). *Understanding institutional diversity.* Princeton, NJ: Princeton University Press.

Ostrom, E., Schroeder, L., & Wynne, S. (1993). *Institutional incentives and sustainable development: Infrastructure policies in perspective.* Boulder, CO: Westview Press.

Scholz, J. T., & Lubell, M. (1998). Trust and taxpaying: Testing the Heuristic approach to collective action. *American Journal of Political Science, 42*, 398–417.

Shepsle, K. (2006). Rational choice institutionalism. In R. A. W. Rhodes, S. A. Binder, & B. A. Rockman (Eds.), *The Oxford handbook of political institutions* (pp. 23–38). New York, NY: Oxford University Press.

Sutinen, J. G., & Kuperan, K. (1999). A socio-economic theory of regulatory compliance. *International Journal of Social Economics, 26*, 174–193.

Virginia Marine Resources Commission. (2011). *Shellfish aquaculture, farming, and gardening.* Retrieved from www.mrc.state.va.us/Shellfish_Aquaculture.shtm

3 What Comes After Marijuana Legalization?

An Exploratory Assessment of Users' Attitudes Towards Rule Compliance

Salvador Espinosa[1]

Introduction

Marijuana legalization is gaining momentum in the United States, as a growing number of states have enacted, or are in the process of enacting legislation to regulate the different uses of marijuana, as well as its stages of production. This has occurred despite the fact that the federal government still considers marijuana an illegal drug. The movement towards decriminalization and legalization is also observed internationally, as attitudes toward the use of marijuana for medical or even recreational purposes are starting to shift.

The trend towards decriminalization and legalization is partly fueled by mounting evidence pointing to the failure of drug policies based on prohibition and the criminalization of consumption (Zedillo & Wheeler, 2012). Additional evidence supporting legalization comes from scientific studies documenting the effects and potential benefits of medical marijuana (Choo et al., 2014; Keyes et al., 2016). Numerous discussions that are taking place nowadays highlight the need for policies that focus less on prohibition and criminalization and emphasize strategies that combine legalization and harm reduction strategies.

The possibility that marijuana consumption increases after legalization, however, remains a concern. The UN Office on Drug and Crime reports that (besides alcohol) marijuana is the most widely used drug around the world, with about 183 million users. But while consumption patterns have remained stable worldwide, use in North America has increased. In the United States, the focus of attention in this exploratory study, the peak of marijuana use occurs between 18 and 25 years of age (Center for Behavioral Health Statistics and Quality, 2015).

Why should the increase in marijuana consumption among the youth be of concern? While a consensus on the negative effects of marijuana is far from being reached, research shows that ". . . exposure to cannabinoids during early puberty can interfere with brain development and cause long-lasting neurological alterations" (Esgate & Groome, 2005:186). Indeed,

> [a]ccumulating evidence from both animal and human studies suggests that regular heavy use during this period is associated with more severe

and persistent negative outcomes than use during adulthood, suggesting that the adolescent brain may be particularly vulnerable to the effects of cannabis exposure.

(Lubman, Cheetham, & Yucel, 2015:1)

So regardless of the views that one may have on the pertinence of marijuana legalization, it is important to highlight that if consumed regularly at an early age, there is a potential public health problem that should not be ignored. The issue deserves careful discussion, especially in the context of recent efforts to create regulated markets that permit the legal use of the drug.

The chapter contributes to ongoing and upcoming debates on the future of marijuana regulation by building on the idea that marijuana users could be persuaded to comply voluntarily with rules or policy initiatives seeking to curb consumption. Exploring the potential for the use of persuasion as a tool to encourage voluntary compliance calls for a careful assessment of the interconnection among rules or public policies, the behavior of the target audience, and the outcomes that one expects to obtain. In all this, having a good understanding of the attitudes and perceptions of the individual whose behavior one tries to influence becomes of utmost importance.

Attitudes and perceptions are closely related terms. An attitude is "a mindset or a tendency to act in a particular way due to both an individual's experience and temperament" (Pickens, 2005:44). Perception, on the other hand, refers to ". . . the process by which organisms interpret and organize sensation to produce a meaningful experience of the world" (Lindsay & Norman, 1977, as cited in Pickens, 2005:52). The significance of perception for a study linking persuasion and voluntary compliance has to do with the cognitive process that occurs when an individual faces multiple scenarios and is asked to make a choice from this menu of possibilities.

One way in which this cognitive process can be studied is by exposing individuals to a particular situation or stimulus (e.g., a visual cue with a message recommending a course of action). The individual then interprets the situation or stimuli, and turns it into something meaningful based on prior experiences. This adds to biographical and psychological pre-disposition accumulated through environmental and situational contexts. However, what an individual interprets or perceives may be substantially different from reality (Pickens, 2005). It is precisely the potential divergence between what rules or policy programs seek and how the individuals perceive such rules and policy programs that motivates this research study. This approach to public policy design has been particularly salient in efforts to tackle public health issues such as obesity (Ammerman, Hartman, & DeMarco, 2017), diabetes (Bradley & Speight, 2002; O'Brien, Moran, & Tang, 2016), and tobacco use (Boynton et al., 2016), among others. The discussion that follows contributes to a growing literature seeking to incorporate insights from cognitive and behavioral sciences into public policy design (Lunn, 2014; OECD, 2017; World Bank, 2015), but more specifically, to an evolving literature advocating for the use of behavior-informed policies to try to encourage demand for healthy choices.

Under what conditions can marijuana users be persuaded to comply with a rule or policy program whose ultimate goal is to discourage consumption? It is argued here that unveiling the link that exists among individual attitudes and compliance decisions is at the crux of any analysis, as it will be a crucial determinant of the effectiveness of a rule or policy program.

Psychologists have extensively studied the role of persuasion in compliance. A branch of the literature in this field considers that certain individual motivators tend to drive cognitions and behaviors, which end up affecting compliance and conformity (R. Cialdini & Trost, 1998; R. B. Cialdini & Goldstein, 2004; Wood, 2000). A core idea in this line of research is the possibility that individuals (i.e., the targets or clients of a policy intervention) ". . . are motivated to form accurate perceptions of reality and react accordingly, to develop and preserve meaningful social relationships, and to maintain a favorable self-concept" (R. B. Cialdini & Goldstein, 2004:591). Such an approach explores how susceptible one is to an external cue or influence, and the behavior that may result from it.

The research questions driving this exploratory study are as follows:

1. What are the attitudes of marijuana users towards its use and the consequences of using it?
2. Given these attitudes, under what conditions would marijuana users be more willing to comply with a rule or policy program aimed at discouraging consumption?
3. What are the implications in terms of a rule and/or policy design that one can derive from answering the preceding questions?

This research has a clear connection with the subject matter of the book. As stated in Chapter 1, compliance can be defined as a behavioral state where individuals are expected to conform to directives embodied in laws, social norms, or organizational policies. This approach to the study of compliance is relevant in the context of drug policy design because the effectiveness of any policy measure seeking to modify consumption choices will depend upon the users' willingness to adhere to the established directives. And such willingness will not be a direct consequence of the directive but the outcome of a more complex cognitive mental process by which individuals interpret and internalize the information embedded in a rule or policy, and react to it. Given that the causal connection among rules, behavior, and expected policy outcomes is not straightforward, the point of departure for this study of compliance is a research design focusing on the behavior of an individual (i.e., a micro-level approach), the factors that could be associated with his/her willingness to comply or deviate with the policy objective, and how this knowledge can contribute to enhance drug policy effectiveness.

Chapter 1 states that compliance can be studied descriptively, diagnostically, and/or normatively. The discussion that takes place in the following pages combines description and diagnosis, as it constitutes the first attempt to further knowledge on the marijuana users' attitudes, the factors driving consumption of this drug, and the extent to which they would be prone to comply with policies seeking a voluntary reduction in consumption. The diagnostic will contribute to a better understanding of the factors animating marijuana use among the youth, as well as factors that could increase the likelihood of compliance with new rules or policy programs aimed at reducing marijuana use. Description, on the other hand, will provide readers with background information to engage in a research project that starts with an exploration of drug policy, but whose long-term objective is to contribute to ongoing and future debates on the use of cognitive and behavioral sciences to inform regulatory and policy design.

The rest of the chapter is organized as follows: The next section sets the context for the discussion by reviewing the pertinent literature on the determinants of marijuana use and the literature relating attitudes, perceptions, persuasion, and compliance. The chapter then discusses the chosen theoretical approach and the empirical strategy to answer the research questions formulated earlier, and reports the findings of a pilot study conducted among marijuana users between 18 and 24 years old living in the San Diego (California) region. All of this is then used as a starting point to reflect on the implications of these findings and to highlight the elements of a research agenda that incorporates a behavioral perspective to drug policy and regulatory design.

Background Literature

In spite of the alleged benefits of moderate marijuana use, evidence shows that consumption during adolescence can be associated with higher health risks than if consumed during adulthood, as effects can be more persistent and severe (Lubman et al., 2015). The epidemiological and clinical literature documents the link between cannabis use, brain development, and mental health. Tetrahydrocannabinol (THC), the main psychoactive component in cannabis sativa (a variety of marijuana), can increase the risk of adverse psychological outcomes such as depression and anxiety (Degenhardt, Hall, & Lynskey, 2003; Moore et al., 2007), impairments in learning and memory (Solowij & Battisti, 2008), or deficits in executive functions such as decision making or attention (Crean, Crane, & Mason, 2011).

The literature on the subject matter includes studies focusing on the youth, a segment of the population that can be particularly affected if they choose to use marijuana regularly (Pearson, Liese, & Dvorak, 2017; Suerken et al., 2014). Suerken et al. (2014:302), for example, identify predictors of marijuana use among first and second semester students in colleges located in North Carolina and Virginia (USA). About one-third of respondents were using marijuana when this study was conducted, and 8.5% of respondents accepted that their first use occurred in their first year of college. Participants also acknowledged that

> . . . having at least $100 per month in spending money; attending church rarely or never; current use of cigarettes, alcohol, and hookah tobacco;

> lifetime use of other illicit drugs; and a higher propensity toward sensation seeking were associated with a higher likelihood of having used marijuana at least once in college. Hispanic ethnicity, living on campus, and current use of cigarettes and alcohol were associated with a higher likelihood of initiating marijuana use during freshmen year.

Pearson et al. (2017) studied the prevalence of marijuana use and its consequences using a bigger sample (n = 8,141 students from 11 universities throughout the United States). Findings relating to consumption rates were similar to other studies using representative samples. However, the authors observed large differences in the reported consequences of marijuana use. The study listed 50 items reflecting eight dimensions associated with such consequences (social-interpersonal consequences, impaired control, negative self-perception, self-care, risk behaviors, academic/occupational consequences, physical dependence, and blackout use). On average, respondents experienced eight negative consequences, the most common being driving a vehicle under the influence of the drug, saying or doing embarrassing things, unplanned use of the drug, and feeling ill the morning after use.

The role that peers play in first use of the drug has long been established (Kandel, 1973). Recent research, nevertheless, highlights that on many occasions marijuana use among college students is influenced by incorrect perceptions about friends' norms of use (Kilmer et al., 2006). Although friends do play a role in first-time use of marijuana, other factors influence perceptions. Bachman, Johnson, and O'Malley (1998) review historic trends among high school seniors in the United States and show that changes in the society's views are correlated with patterns of use. The results of their quantitative analysis of large samples of users (ranging between 61,000 and 82,475) allow them to conclude that individual lifestyle factors such as grades, religious commitment, or truancy do not explain historic trends. However, factors such as the perceived risk of harmfulness and disapproval can be considered as salient (Bachman et al., 1998).

A central tenet in this chapter is to explore individual-level factors driving marijuana use among young consumers, to learn about circumstances that would motivate them to reduce consumption, as well as factors that would increase their willingness to comply with rules of policy programs seeking to curb consumption. This exploration is a necessary first step to inform debates on the design of drug policies that are no longer anchored in the notions of criminalization and prohibition but on persuasion.

The notion of persuasion is a core element in the literature on social influence (R. B. Cialdini & Goldstein, 2004; Wood, 2000), the literature on self-regulatory behavior (Bandura, 1991, 2015; Binswanger, 1991), and the literature linking behavior to public policy (Oliver, 2013; Shafir, 2013; Thaler & Sunstein, 2009).

Cialdini and Goldstein (2004) review some of the works pertaining to the so-called social-cognitive movement written between 1997 and 2002. Researchers in this movement consider that individuals have implicit or explicit goals, and that these goals affect the way in which they process information and make decisions. For Cialdini and Goldstein, cognition and decision making in compliance and conformity situations are driven by three core objectives: accuracy, which has to do with the motivation of an individual to attain his/her goals in the most effective and rewarding way; affiliation, which is related to the motivation to create and maintain meaningful social relations with others; and the goal of maintaining a positive self-concept (a notion of particular relevance in the study of compliance, especially when the role of self-perception is evaluated). In this literature, compliance involves acquiescence, in other words, a voluntary agreement with a particular kind of communication or objective. Compliance is then conceived as the consequential response to a particular cue (such cue can be devised as a tactic, directive, or activity).

The notion of self-regulatory behavior allows one to start thinking about the subject matter of this research study from a theoretical standpoint. As Bandura (1991) explains, human behavior is extensively motivated and regulated by self-influence. This behavior operates through continuous self-monitoring of one's behavior, the judgment of one's behavior in relation to personal standards and environmental circumstances, and affective self-reaction. This approach assumes that individuals' actions follow a purpose and are regulated by forethought. Consequently, "people form beliefs about what they can do, they anticipate the likely consequences of prospective actions, they set goals for themselves, and plan actions that are intended to produce the desired outcomes" (p. 248). These assumptions about individual behavior have been a reference point for studies exploring drug use among diverse segments of the population (Armitage, Conner, Loach, & Willetts, 1999; Kam, Matsunaga, Hecht, & Ndiaye, 2009).

The literature overviewed earlier can be linked to a line of work advocating for the use of behavior-informed theories and methods to improve regulatory and policy effectiveness. Proponents of this approach consider that one can devise specific, cost-effective interventions, aimed at encouraging or discouraging actions or behaviors (Thaler & Sunstein, 2009). The theoretical knowledge supporting such interventions can be applied to drug policy design, more specifically, in the crafting of rules or policy programs seeking to modify consumption patterns in a context of legalization and freedom of choice. But to do so it is necessary to have a better understanding of the factors that may determine the success or failure of an intended policy intervention. Some of those factors will be closely connected with the individual, his/her perceptions about the world, or the environment where his/her interactions take place.

As the previously mentioned literature shows, marijuana use is a complex and multidimensional problem. What the framework introduced in Chapter 1 does is then to facilitate the contextualization of the issue, facilitating the classification of the determinants of marijuana use. Breaking a clearly complex problem into manageable pieces allows one to study a particular aspect of marijuana use and, later on, to expand the scope of the analysis and explore the inter-connections among individual, group, and system-level variables. While it is clear that the design of policies to address issues pertaining to marijuana use must take into consideration such inter-connections, the exploratory work that follows starts with a close look at the attitudes of individuals, leaving the analysis of the group where they interact, or the broader social and institutional context, for a subsequent inquiry.

Research Design

Let us assume that the goal of an exogenously determined rule or policy is to persuade an individual to voluntarily reduce his/her consumption of marijuana. This chapter posits that the success of those rules or policies will depend upon the attitudes of the individual towards various factors, such as the perceived consequences of using the drug, or their perceptions about the entity in charge of the design or enforcement of the behavioral directive. A systematic study of these factors is a necessary precondition to understand what animates compliance among marijuana users.

The connection between attitudes and compliance with (or adherence to) an exogenously determined behavioral directive is studied here by developing a research protocol combining semi-structured interviews and a method known as Q-sorting (McKeown & Thomas, 2013; Watts & Stenner, 2012). This method allows researchers to learn about ". . . people's perceptions of their world from the vantage point of self-reference" (McKeown & Thomas, 2013:1). Contrary to methods such as surveys and opinion polls (where questions are asked sequentially), Q-sorting presents all the information related to a topic at the same time, leaving users with the task of organizing each piece of information based on the perceived relevance that they give to each element. By doing so, participants disclose valuable information about their views about a particular topic, their preferences, or the issues that they deem relevant. In the context of a study on compliance and marijuana policy, Q-sorting allows a researcher to explore, for example, if the attitudes towards regulation will be similar among individuals with diverse characteristics or backgrounds.

This exploratory research study uses Q-sorting to gather information about the attitudes of young marijuana users towards marijuana use, the perceived consequences of using the drug, the circumstances under which users would consider reducing marijuana consumption, and their attitudes towards rule compliance.

Four envelopes were created to conduct the Q-sorting exercise for this study. Each envelope contained a deck of cards. In each card, there was a phrase describing a situation related to each of the dimensions of consumption mentioned earlier. Each card was associated with a letter, which was written on the back.[2]

After determining eligibility for the study and answering background questions, the researcher met with participants individually. Participants received the first envelope and were asked to sort the cards by using a template like the one shown in Figure 3.1 as a guide (the number of spaces available varied in each Q-sorting exercise to reflect the number of statements that each envelope contained).

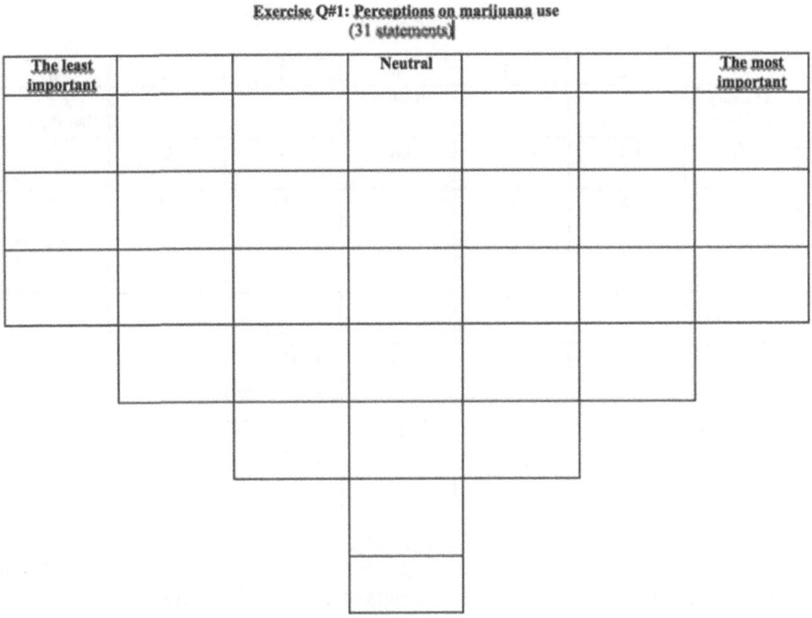

Figure 3.1 Template for a Q-sorting Exercise

The cards in each deck were sorted based on the importance that participants gave to each statement (i.e., from the least to the most important). There was no time limit to complete the exercise. The method required participants to make choices about the relative importance that they assigned to each statement.

Upon completion of the exercise, the interviewer turned the cards and recorded the letters appearing in the back of each card. Figure 3.2 shows a sample of a completed Q-sorting exercise.

The cards in each envelope were aimed at gathering data on a particular dimension of marijuana use. The first envelope sought to gather information on the reasons why marijuana was being used; the second, on the perceived consequences of marijuana use; the third, on the circumstances in which the respondent would consider using less marijuana; and the fourth envelope, on the factors that would increase the respondents' willingness to comply with an unspecified rule or policy directive.

To be able to analyze the answers, each column was assigned a number ranging from 3 (the most important) to −3 (the least important). Each letter was paired with a number based on the column where participants placed the card. The numbers were recorded in a dataset for further analysis.

Users willing to move to the second phase of the study participated in a semi-structured interview; elaborated on the motivations for their answers; and talked about their consumption habits, attitudes toward regulation, as well as

Exercise Q#1: Perceptions on marijuana use
(31 statements)

-3	-2	-1	0	1	2	3
The least important			Neutral			The most important
A	CC	F	DD	I	L	C
P	J	S	B	D	O	R
X	M	N	G	E	W	H
	Y	Z	K	T	V	
		AA	Q	BB		
			U			
			EE			

Figure 3.2 Example: Recording of the Results of a Q-sorting Exercise

factors that would enhance their willingness to comply with hypothetical rules, norms, or programs aimed at discouraging consumption.

The focus of attention in this exploratory study was on college-age individuals between 18 and 24 years old who were active marijuana users. Study participants were recruited on the campus of two public universities located in San Diego, California (USA). A total of 20 individuals qualified for the study and agreed to participate (9 females and 11 males). At the time of the interview, all participants were enrolled in college and declared to be using marijuana. All but two respondents declared that, under certain circumstances, they would be willing to reduce current consumption levels.

Though admittedly low, this sample was deemed sufficient to start developing a narrative reflecting the attitudes of a segment of the population of marijuana users. This is a necessary first step to gain a better understanding of aspects that would animate compliance with alternative regulatory scenarios and policies seeking a voluntary reduction in the consumption of the drug.

The results of the Q-sorting exercise and the lessons that can be drawn from the one-on-one interviews are discussed in the following section of this chapter.

Findings and Discussion

What are the attitudes of respondents towards marijuana use, the consequences of marijuana consumption, the circumstances that would motivate a reduction in use, and the circumstances that would increase compliance? This exploratory study focused on the statements receiving the highest rankings (i.e., statements placed in columns 2 and 3, as shown in Figure 3.2). The statements that appeared most frequently in the top-ranking categories, along with the percentage of respondents assigning those rankings, are depicted in Figure 3.3. Looking at these responses allows one to get an interesting perspective of the attitudes toward marijuana use and rule compliance among young college-age consumers.

Notice that for about a third of participants marijuana is a product that helps them relax, sleep, or reduce stress. For the majority of participants, marijuana is also perceived as a product that enhances creativity. The use of marijuana is associated with positive feelings that contribute to respondents' sense of well-being.

I use marijuana because...

Top choices *(Coded as 3)*	***Responses*** *(%)*
It helps me relax	35
I feel creative and have interesting thoughts	30
It helps me sleep	30

2nd best *(Coded as 2)*	***Responses*** *(%)*
It helps me feel good	40
It helps me reduce stress	40
I feel creative and have interesting thoughts	35

The main consequences that I have experienced from using it are...

Top choices *(Coded as 3)*	***Responses*** *(%)*
I feel more hungry	55
I have trouble remembering things	35
I cough and have respiratory problems	30

2nd best *(Coded as 2)*	***Responses*** *(%)*
I don't finish the activities that I start	60
I have trouble remembering things	45
I used more marijuana than I had planned	45

The circumstances that would motivate me to reduce my current level of consumption are...

Top choices *(Coded as 3)*	***Responses*** *(%)*
If anti-doping tests are conducted at my workplace	35
If I know it has dangerous or disgusting ingredients	35
If I find better ways to relax	30

2nd best *(Coded as 2)*	***Responses*** *(%)*
If I am presented with convincing evidence of the damages that marijuana causes	35
If anti-doping tests are conducted at my workplace	35
If the price of marijuana is too high	30
If the price of marijuana starts increasing	30

The circumstance that would motivate me to comply with rules pertaining to the purchase and use of marijuana are...

Top choices *(Coded as 3)*	***Responses*** *(%)*
Police do not arrest me for being a consumer	35
The rules are fair	25
I can legally purchase good-quality marijuana	25

2nd best *(Coded as 2)*	***Responses*** *(%)*
I am not detained by police	30
The government does not keep records showing that I am a user	30
Penalties for not complying are reasonable	25
Authorities do not treat me like a criminal	25
Strategies dealing with marijuana consumption are similar to the existing ones for tobacco or alcohol	25
Community tolerates responsible consumption	25

Figure 3.3 Top Choices in the Q-sorting

When asked about the consequences associated with marijuana use, a substantial number of participants acknowledged that it makes them feel hungrier than normal, that it affects their memory (i.e., having trouble remembering things or being unable to finish activities that they started), and that they usually end up having more respiratory problems than usual. About half of participants also acknowledged that it was common to observe that their levels of consumption were larger than what they originally planned.

The third and fourth questions in the Q-sorting exercise addressed issues of particular importance for this book. Participants were asked about the circumstances that would motivate a voluntary reduction in their current levels of consumption. For the majority (70%), the possibility that drug tests were conducted in their workplace would be determinant in their consumption decisions. This fact shows the concern of college-age users for the existence of monitoring mechanisms that could make their consumption habits public, or that may have implications in their professional careers.

About a third of respondents would consider reducing or eliminating marijuana use if credible information about the contents of the drug that they were using, or the health risks associated with use was available. More than half of respondents also highlighted the role that the price of marijuana has in their purchasing and consumption decisions.

For the fourth Q-sorting exercise participants were asked the following question: Under what circumstances would you be more willing to comply with regulations pertaining to the purchase and consumption of marijuana? When the statements that were more frequently chosen in this Q-sorting exercise are considered altogether, one notices that for young marijuana users participating in this study, avoiding unwanted interactions with police, respect for their privacy, tolerance for what they envision as responsible consumption, fair and reasonable rules, and legal access to good-quality marijuana are factors that would encourage them to comply with rules pertaining to the purchase and use of the drug.

Avoiding unwanted interactions with police is a significant aspect for the majority of participants. About two-thirds of them stated that their incentive to comply would be due to their concern with arrest or detention. Perhaps this desire to avoid law enforcement agencies is correlated with the desire to maintain consumption private, and more specifically with a demand that governments do not keep records showing that a person is a consumer.

There were several statements aimed at capturing information about users' perceptions towards rules and failure to comply with them. However, the two appearing in the top rankings more often were "the rules are fair" and "penalties for not complying are reasonable." But what do participants consider fair and reasonable? Since the Q-sorting exercise by itself was not sufficient to delve into this type of question, semi-guided interviews were conducted with participants willing to meet again with the interviewer.

Before each interview participants received a report showing their top choices in each of the Q-sorting exercises, and a copy of the results reported in shown in Figure 3.3. Each conversation started with a review of participants' top choices but with an emphasis on the circumstances that would motivate a change in their consumption patterns, and the factors that would increase their willingness to comply with rules pertaining to the purchase and use of marijuana.

Two recurrent topics in these conversations were the interactions with law enforcement agencies and the possibility that drug tests could be conducted at the workplace. When asked why these statements seemed to be so important for participants, many answered that since they were about to start looking for jobs, they did not want their use of marijuana to affect their career opportunities or their reputations. This was also related to their desire to keep interactions with police at a minimum.

There were two issues stemming from these conversations that caught the interviewer's attention, both of which can be related to young users' attitudes toward rule compliance. The first issue is their perceived capacity to exert self-restraint. When asked about a hypothetical regulatory scenario aimed at curbing consumption, all but one thought that they would be able to stop using marijuana without problems. More than one even said that they were using it because they liked the effects, that the drug helped them cope with stressful situations, or simply to socialize. All except for two participants agreed that they did not really need it and were confident about their ability to quit use.

A second issue was the apparent disconnection between attitudes toward rule compliance and the actions of some participants. Are young marijuana users truly willing to abide by rules targeting the use of something that contributes to their perceived well-being? Because even though some participants see a respect to privacy (e.g., by not conducting drug tests or keeping records identifying an individual as a consumer) or safe access to legal, good-quality marijuana as factors that would animate them to comply, when asked if they were violating current laws, most of them nodded (e.g., when the study took place, it was still illegal in the state of California to purchase marijuana without a medical card and a prescription issue from a licensed doctor). The majority of interviewees were familiar with current regulations pertaining to the purchase and use of marijuana, but seemed unable to establish a clear connection between a mandate, the consequences for noncompliance, and themselves.

This exploratory study is useful to reflect on the connection between the topic of this chapter and the overreaching theme of the book. The objective, as stated in Chapter 1, is to inquire about the factors influencing decisions to comply (or not) with a rule or norm. A framework is then presented to guide research efforts in an interdisciplinary setting. Such a framework, which should be seen as a map to facilitate theory development and the formulation of models, can facilitate the study of complex topics, like the attitudes and perceptions of users of illicit drugs.

The compliance framework described in the opening chapter of the book refers to three levels of compliance behavior (i.e., individual, group/

organization, and social). This element of the framework allows one to devise a general classification of the factors animating compliance (or the lack of it). Drug consumption, as a multidimensional problem, can be best addressed if analyzed in stages. The Q-sorting exercise included scenarios to gain a better understanding of the compliance phenomenon but taking into account the perspective of individual users. Aspects such as interpersonal connections or the influence of the social environment were not considered.

The framework also highlights the need to think about the compliance context, as this will ease the classification of factors into categories. Doing so is important because when studying the drug use phenomenon, it may well be the case that the compliance dynamic varies across levels of analysis. A micro-level approach that focuses on individual behavior allows one to pay close attention to cognitive processes, judgments, motivations, or environmental factors that users themselves consider salient in their choices to use (or not) a drug, as well as their willingness to follow directives seeking to modify their behavior.

Given the preceding results, what can one say about rule compliance among young marijuana users? What needs to be taken into account if the aim of a rule or policy program is to encourage voluntary reductions in the users' consumption patterns? Once the level of analysis is set, one can focus on the selection of a theoretical approach to guide the crafting of working hypotheses.

Halpern and Bates overview individual level theories that can be used to look at the influences and processes involved in decision making (Halpern et al., 2004). These theories include instrumental and classical conditioning, which assume that behavioral change can be attained through measures that encourage individuals to learn new associations among stimuli (Pavlov, 1927); heuristics and the consumer information-processing model, which argues that human cognition processes include "mental shortcuts" that may induce systematic misjudgments of events (Tversky & Kahneman, 1974, 1981); theories and models based on the notion of "stages of change," whose central tenet is that an individual's behavioral change is a process of increasing readiness (Prochaska & DiClemente, 1983); or the theory of planned behavior, which holds that attitudes, subjective norms, and perceived control influence people's intentions to modify their behavior (Ajzen, 1991; Armitage et al., 1999).

There is, however, an alternative theory that seems to be more in line with what participants in the Q-sorting decision-making exercise reported: the cognitive consistency and dissonance theory (Festinger, 1957; Harmon-Jones, Harmon-Jones, & Levy, 2015). As Halpern et al. (2004) explain, the theory of cognitive dissonance, or cognitive consistency theory, argues that in some situations there is a discrepancy among people's attitudes (or values) and their actions. People try to resolve this discrepancy by adapting their attitudes rather than their behavior. By doing so, the person feels a reduction in the tension or discomfort that the discrepancy creates. For example, during the interviews study participants were asked why they thought that avoiding unwanted interactions with police appeared to be so important. Various participants referred to the impact that an arrest could have on their job search, or on the reputation that they would develop among peers and relatives. Some of those respondents, however, acknowledged that they did not have a medical marijuana card (which at the time of the interview was needed to purchase marijuana legally in the state of California). They knew they were violating state law. Most of them were also aware that under federal law, purchasing and consuming marijuana is also illegal. Evidently, there was a disjoint between their attitudes toward rule compliance and their actions.

The preceding example illustrates an important aspect to consider when thinking about regulatory or policy interventions to persuade users to change their consumption patterns. Any behavioral directive, either in the form of a rule or policy program, should try to align attitudes and behavior so that users act according to their beliefs, rather than making such beliefs adapt to their actions.

This chapter is the first attempt to understand aspects about the attitudes of marijuana users that may contribute to the success or failure of rules or policies seeking a voluntary reduction of consumption. This exploratory analysis addresses the issue by analyzing attitudes towards compliance at the individual level, although there are other elements of the framework introduced in Chapter that can be incorporated in the development of hypotheses.

The data for this exploratory study were gathered from marijuana users whose age was between 18 and 24 years old. The small sample used in this exploratory assessment unveiled useful information about aspects of consumption and compliance that users deem relevant. One should keep in mind, however, that the context that each participant faces, the characteristics of their biophysical environment (e.g., whether they live at a dormitory on a college campus or with their family), the characteristics of the community where users interact (e.g., urban versus rural colleges), or the monitoring and enforcement structures, can play a role in the way in which an individual will weigh the costs and benefits associated with consumption and compliance.

The effectiveness of a rule or policy program seeking a voluntary reduction in marijuana use can increase if one gains an adequate understanding of the attitudes of the specific segment of the population that the rule or policy program is trying to influence. This chapter is the initial step in a research agenda that will apply theories and methods from cognitive and behavioral sciences to drug policy design. The compliance framework introduced in the opening chapter of the book is a useful guideline to structure inquiries on a topic of great relevance and timeliness. Readers are invited to engage in the conversation by furthering the initial findings reported in this chapter and think about the extent to which marijuana users' attitudes toward compliance can impact the effectiveness of rules or policies aimed at encouraging voluntary reductions in consumption.

Notes

1 The Institutional Review Board at San Diego State University reviewed and approved the research protocol for this study (IRB #1979099). Dr. Espinosa thanks participants for their willingness to speak openly and about their experiences with marijuana consumption.

2 The phrases that were used in the preparation of the Q-sorting exercise were adapted from the Marijuana E-Checkup Program used at San Diego State University (see http://go.sdsu.edu/student_affairs/cps/echug-marijuana.aspx. Last retrieved 7/1/2017), as well as from suggestions from marijuana users interviewed during the preparation of the research protocol.

References

Ajzen, I. (1991). The theory of planned behavior. *Organizational Behavior and Human Decision Processes*, *50*(2).

Ammerman, A. S., Hartman, T., & Demarco, M. M. (2017). Behavioral economics and the supplemental nutrition assistance program: Making the healthy choices the easy choice. *American Journal of Preventative Medicine*, *52*(2), S145–S150.

Armitage, C. J., Conner, M., Loach, J., & Willetts, D. (1999). Difference perceptions of control: Applying an extended theory of planned behavior to legal and illegal drug use. *Basic and Applied Social Psychology*, *21*(4), 301–316.

Bachman, J., Johnson, L., & O'Malley, P. (1998). Explaining recent increases in students' marijuana use: Impacts of perceived risks and disapproval, 1976 through 1996. *American Journal of Public Health*, *88*(6), 887–892.

Bandura, A. (1991). Social cognitive theory of self-regulation. *Organizational Behavior and Human Decision Processes*, *50*(2), 248–287.

Bandura, A. (2015). On deconstructing commentaries regarding alternative theories of self-regulation. *Journal of Management*, *41*(4), 1025–1044.

Binswanger, H. (1991). Volition as cognitive self-regulation. *Organizational Behavior and Human Decision Processes*, *50*(2):154–178.

Boynton, M. H., Agans, R. P., Bowling, J. M., Brewer, N. T., Sutfin, E. L., Goldstein, A. O., & Ribisl, K. M. (2016). Understanding how perceptions of tobacco constituents and FDA relate to effective and credible tobacco risk messaging: A national phone survey of US adults, 2014–2015. *BMC Public Health*, *16*.

Bradley, C., & Speight, J. (2002). Patient perceptions of diabetes and diabetes therapy: Assessing quality of life. *Diabetes Metabolism Research and Reviews*, *18* (Supplement S3), S64–S69.

Center for Behavioral Health Statistics and Quality. (2015). *National survey on drug use and health 2014*. Rockville, MD: Center for Behavioral Health Statistics and Quality.

Choo, E. K., Benz, M., Zaller, N., Warren, O., Rising, K. L., & McConnell, J. (2014). The impact of state medical marijuana legislation on adolescent marijuana use. *Journal of Adolescent Health*, *55*(2), 160–166.

Cialdini, R. B., & Goldstein, N. J. (2004). Social influence: Compliance and conformity. *Annual Review of Psychology*, *55*, 591–621.

Cialdini, R., & Trost, M. R. (1998). Social influence: Social norms, conformity, and compliance. In D. T. Gilbert, S. T. Fiske, & G. Lindsey (Eds.), *Handbook of social psychology* (Vol. 2, pp. 151–192). Boston, MA: McGraw Hill.

Crean, R. D., Crane, N. A., & Mason, B. J. (2011). An evidence based review of acute and long-term effects of cannabis use on executive cognitive functions. *Journal of Addiction Medicine*, *5*(1), 1–8.

Degenhardt, L., Hall, W., & Lynskey, M. (2003). Exploring the association between cannabis use and depression. *Addiction*, *98*(11), 1493–1504.

Esgate, A., & Groome, D. (2005). Drugs and cognitive performance (Chapter 8). In *An introduction to applied cognitive psychology*. East Sussex, UK & New York, USA: Psychology Press.

Festinger, L. (1957). *A theory of cognitive dissonance*. Stanford, CA: Stanford University Press.

Halpern, D., Bates, C., Mulgan, G., Aldridge, S., Beales, G., & Heathfield, A. (2004). *Personal responsibility and changing behavior: The state of knowledge and its implications for public policy*. London, UK: Prime Minister's Strategy Unit. Cabinet Office.

Harmon-Jones, E., Harmon-Jones, C., & Levy, N. (2015). An action-based model of cognitive dissonance processes. *Current Directions in Psychological Science*, *24*(3), 184–189.

Kam, J., Matsunaga, M., Hecht, M. L., & Ndiaye, K. (2009). Extending the theory of planned behavior to predict alcohol: Tobacco, and marijuana use among youth of Mexican heritage. *Prevention Science*, *10*, 41–53.

Kandel, D. (1973). Adolescent marijuana use: Role of parents and peers. *Science*, *181*, 1067–1070.

Keyes, K. M., Wall, M., Cerda, M., Shulenberg, J., O'Malley, P. M., Galea, S., & Hasin, D. S. (2016). How does marijuana policy affect US youth? Medical marijuana laws, marijuana use and perceived harmfulness: 1991–2014. *Addiction*, *111*, 20177–22195.

Kilmer, J. R., Walker, D. D., Christine, M., Lee, R. S. P., Mallett, K. A., Fabiano, P., & Larimer, M. E. (2006). Misperceptions of college student marijuana use: Implications for prevention. *Journal for Studies on Alcohol and Drugs*, *67*(2), 277–281.

Lindsay, P., & Norman, D. A. (1977). *Human information processing: An introduction to psychology*. New York, USA: Academic Press.

Lubman, D. I., Cheetham, A., & Yucel, M. (2015). Cannabis and adolescent brain development. *Pharmacology & Therapeutics*, *148*, 1–16.

Lunn, P. (2014). *Regulatory policy and behavioural economics*. Paris: OECD Publishing.

McKeown, B., & Thomas, D. B. (2013). *Q methodology* (2nd ed.). Thousand Oaks, CA: Sage Publications.

Moore, T. H. M., Zammit, S., Lingford-Huges, A., Barnes, T. R. E., Jones, P. B., & Burke, M. (2007). Cannabis use and risk of psychotic or affective mental health outcomes: Systematic review. *Lancet*, *370*(9584), 319–328.

O'Brien, M. J., Moran, M. R., & Tang, J. W. (2016). Patient perceptions about prediabetes and preferences for diabetes prevention. *The Diabetes Educator*, *42*(6).

OECD. (2017). *Behavioural insights and public policy: Lessons from around the world*. Paris: OECD Publishing.

Oliver, A. (Ed.). (2013). *Behavioural public policy*. Cambridge and New York, NY: Cambridge University Press.

Pavlov, L. P. (1927). *Conditional reflexes*. London: Oxford University Press.

Pearson, M. R., Liese, B. S., & Dvorak, R. D. (2017). College student marijuana involvement: Perceptions, use, and consequences across 11 college campuses. *Addictive Behaviors*, *66*, 83–89.

Pickens, J. (2005). Attitudes and perceptions. In N. Borkowski (Ed.), *Organizational behavior in health care* (pp. 43–76). Sudbury, MA: Jones and Bartlett.

Prochaska, J. O., & DiClemente, C. C. (1983). Stages and processes of self-change of smoking: Toward and integrative model of change. *Journal of Consulting and Clinical Psychology*, *51*(3), 390–395.

Shafir, E. (Ed.). (2013). *The behavioral foundations of public policy*. Princeton, NJ: Princeton University Press.

Solowij, N., & Battisti, R. (2008). The chronic effects of cannabis on memory in humans: A review. *Current Drug Abuse Review*, *1*(1), 81–98.

Suerken, C. K., Reboussin, B. A., Sutfin, E. L., Wagoner, K. G., Spangler, J., & Wolfson, M. (2014). Prevalence of marijuana use at college entry and risk factors for initiation during freshman year. *Addictive Behaviors*, *39*(1), 302–307.

Thaler, R. H., & Sunstein, C. R. (2009). *Nudge: Improving decision about health, wealth and happiness*. London: Penguin Books.

Tversky, A., & Kahneman, D. (1974). Judgment under uncertainty: Heuristics and biases. *Science*, *185*, 1124–1131.

Tversky, A., & Kahneman, D. (1981). The framing of decisions and the psychology of choice. *Science*, *211*(4481), 453–458.

Watts, S., & Stenner, P. (2012). *Doing Q methodological research: Theory, method and interpretation*. Thousand Oaks, CA: Sage Publications.

Wood, W. (2000). Attitude change: Persuasion and social influence. *Annual Review of Psychology*, *51*, 539–570.

World Bank. (2015). *World development report 2015: Mind, society, and behavior*. Washington, DC. Retrieved from www.amaxon.com/dp/1464803420/ref=wl_it_dp_o_pd_S_ttl?_encoding=UTF8&OLID=21KJ54FNQV5GP&coliid=I27i11udrn8076

Zedillo, E., & Wheeler, H. (Eds.). (2012). *Rethinking the "War on Drugs" through the US-Mexico prism*. New Haven, CT: Yale Center for the Study of Globalization.

4 Voluntary Compliance in Environmental Programs

Cali Curley and William L. Swann

Background

Because of monitoring and enforcement costs and the adverse, unintended consequences associated with mandatory compliance, policymakers sometimes turn to alternatives to regulation that encourage actors to volunteer themselves to be regulated despite potential punishments for noncompliance. Even though such alternatives cannot mandate desired behavior, they can still alter the benefits and risks associated with complying (or failing to comply), and aid in the achievement of policy goals. In this chapter, we use the term "voluntary compliance" to describe this phenomenon.

Voluntary compliance is a special form of compliance whereby individual and organizational actors willingly choose to cooperate with an agreed upon set of rules, norms, and behavioral expectations that are not legally imposed upon them. *Noncompliance* is therefore deciding not to conform to such rules, norms, and expectations. Voluntary compliance occurs in two ways: the act of "opting-in," which requires some form of upfront behavioral change or commitment, and the maintenance of association with sustained behavioral change requirements. While actors are subjected to tangible sanctions such as fines, lawsuits, or imprisonment when failing to comply with traditional regulation, the sanctions for actors in noncompliance with voluntary programs can include losing face and legitimacy, economic opportunities, and favorable future regulatory treatment.

Voluntary compliance is intended to reduce the monitoring and enforcement costs of regulation and encourage actors to mitigate activity that makes others worse off, which can produce positive externalities or benefits enjoyed by third parties. For example, policymakers often incentivize individuals and firms to participate in voluntary programs designed to promote pro-environmental behavior by providing technical assistance and financial incentives. However, individuals and firms also join voluntary programs for legitimacy purposes and sometimes symbolically cooperate with programmatic expectations in the absence of explicit sanctions (Delmas & Montes-Sancho, 2010; King & Lenox, 2000). Teasing out what motivates actors to comply voluntarily thus has important consequences for policy design and research.

Research Questions and Study Contexts

In this chapter, we explore two related questions: (1) Why do actors choose to cooperate in voluntary programs, and at different levels of commitment? (2) How do compliance decisions change based on the structure of the compliance scenario (i.e., the specific voluntary initiative)? We tackle these questions by drawing on theories of individual motivation to empirically explain voluntary compliance decisions in two cases of environmental programs at the micro and meso levels.

At the micro level, we examine what drives voluntary compliance in residential energy programs offered to customers of a municipally owned utility in Tallahassee, Florida. Tallahassee is a mid-sized city that has repeatedly been ranked as a top municipal utility in the United States. It offers a unique opportunity to investigate the programs of a city that is looked to nationally for best practices in demand-side energy management. These programs include low-interest loans, audits, and rebates, each offering a different financial incentive. However, participation may also be driven by social factors such as neighbors learning about, witnessing, and legitimizing behavioral change.

At the meso level, we analyze the environmental commitment of lodging facilities in the long-established Florida Green Lodging Program to understand what factors motivate higher levels of voluntary compliance. This program was established by the state of Florida to encourage lodging facilities to improve their environmental performance and receive special recognition and eligibility for holding competitive state conferences, as well as to reduce their operational costs.

These two study contexts provide an opportunity to understand the design, incentive structure, and motivational factors of voluntary compliance across different levels of scale and complexity, which allows for the development of more diverse and effective policy tools.

Theoretical Approach

We apply the theoretical framework from Chapter 1 to identify the motivational factors of compliance in scenarios where there are no required mandates. We discuss the specific motivations that shape actors' choices to opt into situations where they face a wide array of adverse consequences for deviating from expected behavior. In some cases, these consequences will be similar to traditional regulation; however, since voluntary compliance is not enforced nor monitored closely, it relies more on sanctions, incentives, and motivations that are different from mandatory compliance scenarios.

Like traditional regulation, the rules that make up a voluntary compliance scenario should have a direct effect on the decisions and behavior of actors. However, the greatest threat in most voluntary compliance scenarios is loss of exclusive group or brand recognition status (Prakash & Potoski, 2007). Thus, an implicit goal for most voluntary programs is to encourage norming of specific behavior that creates peer pressure to conform. We elaborate on these rewards, punishments, and motivations in the following sections.

Motivational Pathways of Voluntary Compliance

Previous research on voluntary programs suggests participant motivations include economic incentives such as reducing operational costs (Porter & van der Linde, 1995) or staving off future regulation (Maxwell, Lyon, & Hackett, 2000); forms of altruistic intent to further a collective benefit (Clark, Kotchen, & Moore, 2003); or pressure to maintain a reputation and achieve legitimacy or some social status benefit (Delmas & Montes-Sancho, 2010; King & Lenox, 2000). These explanations align with Sharp's (1978) use of *material*, *expressive*, and *solidary* motives, originally advanced by Clark and Wilson (1961), to explain behavioral choices. These motivational pathways can lead to participation in voluntary initiatives that require compliance to be effective.

Material motivations for opting into voluntary compliance include obtaining a pecuniary payoff and/or decreasing economic costs; for instance, using a deposit-refund system for recycling plastic containers, or preventing future costs such as regulation by complying voluntarily. Extant research suggests firms, for example, opt into environmental compliance scenarios for various material purposes. These include lowering operational costs (Porter & van der Linde, 1995), adjusting to market pressures or new consumer demands (Henriques & Sadorsky, 1996; Moon & deLeon, 2007), gaining exclusive brand recognition and signaling positive information to stakeholders (Prakesh & Potoski, 2007), and reversing a poor track record of environmental performance to prevent future regulation (Khanna & Damon, 1999; Videras & Alberini, 2000).

Expressive motivations, or altruistic and "warm-glow" effects, are also thought to influence voluntary compliance. For example, there may be some personal or cultural belief that induces an actor to willingly comply in a voluntary rule setting. Empirical research in environmental economics and psychology finds evidence that altruistic attitudes of consumers increase the likelihood of participating in voluntary green energy programs (Clark et al., 2003; Kotchen & Moore, 2007). Altruistic values also extend to the organizational level. Research on organizational virtuousness suggests organizational members' prosocial emotions and activities spiral upwards and disseminate throughout organizations, creating contagion effects that induce replication of virtuous behavior among organizational members and lead to performance enhancement (Cameron, 2003).

Finally, *solidary* motivations are believed to encourage voluntary compliance. These motives stem from pressure applied in peer groups that form an identity for the participant and deem what is socially legitimate. These include peer pressure and other social forces such as stakeholder expectations and reputational considerations. While peer pressure and social legitimacy have obvious implications at the individual level, these pressures also extend to organizations. Organizations tend to look and behave similarly due to coercive, normative, and mimetic pressures, rather than pure economic interests (DiMaggio & Powell, 1991; Meyer & Rowan, 1977). Research on voluntary environmental programs (VEPs) finds evidence of such pressures influencing voluntary compliance decisions and behavior (Delmas & Montes-Sancho, 2010; King & Lenox, 2000; Moon & deLeon, 2007; Rivera & deLeon, 2004).

Material, expressive, and solidary motives need not be independent, either. Research on voluntary compliance in environmental policy has tended to pit motivational theories against each other (e.g., Moon & deLeon, 2007), but it could be the case that these theories work together to explain voluntary compliance in various forms. For example, heavy-polluting firms join VEPs to clean up a "dirty" reputation (solidary), protect against costly regulation (material), and reduce their contribution to global climate change (expressive) simultaneously. In the next section, we explore these motivations and the compliance scenario within two voluntary programs. We present an overview of the methods used and then explore more detailed methods in each case.

Methods

Each case is composed of two parts: a descriptive probe into the compliance situation context and a quantitative investigation of participation in and commitment to the voluntary initiative. The descriptive investigation will discuss the four elements identified as part of the compliance situation context in Chapter 1: (1) degree and type of monitoring/enforcement; (2) design of specific rules; (3) capacity, relative to required behavioral change; and (4) individual psychological factors. Both cases will then use descriptive and quantitative evidence to answer our research questions.

Case 1: Residential Compliance in Energy Programs

Energy programs for residential properties are typically voluntary in nature. But there is often some aspect of compliance required for participants to experience consumption reductions from programmatic activities. Previous research suggests that White, upper middle class, and more educated individuals have a higher likelihood of participating in these initiatives (Berry, 1990; Powers, Swan, & Lee, 1992). Beyond these findings there is limited understanding of why actors participate voluntarily at different levels of commitment.

Energy programs are usually offered by local governments and/or utilities. Their focus is to decrease peak demand and delay the need for generating additional capacity. They typically offer a wide array of programs that make up a demand-side management strategy, including, but not limited to, free energy audits, rebates for appliances, and low-interest loans for larger ticket items.

Each program faces a different compliance scenario which may change the subset of participants willing to participate in the program.

Compliance Situation Context Investigations

Degree and Type of Monitoring/Enforcement

The monitoring and enforcement of residential energy programs is minimal but substantially different depending on the type of program. The audit program does not have a formal monitoring or enforcement mechanism. Once auditors enter the home, they begin their work—caulking windows, changing light bulbs, installing low-flow shower heads, adjusting thermostat settings, testing energy loss, etc. The only follow-up mechanism used is a phone call that the utility makes at random asking about the audit experience.

The loan program, however, has a more formal monitoring mechanism that ensures the city's limited budget to make loans is being utilized efficiently and appropriately. This mechanism includes a receipt provision—the customer must provide a copy of the receipt for the purchase of the high energy efficient material the loan was approved to purchase. This program also has random follow-up inspections after installation, as auditors revisit the home to ensure the installation was completed properly by contractors.

Design of Specific Rules

The rules of both programs are designed with material incentives in mind. In the audit program, participation is free and incentivized through potential energy savings from participation. The audit is also used as an entry-level program, as participants are told about the loan program during the audit itself. Typically, before a customer can participate in the loan program, they need to have an audit conducted. The audit program has minimal requirements; it asks only for the participant to be present during the time of the audit. There are no sanctions in place. The customer can fail to present for an audit and request a follow-up appointment without fear of sanction. There are also no sanctions in place if the participant were to remove low-flow shower heads or new light bulbs.

The low-interest loan program operates similarly on a material incentive—the utility offers an interest rate lower than market value but requires the purchase of higher-rated energy efficient materials (e.g., appliances). This helps the customer obtain material gains in two ways: (1) reduced long-run interest costs and (2) energy savings. Sanctions, such as withholding electricity or adjusting payment plans, are put in place only if the customer fails to repay their loan, does not allow for follow-up inspection, or purchases equipment failing to meet energy efficiency standards. However, the loan program requires a financial commitment from the homeowner in the form of interest payments.

Capacity, Relative to Required Behavior Change

Lack of knowledge and incentives are common barriers to enhance residential energy efficiency. Many households do not have adequate knowledge and information about how to increase energy savings in the home. And even when households understand the value of energy savings, they may not have the immediate financial capacity to change their behavior. The audit and loan programs educate households about energy savings and help them overcome financial burdens associated with behavioral change. Leaning on the experience and knowledge of utility experts allows utility customers to make more informed decisions regarding their energy-related behavior. It also ensures that they are informed prior to enrolling into a situation of voluntary compliance.

Individual Psychological Factors

Voluntary compliance, like traditional compliance, requires an understanding of the individual psychological factors that come into play. Earlier, we discussed the three primary motives that can shape decisions of voluntary participation, however no single motivating factor is dominant, and they may rely on other important factors such as trust. In residential energy programs, the decision to opt-in might be motivated by a material rationale (e.g., reduced monthly energy bills, decreased costs of new appliances through incentives, etc.). However, there may also be a solidary motive at play, particularly in how information diffuses in groups. Consider the installation of residential solar panels: one neighbor in a cul de sac places solar panels on the roof using the loan program, which provides information to another neighbor who in turn makes a similar decision. These neighbors begin to build a new identity in their neighborhood and share information with other neighbors, which further encourages participation and compliance in the loan program.

In addition, the need for trust with the organization that is establishing and managing the program is important. Actors generally receive information about energy efficiency from three sources: government agencies offering the program or policy, private companies selling the equipment, and personal relationships. However, previous research suggests that more trustworthy information about energy conservation is derived primarily from acquaintances and non-experts (Darley, 1978; Leonard-Barton, 1981; Stern, 1992).

Actors are psychologically complex. In the audit program, energy auditors change light bulbs and showerheads, caulk windows, alter thermostats, and discuss other programs to help customers save money. Here there is a strong material incentive for cost minimization that encourages participant compliance (e.g., keeping new light bulbs and showerheads in place). However, anecdotal evidence from discussions with utility representatives reveals that some audit participants remove light bulbs and showerheads almost immediately after their audit. Thus, understanding the motives and psychological factors affecting voluntary compliance choices are important for informing program design and implementation.

Case Specific Data and Methods

To explore the choice to participate quantitatively, we use data on programmatic participation and residential energy consumption from the City of Tallahassee Utilities. We also draw data from the 2010 U.S. Census at the block level to incorporate the characteristics of individuals living within these homes. These data were merged with Leon County property tax appraisal data to describe the housing stock characteristics of the homes in question. Here we compare these characteristics across programs to understand the differences in decisions to opt into compliance scenarios by utility customers living in owner-occupied homes. While these data are available for the entire population, we selected a sample of 443 households that maintains the population level participation rates of loans and audit programs.

The dependent variable—the choice to not participate, participate in the audit program only, or participate in the loan and audit program—is built from understanding the *degree and type of monitoring/enforcement* as well as the *design of specific rules*. These contextual characteristics helped identify that participating in loan and audit signified a higher-level commitment to energy savings relative to participating in the audit only. The *individual psychological factors* related to participation and the *capacity, relative to required behavior change* are used to inform the independent variables. These contexts suggest what types of information are required to understand individual compliance decisions.

Table 4.1 summarizes the differences between household-level characteristics between the groups that comply with their energy auditors' request that they participate in the low-interest loan program after receiving an audit compared to those who receive an audit but do not opt into the loan program. Participation rates across the city are 7% in the audit program, and roughly 1% in the loan program, suggesting many audit participants do not proceed to the

Table 4.1 Differences in Characteristics of Loan Versus Audit-Only Participants

Characteristics	*Loan Participants*	*Audit-Only Participants*	*Difference*
Mean value of home	$160,047	$155,169	$4,878
Age of home	35.2 years	31.1 years	4.1 years
Home size (sq. ft.)	1,926	1,825.8	100.2
Educational level†	14.9 years	14.6 years	0.3 years
Number of occupants†	2.39	2.21	0.18
Minority (%)†	25.7%	31.1%	−5.4%

Note: † data measured at the census block level.

loan program. Larger, older, and more expensive homes tend to have owners who comply with the auditor's request for participation in the loan program and demonstrate higher levels of commitment to energy savings.

The following analysis examines differences in characteristics between those choosing not to participate in any program (non-participants), those opting into only the audit program (low-compliance context), and those opting into the audit and loan program (higher-compliance context). We utilize a multinomial logit model to compare both options (1) audit participation only and (2) loan and audit participation to the base outcome (0) of no participation. We can thus interpret the differences between those who choose to participate at a level of compliance and those who choose not to participate at all.

Proxy variables, measured at the census block level, are included for factors identified as important in the literature: percentage of racial minorities, median income, and percentage with a bachelor's degree (Berry, 1990; Powers et al., 1992). Other variables inform participation decisions: high bill complaints (a dummy variable equal to 1 if a customer filed a complaint), household energy use (lagged one year), and the percentage of renters in the area. We added measures for home characteristics, including home market value and age (and a squared term to capture curvilinear effects associated with home age). We also controlled for years, as external economic climates may shape participation decisions, as well as summer and winter months to capture seasonal effects associated with participation.

Findings

Table 4.2 reports the multinomial logistic regression results, which suggest clear differences between non-participants, audit-only participants, and loan-and-audit participants. Compared to the non-participants, those opting into the audit program are likely to participate if they live in areas with older homes. This finding appears to align with material motives. For instance, older homes tend to have greater energy loss, and audits can determine where residents can improve energy savings. Residents in older homes thus likely have a strong material motivation to participate in the audit program and presumably lower their energy bills. However, as indicated by the statistically significant squared term, this effect diminishes as the age of the home increases.

Other significant predictors align more with solidary motives. Those living in areas with higher levels of education are more likely to participate in the audit program, which is consistent with previous research. Surprisingly, however, the model suggests households in neighborhoods with a greater percentage of racial minorities tend to participate more in the audit program. This may indicate a peer effect within Black/African American and other minority neighborhoods in Tallahassee. While minorities in urban areas have been traditionally disadvantaged in accessing opportunities (Loury, 1977), minority groups are also known to cultivate strong social institutions (e.g., churches,

Table 4.2 Multinomial Logit Model Examining Levels of Compliance Relative to Baseline of Non-Participation

Variables	*(1)* *Audit Participation Only*	*(2)* *Loan and Audit Participation*
Percent renters	−0.003	−0.016
Home age	0.030***	0.062
Home age^2	−0.0004***	−0.0003
Market value	−5.09e-07	3.40e-06
Base square feet	0.00007	−0.002***
2006	−3.678***	−18.49***
2007	−2.126***	−3.530***
2008	−1.078***	−2.162***
2009	−0.363***	−1.234**
2010	−0.102***	0.038
Winter	−0.083***	0.061
Summer	−0.037***	0.006
Percent minority	0.005**	−0.002
Percent bachelor's	0.013***	0.030
Median income	−5.56e-06	0.00004***
E-bill	−0.108	0.367
High bill complaint	0.158	−16.99***
Lagged energy use	0.00006	0.0004
Constant	−2.68***	−8.14***
Observations	175,375	
Groups	443	
Prob > chi^2	0.0000	

Note: ***$p < 0.01$, **$p < 0.05$, *$p < 0.10$.

civic groups, etc.) that promote opportunities for individual and communal advancement (Putnam, 1993). Moreover, since the trustworthiness of information is thought to be higher from acquaintances, it may be less surprising that minority neighborhoods in Tallahassee participate more in the audit program, controlling for income and other relevant factors, assuming such neighborhoods have developed stronger social networks.

We see different trends when comparing non-participants to those participating in loan programs. Loan participants tend to live in smaller homes (controlling for home value and age), higher income areas, and in households that did not file a high bill complaint. Calling the utility with a high bill complaint is negatively associated with higher levels of compliance. This is likely because high bill complaints usually intend to reduce energy bills and not reflect interests in making energy efficiency investments. The results also suggest that those with higher median incomes tend to participate in programs with higher compliance requirements. This is likely because of the financial costs associated with participation in the loan program, which means they may be more willing to commit to energy efficiency if they have the economic means to do so.

Summary

In the case of residential energy programs, we see the importance of household characteristics and policy design in shaping voluntary compliance. The compliance context reveals some of the underlying motivations and design mechanisms that might influence voluntary compliance decisions, such as financial incentives (material), neighbor effects (solidary), and costs of compliance. From the statistical model, we find support for these material and solidary motivations and observe significant differences in the characteristics of households choosing to comply with voluntary programs that have different costs of compliance. These findings demonstrate the practical value of having more targeted marketing, using motivational strategies to encourage participation in these programs. Specifically, we find that material motives such as cost savings to older homes and making public presentations in the neighborhoods should encourage participation in the audit program; and finding ways to reduce compliance costs for lower-income households in the loan program would encourage participation, as they appear more resistant to the higher-level costs. One question that remains is whether this multifaceted motivational structure of voluntary compliance holds at the meso and macro levels.

Case 2: Firm Compliance in a VEP

VEPs are defined as "collaborative arrangements between firms and regulators in which firms voluntarily commit to actions that improve the natural environment" (Delmas & Terlaak, 2001, p. 44). VEPs typically involve legally non-binding agreements without penalties for non-performance other than dismissal from the program. Most VEPs offer selective benefits to participants in the form of technical assistance, analytical tools, information subsidies, brand enhancement, and public recognition (Koehler, 2007). VEPs can be found across various industries at all levels of government in the United States and internationally.

This case focuses on Florida's Green Lodging Program, a voluntary initiative in which lodging facilities in the state can opt into a compliance scenario that calls for increased environmental standards in lodging operations. Launched in 2004 by the Florida Department of Environmental Protection (FDEP), the Green Lodging Program designates and recognizes lodging facilities that commit to conserving and protecting the state's natural resources. The program permits self-regulation and allows facilities to evaluate their own operations via self-reporting forms. The program allows facilities to set environmental goals and take actions to continuously improve their environmental performance. Participating facilities can reduce their operational costs by generating less waste and reducing their consumption of energy and water, receive technical and marketing assistance from the state, and are given legislative preference for hosting state government meetings and conferences. As of fall 2017, there were 432 active facilities in the program.

Compliance Situation Context Investigations

Degree and Type of Monitoring/Enforcement

To opt into in the program, FDEP requires facilities to conduct a thorough property assessment and implement environmental practices in five operational areas: (1) energy efficiency; (2) water conservation; (3) waste reduction, reuse, and recycling; (4) indoor air quality; and (5) communication and education (for guests, employees, and the public). Participants are required to report the environmental practices they have implemented along with their environmental performance data on water consumption, electricity use, and waste generated. The program is administered primarily online and involves minimal government oversight of participants, relying on facilities to self-report. However, the program conducts random spot checks and provides an online survey to guests who have stayed in designated facilities that asks questions about the facilities' compliance with programmatic aims.

Design of Specific Rules

The program assigns different weights of potential positive environmental impact to designated facilities. Designation levels are set on a four-level tiered basis, "Palm Levels," in which participating facilities must commit to a minimum level of points before being designated. Facilities must commit to implementing a minimum number of environmental practices that would qualify at one of four Palm Levels (1–4, with 4 being the highest designation). Examples of qualifying practices include, among other things, encouraging guests to reuse towels and bed sheets; educating guests and employees about recycling; instituting environmentally friendly purchasing policies; composting excess food and landscape trimmings; developing an onsite recycling program; reminding guests about conserving water; installing low-flow water fixtures and energy-efficient lighting; and having a written environmental action plan. Designation in the program is valid for three years. To maintain designation, facilities must report their annual environmental performance data and implement at least two new environmental practices per year from any of the five operational areas mentioned in the preceding paragraph.

Capacity, Relative to Required Behavior Change

The program offers participating facilities free marketing and technical assistance as well as a guide for best management practices through its website and onsite visits to help ensure designated facilities maximize their environmental and financial performance. Often these lodging facilities lack the knowledge, training, and confidence to improve their environmental performance without sacrificing their bottom line. Online assistance and onsite consultations inform and educate designated facilities about the complementary aspects of environmental and financial performance.

Individual Psychological Factors

Facility operators have several likely motives for opting into and maintaining membership in the program. Materially, designation enables facilities to gain legislative preference for hosting state meetings. Facilities can also use the program as an opportunity to identify costly production processes such as overconsumption of natural resources and generation of waste. As for expressive motives, some facilities may be inclined to reduce their environmental footprint and help preserve the natural beauty of their state. The fact that even smaller facilities opt into the program, knowing their behavioral changes have little impact on their bottom lines or ability to attract new clientele, may be indicative of some altruistic intent to preserve natural resources. Finally, solidary motives are also likely at play, as facilities may join and comply with program expectations because doing so could be perceived as a legitimate practice. However, facilities may do the bare minimum to receive designation and then symbolically comply with the program to satisfy legitimacy requirements but not go through with the commitments to reduce their environmental impact.

Case-Specific Data and Methods

To determine which motivational factors explain variation in programmatic commitment of participating facilities, data were obtained from 362 Green Lodging applications or renewals during the period 2011–2017. Although the program had been in place since 2004, FDEP moved to a new points system in 2011. These applications and renewals included information on facilities' location, region, size, type (e.g., hotel-motel, condo-hotel/timeshare, etc.), and amenities such as the number of restaurants and conference rooms; baseline performance data that included volume of waste generated, volume recycled, volume of water used, kilowatt hours (kWh) of electricity and natural gas used, and the total waste, water, and energy costs; as well as the total environmental points across the five environmental areas mentioned earlier, which were used to determine Palm Tree designation.[1]

For the dependent variable, we used the total environmental points combined from the subtotals for each of the five environmental categories: energy efficiency; water conservation; waste reduction, reuse, and recycling; indoor air quality; and communication and education. This dependent variable captures the extent to which facility participants committed to the goals of the program.[2]

For independent variables, we included three measures capturing material motivations: total costs of waste, water, and energy. We anticipate lodging facilities incurring higher costs have more financial incentive to commit to higher levels of environmental protection to reduce costs and enhance their bottom line.

We also included predictors capturing solidary influences. We included two measures of facility size (total building square footage and number of guest rooms). Larger organizations tend to have more rationally formalized structures based on legitimate practices (Meyer & Rowan, 1977), and are better equipped to take opportunities for change (Haveman, 1993). We expect larger facilities will face greater pressure to conform to increased industry environmental standards, and have the ability to do so, thus scoring higher in environmental protection.

As a proxy measure for facility quality and service level, we used Expedia's five-point star rating system (Expedia, 2017). Star ratings are a consistent predictor of room price and guest satisfaction in the hospitality literature (Israeli, 2002; Jeong & Jeon, 2008). Since star ratings attempt to standardize the level of service quality in the industry, lodging facilities in the same class should tend to offer similar service-amenity packages. Hoteliers, particularly with larger properties, utilize star ratings as a marketing tool to differentiate themselves and may voluntarily adopt environmental practices to conform to external forces (Kasim, 2007). Larger, 3–5 star facilities have been found to adopt more environmental practices than their smaller, 1–2 star counterparts (Mensah, 2006; Nicholls & Kang, 2012).

To capture geographical proximity peer effects associated with solidary motives, we included dummy variables for each of the six FDEP-designated regions in the state (southeast, southwest, south, central, northeast, and northwest). The central district, which includes the Orlando area, had the highest mean total environmental points (445.61), followed by the south (432.75) and southeast (431.77). The northwest district, which includes the Florida panhandle, had the lowest mean (363.43). A one-way analysis of variance (ANOVA) indicated the difference for at least one of the means was statistically significant: $F\ (5{,}332) = 3.60$, $p < 0.01$. The differences in means between the northwest and the central, south, and southeast districts were all significant at the 0.05 level. The clustering of environmental commitment may indicate a peer effect within regions. For example, as hoteliers learn more about what their neighboring facilities are doing in terms of environmental practices, they may imitate such behavior and implement green practices within their own facility.

Finally, to isolate the effect of star rating, we controlled for the number of restaurants and conference rooms since these amenities could explain whether facilities engage more in some specific environmental areas such as water conservation and energy efficiency, respectively, to save costs. Table 4.3 reports the summary statistics for all variables.

We estimated three linear regression models of total environmental points. The first model included only the economic cost variables capturing material motivations; the second model included only the sociological factors capturing solidary motivations; and the third model combined both sets of variables.[3] Due to missing data, our sample size was reduced to 198 in the combined model.

Table 4.3 Summary Statistics

Variable	*Obs.*	*Mean*	*SD*	*Min*	*Max*
Total environmental points	362	424.76	101.67	233	789
Total waste cost	253	36,861.14	51,031.06	110	338,146
Total water cost	314	134,995	199,396	12	1,885,396
Total energy cost	315	481,326.3	706,338.8	500	5,892,588
Guest rooms	362	253.51	283.42	1	1800
Total bldg. sq. ft.	337	261,006.5	363,570.2	400	2,129,885
Meeting rooms	356	6.54	10.34	0	76
Restaurants	356	1.44	1.9	0	15
Star rating	330	3.36	0.66	2	5
Southeast	362	0.25	0.43	0	1
Southwest	362	0.14	0.35	0	1
South	362	0.15	0.36	0	1
Central	362	0.27	0.45	0	1
Northeast	362	0.11	0.31	0	1
Northwest	362	0.08	0.27	0	1

Findings

Table 4.4 displays the model results. To improve the normality of our data, we used natural log transformations of the dependent variable, total environmental points, and the independent variables for total costs of waste, water, and energy, and the number of guest rooms and total building square footage. In total, our combined model explains about 20% of the variance in environmental commitment with the independent variables.

In model 1, we see that only one material motivation, total cost of energy, significantly predicts the level of voluntary compliance in the direction expected. Facilities spending more on energy costs tend to have greater commitment to environmental goals based on their practices in place, presumably because they could reduce energy costs in the long run by improving their energy efficiency.

Model 2 considers only the solidary motives (i.e., facility size, service amenities/quality, and geographic location) and finds positive correlations between total environmental commitment and total building square footage, star rating, and all but one of the regional districts. Consistent with extant research (Mensah, 2006; Nicholls & Kang, 2012), larger facilities and those offering more upscale service-amenity packages appear to commit more to environmental goals.

However, after combining material and solidary motives in model 3, we observe that only star rating and the northeast district remain statistically significant. Even after controlling for consumption costs, facility size, regional district, and other amenities, star rating significantly predicts facilities' environmental commitment. While nothing suggests that facilities must engage in environmental practices to receive a higher star rating (Expedia, 2017),

Table 4.4 Regression Models for Total Environmental Points (Logged)

	Model 1 (*Material*)	*Model 2* (*Solidary*)	*Model 3* (*Combined*)
Consumption costs			
Total waste cost (logged)	0.004		−0.003
	(0.018)		(0.020)
Total water cost (logged)	0.014		−0.006
	(0.017)		(0.021)
Total energy cost (logged)	0.061***		0.008
	(0.019)		(0.033)
Size, services, and quality			
Guest rooms (logged)		0.002	0.011
		(0.028)	(0.048)
Total bldg. sq. ft. (logged)		0.033*	0.031
		(0.020)	(0.026)
Meeting rooms		0.002	0.001
		(0.001)	(0.002)
Restaurants		0.001	−0.006
		(0.009)	(0.013)
Star rating		0.061**	0.090**
		(0.027)	(0.038)
District (reference: northwest)			
Southeast		0.094*	0.045
		(0.054)	(0.068)
Southwest		0.080	0.045
		(0.057)	(0.074)
South		0.159***	0.104
		(0.060)	(0.078)
Central		0.103*	0.074
		(0.054)	(0.067)
Northeast		0.112*	0.139*
		(0.063)	(0.078)
Constant	5.09***	5.323***	5.25***
	(0.129)	(0.153)	(0.260)
R^2	0.20	0.19	0.20
Adjusted R^2	0.19	0.16	0.14
F value	18.20***	6.71***	3.56***
N	227	299	198

Note: standard errors in parentheses; ***$p < 0.01$, **$p < 0.05$, *$p < 0.10$.

higher-star facilities may use increased environmental standards as a marketing tool to differentiate themselves from other lower-rated facilities and, in doing so, legitimize these standards within the industry.

Summary

We conclude that solidary motives appear stronger than material motives to comply voluntarily with the Green Lodging Program. On average, lodging facilities appear more influenced by the activities of their peer organizations, mainly within their service-amenity class, than by material motives to reduce consumption costs. These findings offer insight into policy design. While our descriptive investigation of the compliance scenario suggested program administrators often highlight the potential for participants to improve their bottom lines with increased environmental standards, a complimentary marketing strategy would be to publish more success stories within each region and across different classes of facilities. Administrators could also potentially capitalize on and strengthen peer effects by recognizing top performers within specific regions and/or hotel classes.

Conclusion

In this chapter, we discussed the concept of voluntary compliance and examined how different motivations shape voluntary compliance decisions in two environmental programs: household compliance with residential energy programs and a VEP for lodging facilities. These cases provide insight into how different types of motivations might be activated by variations in voluntary compliance arrangements. Although this chapter suggests there is much to be discovered about the relationship between motivations and willingness to comply with voluntary directives, it offers a useful methodological approach for pairing a detailed descriptive investigation with a quantitative analysis that explains voluntary compliance at multiple levels of scale.

In the first case, we found evidence of a relationship between the degree of voluntary compliance and motivational factors, especially for material incentives. This suggests the compliance scenario and the design of specific rules matters in shaping individual voluntary compliance decisions. In the second case, we learned that solidary motives (legitimacy and peer effects) play an important role in compliance decisions for firms, which speaks to the importance of reputation and identity building for organizational actors. Comparing these cases, we tentatively conclude that solidary motivations may have more influence on the voluntary compliance choices of firms, while material investment and motives may matter more in shaping voluntary compliance at the micro level. While more investigation is needed, these findings may have important implications for understanding how voluntary compliance differs between individual and organizational actors.

Across both cases, however, our analysis is limited in its consideration of expressive motives, as well as in its use of proxy measures for material and solidary motives and reliance on cross-sectional data. Investigating these motivations in a more robust way in the future requires additional research designs, such as surveys or experiments, that can more precisely measure and compare alternative motivations across different compliance scenarios, ideally over time.

Our findings also speak to the importance of policy design and implementation in voluntary compliance. Policymakers might benefit from research on how motivations shape compliance decisions, because they can choose designs that better elicit responses from individuals and firms that might participate in voluntary programs. Understanding the differences between compliers and noncompliers could inform strategies to encourage participation in voluntary programs.

Notes

1 To receive points, a facility must have implemented the practice in at least 50% of the facility, or at least 50% of the time. Specific practices considered a higher-level commitment to environmental protection by FDEP were awarded more points within each subcategory (e.g., within the communication and education subcategory, if a facility had a written strategic environmental action plan, it received five points; if a facility subscribed to environmental informational resources, it received two points).

2 We also estimated separate linear models for each subcategory, and an ordered logit model for Palm Tree designation. However, the results were highly similar with the combined total environmental points model and were therefore not reported.

3 No problems appeared in terms of multicollinearity or heteroscedasticity.

References

Berry, L. (1990). *The market penetration of energy-efficiency programs* (No. ORNL/CON-299). Oak Ridge, TN: Oak Ridge National Lab.

Cameron, K. S. (2003). Organizational virtuousness and performance. In K. S. Cameron, J. Dutton, & R. E. Quinn (Eds.), *Positive organizational scholarship* (pp. 48–65). San Francisco, CA: Berrett-Koehler.

Clark, C. F., Kotchen, M. J., & Moore, M. R. (2003). Internal and external influences on pro-environmental behavior: Participation in a green electricity program. *Journal of Environmental Psychology*, *23*(3), 237–246.

Clark, P. B., & Wilson, J. Q. (1961). Incentive systems: A theory of organizations. *Administrative Science Quarterly*, *6*(2), 129–166.

Darley, J. M. (1978). Energy conservation techniques as innovations, and their diffusion. *Energy and Buildings*, *1*(3), 339–343.

Delmas, M. A., & Montes-Sancho, M. J. (2010). Voluntary agreements to improve environmental quality: Symbolic and substantive cooperation. *Strategic Management Journal*, *31*(6), 575–601.

Delmas, M. A., & Terlaak, A. K. (2001). A framework for analyzing environmental voluntary agreements. *California Management Review*, *43*(3), 44–63.

DiMaggio, P. J., & Powell, W. W. (1991). The new institutionalism in organizational analysis. In P. J. DiMaggio & W. W. Powell (Eds.), *The new institutionalism in organizational analysis*. Chicago, IL: University of Chicago Press.

Expedia. (2017). *Star ratings (hotel class)*. Retrieved from www.expedia.com/Hotel-Star-Rating-Information

Haveman, H. A. (1993). Organizational size and change: Diversification in the savings and loan industry after deregulation. *Administrative Science Quarterly*, *38*(1), 20–50.

Henriques, I., & Sadorsky, P. (1996). The determinants of an environmentally responsive firm: An empirical approach. *Journal of Environmental Economics and Management*, *30*(3), 381–395.

Israeli, A. A. (2002). Star rating and corporate affiliation: Their influence on room price and performance of hotels in Israel. *International Journal of Hospitality Management, 21*(4), 405–424.

Jeong, M., & Mindy Jeon, M. (2008). Customer reviews of hotel experiences through consumer generated media (CGM). *Journal of Hospitality & Leisure Marketing, 17*(1–2), 121–138.

Kasim, A. (2007). Towards a wider adoption of environmental responsibility in the hotel sector. *International Journal of Hospitality & Tourism Administration, 8*(2), 25–49.

Khanna, M., & Damon, L. A. (1999). EPA's voluntary 33/50 program: Impact on toxic releases and economic performance of firms. *Journal of Environmental Economics and Management, 37*(1), 1–25.

King, A. A., & Lenox, M. J. (2000). Industry self-regulation without sanctions: The chemical industry's responsible care program. *Academy of Management Journal, 43*(4), 698–716.

Koehler, D. A. (2007). The effectiveness of voluntary environmental programs—A policy at a crossroads? *Policy Studies Journal, 35*(4), 689–722.

Kotchen, M. J., & Moore, M. R. (2007). Private provision of environmental public goods: Household participation in green-electricity programs. *Journal of Environmental Economics and Management, 53*(1), 1–16.

Leonard-Barton, D. (1981). Voluntary simplicity lifestyles and energy conservation. *Journal of Consumer Research, 8*(3), 243–252.

Loury, G. (1977). A dynamic theory of racial income differences. In P. A. Wallace & A. M. LaMonde (Eds.), *Women, minorities, and employment discrimination* (pp. 153–186). Lexington, MA: Lexington Books.

Maxwell, J. W., Lyon, T. P., & Hackett, S. C. (2000). Self-regulation and social welfare: The political economy of corporate environmentalism. *The Journal of Law and Economics, 43*(2), 583–618.

Mensah, I. (2006). Environmental management practices among hotels in the greater Accra region. *International Journal of Hospitality Management, 25*(3), 414–431.

Meyer, J. W., & Rowan, B. (1977). Institutionalized organizations: Formal structure as myth and ceremony. *American Journal of Sociology, 83*(2), 340–363.Moon, S. G., & deLeon, P. (2007). Contexts and corporate voluntary environmental behaviors: Examining the EPA's green lights voluntary program. *Organization & Environment, 20*(4), 480–496.

Nicholls, S., & Kang, S. (2012). Going green: The adoption of environmental initiatives in Michigan's lodging sector. *Journal of Sustainable Tourism, 20*(7), 953–974.

Porter, M. E., & van der Linde, C. (1995). Toward a new conception of the environment-competitiveness relationship. *The Journal of Economic Perspectives, 9*(4), 97–118.

Powers, T. L., Swan, J. E., & Lee, S. D. (1992). Identifying and understanding the energy conservation consumer: A macromarketing systems approach. *Journal of Macromarketing, 12*(2), 5–15.

Prakash, A., & Potoski, M. (2007). Collective action through voluntary environmental programs: A club theory perspective. *Policy Studies Journal, 35*(4), 773–792.

Putnam, R. D. (1993). The prosperous community. *The American Prospect, 4*(13), 35–42.

Rivera, J., & deLeon, P. (2004). Is greener whiter? Voluntary environmental performance of western ski areas. *Policy Studies Journal, 32*(3), 417–437.

Sharp, E. B. (1978). Citizen organizations in policing issues and crime prevention: Incentives for participation. *Journal of Voluntary Action Research*, *7*(1–2), 45–58.

Stern, P. C. (1992). Psychological dimensions of global environmental change. *Annual Review of Psychology*, *43*(1), 269–302.

Videras, J., & Alberini, A. (2000). The appeal of voluntary environmental programs: Which firms participate and why? *Contemporary Economic Policy*, *18*(4), 449–460.

5 Procedural Justice and Compliance in Problem-Solving Courts

Bradley Ray and Cindy Brooks Dollar

Introduction

Generally speaking, the criminal justice system attempts to achieve compliance through the threat of punishment, which is arguably aimed at deterring people from committing criminal or antisocial behaviors (Nagin, 1998). While most people are compliant with the law most of the time, some are not. Criminal justice personnel and policymakers suggest that for these individuals noncompliance may be rooted in underlying factors that need to be addressed to encourage legal compliance. This perspective underlies the current problem-solving court movement in the United States.

Problem-solving courts, also called specialty courts, are an alternative to traditional criminal court processing. The overarching goal of these courts is to reduce criminal recidivism and improve defendants' quality of life by linking them to community-based treatments and services that are aimed at addressing the underlying causes of their criminal behavior (Miller & Johnson, 2009; Porter, Rempel, & Mansky, 2010). Rather than emphasizing punishment, problem-solving courts focus on ways to reduce future criminal participation by using judicial authority to hold offenders accountable for criminal behaviors while simultaneously offering incentives that encourage pro-social behaviors. Thus, problem-solving courts attempt to elicit compliance among those who have already been noncompliant with the law but whom they also deem as requiring additional intervention to achieve compliance.

The problem-solving court movement largely grew out of the "war on drugs" policies of the 1980s, which led to significant increases in arrest, prosecution, and incarceration of drug-related offenses (Clear & Frost, 2014). The mass incarceration of persons convicted of drug-related crime resulted in the creation of various diversion programs, including the first drug court, which was established in Dade County, Florida, in 1989 (Nolan, 2001). The drug court model consists of a specialized docket for defendants with a history of substance abuse, and uses extended judicial supervision and a team approach that includes judges, criminal justice and legal personnel, and treatment providers to issue sanctions and incentives that inspire legal compliance. Because of its novelty and personalized success stories, the drug court model was quickly emulated in other jurisdictions. In addition, other forms of problem-solving courts were established, and while these courts serve different populations, they incorporate several of the key components of drug courts. For example, mental health courts, the second type of problem-solving court established, offer an alternative means to handle arrests of persons with mental illness (Petrila, Poythress, McGaha, & Boothroyd, 2001). Like drug courts, mental health courts are based on a holistic model that connects offenders to community-based treatments and resources and provides sanctions to encourage compliance with the law (Lurigio & Snowden, 2009; Winick & Wexler, 2003).

The numbers and types of problem-solving courts continue to proliferate in the U.S. criminal justice system as well as in criminal justice systems abroad (Rossman, Roman, & Zweig, 2011). Today there are nearly 4,000 problem-solving courts in the United States. Although drug courts and mental health courts are the most popular forms of problem-solving courts, the model has been applied to a growing number of social issues such as domestic violence, veteran status, juvenile delinquency, and homelessness (Huddleston & Marlowe, 2011). Much of the research on problem-solving courts has focused on the ability of these courts to increase public safety through increased compliance with law. Researchers generally use administrative data to examine whether those who participate in a problem-solving court are less likely to be rearrested, have fewer rearrests, or serve fewer jail days than groups of similar defendants who did not participate in problem-solving courts. Few studies have been able to use random assignment, so most comparison groups come from quasi-experimental designs. Still, meta-analyses of empirical studies indicate that, compared to defendants in traditional criminal courts, defendants participating in problem-solving courts have lower rates of recidivism both during court supervision and following court completion (GAO, 2005; Mitchell, Wilson, Eggers, & MacKenzie, 2012; Sarteschi, Vaughn, & Kim, 2011; Wilson, Michell, & MacKenzie, 2006).

Since compliance with the law is a key goal of practitioners who work in these programs, it is not surprising that so much of the problem-solving court research has focused on legal compliance (National Association of Drug Court Professionals, 1997; Council of State Governments Justice Center, 2009). Far fewer studies have examined the mechanisms by which the problem-solving court process is associated with positive outcomes. In fact, these mechanisms are often referred to as the "black box" (Goldkamp, White, & Robinson, 2001). To better understand and examine these processes, researchers often turn to available theories and explore their relevance to the problem-solving court model. The theory most often used to explain problem-solving courts' association with legal compliance is procedural justice theory. This theory proposes that compliance with the law is more likely when justice personnel make fair decisions and show defendants respect by giving them both voice and validation (McIvor, 2009; Tyler, 2009; Tyler, Sherman, Strang, Barnes, & Woods, 2007; Tyler & Fagan, 2008). Researchers note procedural justice as an essential factor in explaining compliance with the law in the problem-solving court context (see Rossman et al., 2011).

In this chapter, we review procedural justice theory and research in problem-solving court settings. Following this, we detail the problem-solving court experience by describing how this process plays out for defendants and how compliance is determined in these settings. We then describe a case study where we examine defendant perceptions of procedural justice over time and across three problem-solving court settings to illustrate how procedural justice is associated with compliance, which we operationalize as successful completion of the problem-solving court program. By exploring individual-level attitudes and outcomes across problem-solving courts, we expose an organization context that can vary in a multitude of ways. As such, this chapter highlights the interrelationship between the micro-, meso-, and macro-level factors in understanding compliance. In our case study we measure compliance as successful completion from the problem-solving court which, as described further later in the chapter, requires hard work and dedication by the defendant. However, the defendant's efforts are continually assessed by a problem-solving court team who establishes rules and norms that, whether formal or informal, constitute the meso-level factors by which compliance is determined and noncompliance is sanctioned. Thus, individual-level compliance is nested in an organizational setting, and variations at either level can impact determinations of compliant behaviors. Moreover, as we discuss in our conclusion, problem-solving courts, which represent a meso-level construct, are nested within the broader criminal justice system, which represents a macro-level social system that attempts to enforce the law.

Procedural Justice in Problem-Solving Courts

Procedural justice describes a conflict resolution process that is fair (Lind & Tyler, 1988). Literature concludes widespread support for positive effects of procedural justice. Indeed, procedural fairness explains positive attitudes and behavioral outcomes (i.e., rule-norm compliance) across a variety of contexts. For example, studies find that procedural justice boosts job performance (Aryee, Chen, & Budhwar, 2004; Cohen, Charash, & Spector, 2001; Podsakoff and MacKenzie, 1997; Zapata Phelan, 2009), workplace satisfaction (Hosmer & Kiewitz, 2005; Nowakowski & Conlon, 2005), and intra- and inter-organizational commitment and cooperation (Griffith, Harvey, & Lusch, 2006; Konovsky, 2000; van Dijke, DeCremer, Mayer, & Quaquebeke, 2012). Research on procedural justice in criminal justice settings is similarly supportive as studies consistently indicate that the presence of procedural justice can result in greater compliance with legal authorities and engagement in law abiding behaviors (Lind & Tyler, 1988; Tyler, 2006). While procedural justice has relevance beyond the court system (e.g., Barkworth & Murphy, 2015; Braga, Papachristos, & Hureau, 2014; Tyler et al., 2007; Watson & Angell, 2007), court-based models highlight the fairness with which court processes can be handled. Specifically, procedurally just court encounters are often characterized as treating parties with dignity and respect, giving the persons involved an opportunity to explain their position and express their views, and emphasizing transparency in decision making. Each of these features is expected to produce perceptions of court authority and legitimacy, which results in greater compliance with the court's instructions (Lind & Tyler, 1988; Thibaut & Walker, 1975; Tyler, 1984;2006; 2009; also see Beetham, 1991).

The procedural justice framework helps shed light on the "black box" of problem-solving court processes and provides a theoretical mechanism by which to explain defendants' compliance with the law (Goldkamp, 1999; Goldkamp & Irons-Guynn, April, 2000; Gottfredson & Exum, 2002; Poythress, Petrila, McGaha, & Boothroyd, 2002; Wexler & Winick, 1991. Literature examining procedural justice across problem-solving court settings suggests that defendants perceive greater procedural justice in problem-solving courts than in traditional courts or community-based treatments (Munetz et al., 2014; Rossman et al., 2011; Poythress et al., 2002); that perceptions of procedural justice are associated with greater treatment-based outcomes (Kopelovich, Yanos, Pratt, & Koerner, 2013; Ray & Dollar, 2014; Christy, Poythress, Boothroyd, Petrila, & Mehra, 2005; Pratt, Yanos, Kopelovich, Koerner, & Alexander, 2013); and that defendants who perceive the process as procedurally just are more likely to be compliant with court mandates, have lower recidivism, and are more likely to successfully complete the court requirements (Redlich & Han, 2014; Gottfredson, Kearley, Najaka, & Rocha, 2007; Rossman et al., 2011).

These findings illustrate the importance of procedural justice within the problem-solving setting. In fact, defendants who perceive court processes as procedurally just are likely to have better outcomes, including greater compliance. However, compliance is a multifaceted concept in the problem-solving court setting, and it is often determined by consensus among multiple court actors. Moreover, determinations of compliance have ongoing ramifications for how defendants experience the problem-solving court process. Therefore, we aim to further unpack some of the problem-solving court experience to articulate how compliance is determined.

Compliance in Problem-Solving Courts

Problem-solving courts are local innovations, developed to fit the needs of the particular jurisdiction, so policies and procedures differ depending on legal statues, available services, and the populations they serve (i.e., drug users, persons with mental illness, veterans, etc.) Despite differences, there are some commonalities across problem-solving courts that distinguish them from traditional criminal courts (Huddleston & Marlowe, 2011; Berman & Feinblatt, 2005). Unlike traditional courts, participation in the problem-solving court process is usually voluntary, although some jurisdictions may order drug court as a condition of probation. Defendants are offered the opportunity to participate based on the court's previously determined eligibility criteria, which discerns whether the underlying cause of criminal behavior is an issue that the court is designed to address. After enrolling, the defendant must agree to follow the assigned treatment regimen and be monitored by the court's personnel. Failure to do so, or choosing to opt-out, will result in either a return to traditional court or a revocation hearing.

Problem-solving courts use a non-adversarial team approach in which a judge, prosecutor, defense counsel, and other community-based professionals collaborate in the decision-making process. Rather than trying to determine an adequate punishment for a specific criminal offense, the team works together to link an offender to necessary community-based resources in hopes of preventing future criminal offending. Problem-solving courts use extended judicial supervision by relying on court authority to hold the defendant accountable for legal compliance. Defendants must agree to attend a series of status hearings, which are held in open court. The frequency of these hearings varies, but bi-weekly court hearings are common for high risk offenders (NADCP, 2013; Festinger et al., 2002; Marlowe, Festinger, Dugosh, Lee, Benasutti, 2007; Marlowe, Festinger, Lee, Dugosh, & Benasutti, 2006). Before the public status hearings, the court team discusses each defendant's compliance with the court mandates. Status hearings are used to publicly sanction the defendant's behavior. Defendants may receive positive feedback and incentives or negative feedback and punishment. Each of these are used to encourage compliance with the law.

An important feature of the problem-solving process is *noncompletion.* Most problem-solving courts last between 12 and 24 months. As stated earlier, problem-solving courts rely on extended judicial supervision whereby defendants are required to appear in court on a regular basis for status review hearings. Although the determinations about the defendant's progress are made in private compliance audits, the public status hearings provide a venue for the problem-solving court team to publicly announce decisions about the defendant's ongoing engagement in the court, adherence to treatment, and compliance with law and other court mandates. Defendants who are deemed compliant are often rewarded with less frequent court appearances, and if consistently compliant they successfully complete the court process. That said, our prior work reveals that some degree of noncompliance is expected (Ray, Dollar, & Thames, 2011; Dollar & Ray, 2015). Noncompliant behaviors include defendants missing court, missing treatment sessions, or being rearrested. Noncompliance does not result in immediate expulsion, but when it does occur, the problem-solving court team reviews the situation and decides whether or not to terminate the defendant from the process. Even if the defendant is spared termination, noncompliance is usually met with sanctions that are intended to change behaviors and encourage compliance. Continued or excessive noncompliance can result in court termination.

Successful completion comes with one of two awards, which varies depending on whether the courts are organized as pre- or post-adjudication courts.

In pre-adjudication courts, criminal charges are postponed until the problem-solving court process is complete. Upon successful completion, defendant's charges are dismissed. In post-adjudication courts, defendants are required to enter a guilty plea or be convicted prior to beginning the problem-solving court process, but sentences are deferred or suspended while participating. Upon successful completion, the sentence is renounced and the offense may be expunged.

A defendant may be terminated, meaning that he or she does not successfully complete the court process. Again, what happens to the defendant following termination depends on whether the court uses a pre- or post-adjudication approach (Almquist & Dodd, 2009; Redlich, Steadman, Monahan, Petrila, & Griffin, 2005; Redlich et al., 2006; Steadman, Redlich, Griffin, Petrila, & Monahan, 2005). In a pre-adjudication court, the offender is returned to traditional court for prosecution. In a post-adjudication court, the offender is returned to the traditional court system where the original sentence is served out.

In summary, problem-solving courts are a unique criminal justice experience that is designed for certain types of offenses or offenders. Existing research indicates that defendants in problem-solving courts are more likely to experience procedural justice, a concept associated with compliance, than defendants in traditional criminal courts. However, even in the problem-solving court setting, where procedural justice is more likely to be experienced, not everyone is compliant. In fact, nearly half of those who begin the year or longer process do not successfully complete because they are determined to be noncompliant with the law or other court mandates (Strong, Rantala, & Kyckelhahn, 2016). Next, we examine whether defendant perceptions of procedural justice are associated with problem-solving court completion. In doing so, we look at changes in defendant perceptions of procedural justice at different times and across multiple problem-solving court settings. We also examine whether or not perceptual changes are associated with compliant or noncompliant outcomes.

Case Study of Procedural Justice and Compliance

Data Collection and Measures

We worked with the Indiana Office of Court Services to select and administer surveys with problem-solving court defendants. These courts are located in different counties across the state. Court A is located in an urban area and has a population of over 350,000. Court B is located a suburban area and has a population of approximately 275,000, and Court C is located in a rural area and has a population of approximately 20,000. The Indiana Office of Court Services has certified each court as practicing the essential elements of a problem-solving court model and maintaining practices consistent with state and federal statutes (Council of State Governments, 2009).

The following analysis is based on a one-year cohort of defendants who entered these courts between April 2014 and December 2015. Defendants completed a survey about their court experiences at two time points: after defendants' first appearance in the problem-solving court (baseline) and again three months later (follow-up). The full sample includes 109 defendants who completed the baseline survey and 81 defendants who completed the three-month follow-up survey. Attrition was due to court termination; thus 28 defendants were terminated from the court process prior to the three-month follow-up period. For this case study, we focus only on those respondents where we have both baseline and follow-up data (N = 81), resulting in 29 defendants from Court A, 24 defendants from Court B, and 28 defendants from Court C.

Our measure of procedural justice comes from the Multisite Adult Drug Court Evaluation (MADCE) study (Rossman et al., 2011) and consists of eight items which ask about the extent to which defendants experienced procedurally just interactions with the judge. Specifically, these survey items were designed to assess the judge's willingness to listen to and validate the defendant's point of view, the judge's knowledge about the defendant and his or her case, the judge's emphasis on assisting and helping the defendant, and the defendant's feelings about being treated fairly and respectfully. Each item relied on a five-point Likert-scale response option ranging from "strongly disagree" to "strongly agree." We focus on measures of procedural justice with the judge because the research highlights judges as the people most likely to convey procedural justice (Marlowe et al., 2007; 2006; Wales, Hiday, & Ray, 2010). We also include demographics characteristics (age, gender, and race/ethnicity), the defendant's key arrest type (i.e., felony or misdemeanor), self-reported lifetime number of prior arrests, and a "risk score" from the Indiana Risk Assessment System. Finally, our outcome of interest is compliance, which we operationalize dichotomously and measure using administrative data from the courts determining whether the defendant successfully completed the court (completion = 1) or was unsuccessfully terminated from the court (termination = 0).

Results

Table 5.1 shows defendant responses to each of the procedural justice items. Unfortunately, we do not have a traditional criminal court sample with which to compare these responses; however, as illustrated, defendants had overwhelmingly positive attitudes about their court experience (see Table 5.1). For example, at baseline 93.8% of defendants agreed or strongly agreed the judge treated them fairly and 91.4% indicated that the judge treated them with respect. What is more, the survey responses generally indicate an increase in perceptions of procedural justice at three-month follow up.

The eight-item procedural justice index showed extremely high internal reliability (Cronbach's alpha = .90 at baseline and 0.89 at follow-up) so we combined the procedural justice items into a single index that ranged from 1 to 5 (higher values associated with higher perceived procedural justice). Average responses across the three courts for the baseline sample were not significantly

Table 5.1 Responses From Perceived Procedural Justice Items (N = 81)

	Baseline		*Follow-Up*	
	M (SD)	*% SA/A*	*M (SD)*	*% SA/A*
Your judge is knowledgeable about your case.	4.23 (0.80)	85.2	4.42 (0.93)	91.4
Your judge knows you by name.	4.14 (0.88)	85.2	4.51 (0.81)	92.6
Your judge helps you to succeed.	4.10 (0.77)	80.2	4.48 (0.69)	88.9
Your judge emphasizes the importance of treatment.	4.43 (0.59)	95.1	4.69 (0.49)	98.8
Your judge is intimidating and unapproachable.[a]	2.06 (0.95)	7.4	1.85 (0.90)	4.9
Your judge gives you a chance to tell your side of the story.	4.02 (0.91)	80.2	4.38 (0.81)	91.4
Your judge can be trusted to treat you fairly.	4.19 (0.79)	93.8	4.41 (0.67)	92.6
Your judge treats you with respect.	4.35 (0.64)	91.4	4.58 (0.54)	97.5

Responses ranged from 1, strongly disagree, to 5, strongly agree; [a] item reverse coded for scale; SA/A is strongly agree and agree combined.

different; however, there were increases in procedural justice over time. As illustrated in Figure 5.1, we found significant increases in perceived procedural justice for the overall sample, from 4.17 to 4.45 ($t = 3.21$, df = 80, $p < .01$), and for the Court C, from 4.25 to 4.72 ($t = 4.00$, df = 80, $p < .001$). Courts A and B did not indicate statistically significant increases; both experienced score increases in procedural justice over time.

We examined whether perceptions of procedural justice influence compliance as measured by successful court completion. The overall completion rate is 54.3% ($n = 44$) which is similar to completion rates in other studies (Burns et al., 2012; Redlich et al., 2010; Strong, Rantala, & Kyckelhahn, 2016). In order to look at the association between procedural justice and completion, we created a variable that captures individual-level *change* in perceptions of procedural justice by subtracting each defendant's procedural justice score at follow-up from their respective score at baseline. In doing so we found that those who completed the problem-solving court had a significantly higher rate of change than those who were terminated (a 0.45 and 0.07 increase respectively; $t = 2.291$, df = 79, $p < .05$).

Next, we entered this change variable into logistic regression models to examine if change in procedural justice influenced compliance which, again, is operationalized as a successful or non-successful court outcome. As shown in Table 5.2, individual-level changes in perceptions of procedural justice are positively associated with a defendant's likelihood to successfully complete (i.e., remain compliant). Model 1 reports the results of a baseline model that regresses the change measure for judicial perceptions on court outcome. The data show that defendants who report a positive change in judicial procedural

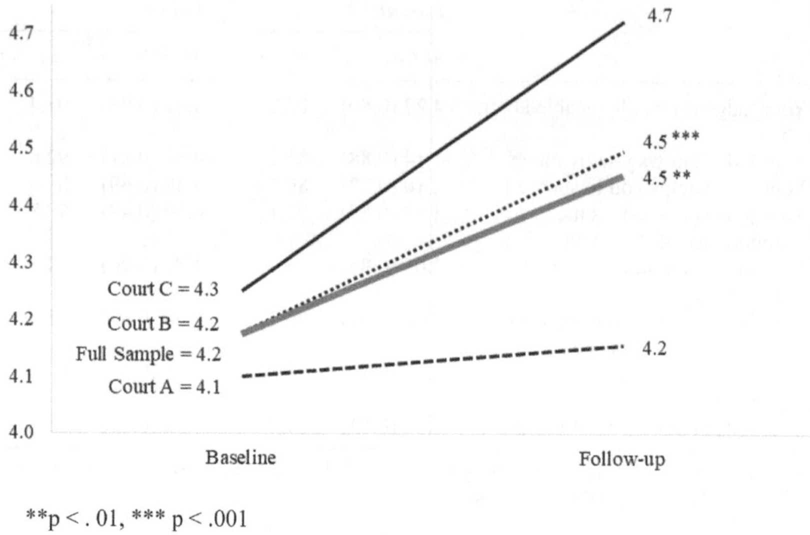

Figure 5.1 Perceived Procedural Justice at Baseline and Follow-Up by Court

Table 5.2 Logistic Regression Predicting Successful Court Completion (N = 81)

	Model 1		*Model 2*	
	B (SE)	*Expb (95% CI)*	*B (SE)*	*Expb (95% CI)*
Change in procedural justice with judge	0.68 (0.31)*	1.97 (1.07–3.60)	0.74 (0.34) *	2.09 (1.06–4.10)
Age			−0.01 (0.02)	0.99 (0.95–1.03)
Female (1 = yes)			−0.83 (0.55)	0.44 (0.15–1.28)
White (1 = yes)			−0.55 (0.88)	0.58 (0.10–3.22)
Felony (1 = yes)			0.16 (1.48)	1.18 (0.06–21.62)
Prior arrests			0.00 (0.04)	1.00 (0.93–1.08)
Risk score			−0.04 (0.04)	0.96 (0.89–1.03)

*p < .05

justice are nearly two times as likely to complete the court process ($b = 0.68$, Exp$b = 1.97$, $p < .05$). In model 2, we control for several demographic and legal covariates (i.e., age, gender, race/ethnicity, felony status, prior arrests, and risk score), none of which are statistically significant but still find a significant association between changes in procedural justice and successful completion. Net of other measures, increases in perceived procedural justice are associated with compliance, as measured by successful completion ($b = 0.74$,

Exp$b = 2.09$, $p < .05$). Therefore, it would appear that as perceptions of procedural justice increase over time, so too does the likelihood that the defendant will remain compliant and successfully complete the problem-solving court process.

The Subjectivity of Compliance in the Criminal Justice System

Consistent with past research on procedural justice in problem-solving courts the case study presented in this chapter demonstrates that defendants in these court programs have high perceptions of procedural justice, and these perceptions are associated with compliance as measured by successful completion from the process. As we mention earlier, successful completion reflects the culmination of numerous compliant status hearings whereby the court team determines the defendant's progress.

We have published a number of studies on problem-solving courts and some of these studies report on long-term observations of the court status hearings and pre-court compliance audits (see Ray, Dollar, & Thames, 2011; Ray & Dollar, 20143;2014; Dollar & Ray, 2015). In these studies, we found that problem-solving court judges often tell new defendants that the team is accepting of, and actually expects, some level of noncompliance early on in the process. Judges tell the defendants that they are willing to forgive minor slip ups (Ray, Dollar, & Thames, 2011). However, we have also found that this forgiveness and the team's perceptions of noncompliance reflect certain biases (Ray & Dollar, 2014). For example, in one of these studies we used a mixed-methods approach that combined both systematic observational data of team meetings and quantitative analysis of administrative data. The data from this study revealed patterned differences in how defendants' compliance was perceived and addressed. Specifically, we found that the defendant's gender and race influenced perceptions such that similar behaviors were differentially deemed compliant or noncompliant. For example, during one team meeting, we noted that the discussion of a female defendant's absence from a court session was explained by pointing to family, housing, and transportation issues, which led to her absence being contextualized and forgiven. During the same meeting, a male defendant's absence was also discussed. While these two defendants had been in the program for a similar period of time, the team was quick to recommend sanctions and termination for the male defendant's absence but forgave the female defendant's absence. This is just one example from our qualitative observations, but we found that males were generally more likely to be perceived as more culpable for noncompliant behaviors than females. Relatedly, the team would spend more time attempting to contextualize female defendants' noncompliance in ways that minimized culpability. Moreover, while race was not mentioned during our observations of the team meetings, our quantitative analysis of the data revealed that it was a significant predictor of program completion. We found that White females were most likely to complete and Black females were least likely to complete (Ray & Dollar, 2013). Thus, although the results reported in this chapter are consistent with the literature on procedural justice in problem-solving courts, our earlier research highlights the difficulty in operationalizing, measuring, and ultimately explaining compliance in this setting.

When compliance is determined by others, their determination may be influenced by preexisting bias. The disparities in compliance determinations that we have identified in our earlier studies might be a function of gender and racial bias, but they might also be accounted for by other variables correlated with these factors, such as employment history, educational attainment, socioeconomic status, and drug use. In fact, some studies find that race effects in problem-solving court decisions may be minimized or eradicated when other factors are considered. For example, drug court research suggests that lower graduation rates for Black participants are attributable to their being younger than other racial groups (Spiropoulos, Salisbury, & Van Voorhis, 2014); less likely to be employed or enrolled in school (Dannerbeck, Harris, Sundet, & Lloyd 2006; DeVall & Lanier, 2012; Gallagher, 2013; Howard, 2014); more likely to be in a lower socioeconomic bracket (Dannerbeck et al., 2006); more likely to live in disadvantaged neighborhoods characterized by high concentrations of poverty, violence, and single-female-headed households (Howard, 2014); or more likely to be experiencing clinically significant levels of anxiety or psychological distress (McKean & Warren-Gordon, 2011; Spiropoulos et al., 2014).

Regardless of the source of this bias, it raises a problematic issue for the study of compliance *and* procedural justice. Some research finds no difference across race-ethnicity in perceptions of procedural justice in traditional courtroom settings (Baker et al., 2013, 2015; Tyler, 2001; Tyler & Huo, 2002; Higgins & Jordan, 2005) and other research indicates that Blacks and Hispanics are less likely than Whites to perceive the court system as fair and just (Higgins, Wolfe, Mahoney, & Walters, 2009; Sun & Wu, 2006). To date, only one study has assessed this in a problem-solving court setting. Atkin-Plunk and colleagues (2017) examined survey data from defendants in a drug court and veteran's court and found that Black defendants had significantly lower perceptions of procedural justice but that these perceptions were not associated with outcomes. Since problem-solving courts operate within the broader justice system, where institutional and individual-level bias has been well-documented (e.g., Alexander, 2010; Chiricos & Crawford, 1995; Crawford et al., 1998; Crutchfield, Skinner, Haggerty, McGlynn, & Catalano, 2009; Mauer, 1999; Spohn, Gruhl, & Welch, 1981; Steffensmeier, Ulmer, & Kramer, 1998), it is plausible that they also employ disproportionate punishment to minorities. The subjective appraisal of compliance likely provides one way of doing so. Our argument, then, is that the extent to which determinations of compliance are influenced by biases, *in any context*, affects the ability to understand and theorize about compliance, as an objective behavior, in that context. What is more, certain individuals may perceive a process to be procedurally just, but those perceptions may also be influenced by external factors and experiences that they bring into that context. In other words, just as variations in how persons are treated may be based on biases, variations in how persons perceive treatment may also take into account that bias treatment.

Understanding the complexity of compliance in the problem-solving court context highlights the need for an interdisciplinary, multi-level framework like the one provided in this book. As a meso-level organization, problem-solving courts take an approach that provides an alternative route to the traditional criminal justice system in achieving compliance. For example, the court team focuses on linking defendants into needed community-based treatments or services and using sanctions and incentives to compel compliance. This occurs over a series of months, whereby the team members develop a personal relationship with the defendant. At the micro level, defendants are offered a unique criminal justice experience, which they often report perceiving as procedurally just (Munetz et al. 2014; Hiday, Wales, & Ray, 2010; Rossman et al., 2011; Poythress et al., 2002). Perhaps due to these perceptions, these programs elicit law-abiding behaviors in persons who had previously been regularly noncompliant with the law (Government Accountability Office, 2005; Mitchell et al., 2012; Sarteschi et al., 2011; Wilson et al., 2006). However, problem-solving courts are ultimately situated within the wider macro-level criminal justice system, and are bound by the policies and practices of this social system.

Disparities in Procedurally Just Opportunities

When acknowledging the subjectivity of compliance operating at multiple levels of interactions, concerns about who is afforded the opportunity to participate in a problem-solving court and experience the procedural justice that comes with this opportunity are raised. For example, in the present study we use data from three problem-solving courts. This included two different types of problem-solving courts (drug court and mental health court) that were located in different parts of the state of Indiana. Two of the courts have county-level populations above 250,000. Data collection occurred over an 18-month period and nearly everyone who participated in the court completed a baseline survey instrument. Only eight of the defendants (approximately 7%) were non-White. Overall, Indiana as a state has a population that is 16% non-White but a prison population that is 35% non-White. Thus, there are *certainly* disparities in incarceration that appear to also be present in the selection of defendants into the problem-solving court context.

These disparities appear to be consistent with other research on racialized selection into problem-solving court (e.g., Huddleston, Marlowe, & Casebolt, 2008) and beg the question: Should there be equity in the opportunity to experience procedural justice? Such equity could be achieved in several ways. We might consider what specific policies are resulting in disparity and, in doing so, create standardized policies around referral and acceptance into the problem-solving court. Perhaps it could simply be a matter of training team members to work with diverse populations, but exclusion of non-White populations is not the only issue. In fact, the types of social problems that we choose to address through problem-solving courts, and thus through creating procedurally just experiences, also contain bias. Drug courts aim to separate those with a substance use disorder from those who deal drugs. Mental health courts focus on those with untreated mental illness, which implicitly suggests non-treatment as a criminogenic factor, contradicting extensive research highlighting other socioeconomic problems. As new courts for veterans, drunk driving, and prisoner re-entry continue to proliferate, the structure of the problem-solving court and the principles of procedural justice are targeted at new populations. By separating out certain kinds of defendants (those with a substance use disorder, untreated mental illness, veteran or ex-prisoner statuses), we are implicitly selecting these groups to have the potential for a procedurally just experience. We could just as easily have selected single parents, the unemployed, or the disabled as a special group worthy of a problem-solving court setting. However, even in doing this, we would only further create boutique court experiences. Thus, given the growing body of literature linking procedural justice to compliance in criminal justice settings (Gottfredson et al., 2007; Kopelovich et al., 2013; Ray & Dollar, 2014; Redlich & Han, 2014; Rossman et al., 2011), the more socially just approach might be to infuse procedural justice principles throughout the criminal justice experience rather than creating separate tracks for certain types of offenses and offenders.

Conclusion

The empirical analysis that we present here demonstrates that defendant perceptions of procedural justice are positively associated with compliance. While this research is congruent with other studies in this area, we raise concerns about the subjective nature compliance and equity in experiences and opportunities that might be more procedurally justice. Our concerns are not meant to suggest that those who participate in problem-solving courts are socially or economically privileged. Through this and our prior work, we have spent time observing and investigating over 16 different problem-solving courts across the United States, and we can attest that this population tends to be relatively disadvantaged in a variety of ways. However, the select group who get to experience the procedurally just problem-solving court experience might be those who are perceived as worthiest and most deserving of this experience rather than those who need it the most.

Chapter 1 identified compliance behavior as potentially occurring at three levels. It may seem obvious that perceptions of procedural justice and its influence on defendants' compliance occurs at the individual level, but our study illustrates the importance of using a multi-level framework. While our case study focuses largely on the micro-level attitudes and behaviors of individual defendants, we contextualize these perceptions within the meso-level organization of the problem-solving court by highlighting the unique nature of these courts. We also discuss how problem-solving courts are bound by the macro-level context of the criminal justice system. Thinking about compliance across these multiple levels raises a variety of issues concerning subjectivity and structural inequalities This multi-level approach also offers a compelling roadmap by which to explore these concerns. Future research should consider exploring the association between perceptions of procedural justice and compliance in a traditional court context. Moreover, a multi-level compliance framework could be used to investigate how variations across court contexts alter perceptions and policies surrounding compliance. Finally, future research may examine how stability and changes in state and federal laws differentially influence perceptions of procedural justice and compliance across social-demographic groups. In this chapter, we have focused on problem-solving courts as an ideal setting to explore the interconnection between levels of analysis to better understand compliance; however, applications for this framework are unlimited, and while the idea of assessing how compliance relates to our socio-political lives at multiple levels may seem daunting, it is arguable that in doing so, we better approximate the complexity of our lived experiences.

References

Alexander, M. (2010). *The new Jim Crow: Mass incarceration in the age of colorblindness*. New York, NY: The New York Press.

Almquist, L., & Dodd, E. (2009) *Mental health courts: A guide to research-informed policy and practice*. The Council of State Governments Justice Center, United States of America. https://www.bja.gov/Publications/CSG_MHC_Research.pdf [accessed 27 April 2018].

Aryee, S., Chen, Z. X., & Budhwar, P. S. (2004). Exchange fairness and employee performance: An examination of the relationship between organizational politics and procedural justice. *Organizational Behavior and Human Decision Processes, 94*, 1–14.

Atkin-Plunk, C. A., Peck, J. H., & Armstrong, G. S. (2017). Do race and ethnicity matter? An examination of racial/ethnic differences in perceptions of procedural justice and recidivism among problem-solving court clients. *Race and Justice*, https://doi.org/10.1177/2153368717691800.

Baker, T., Pelfrey, W. V., Bedard, L. E., Dhungana, K., Gertz, M., & Golden, K. (2013). Female inmates' procedural justice perceptions of the police and courts: Is there a spill-over of police effects? *Criminal Justice and Behavior, 41* (2), 144–162.

Baker, T., Pickett, J. T., Amin, D. M., Golden, K., Dhungana, K., Gertz, M., & Bedard, L. (2015). Shared race/ethnicity, court procedural justice, and self–regulating beliefs: A study of female offenders. *Law & Society Review, 49*(2), 433–466.

Barkworth, J. M., & Murphy, K. (2015). Procedural justice policing and citizen compliance behaviour: the importance of emotion. *Psychology, Crime and Law, 21*, 254–273.

Beetham, D. 1991. *The legitimation of power: Issues in political theory*. London, UK: Palgrave Macmillan.

Berman, G., & Feinblatt, J. (2005). *Good courts: The case for problem-solving justice*. New York, NY: The New York Press.

Braga, A. A., Papachristos, A. V. & Hureau, D. M. (2014). The effects of hot spots policing on crime: An updated systematic review and meta-analysis. *Justice Quarterly*, *31*(4), 633–663.

Burns, P. J., Hiday, V. A., & Ray, B. (2013). Effectiveness 2 years postexit of a recently established mental health court. *American Behavioral Scientist*, *57*(2), 189–208.

Chiricos, T., & Crawford, C. (1995). *Ethnicity race and crime: Perspectives among time and place*. New York, NY: State University of New York Press.

Christy, A., Poythress, N. G., Boothroyd, R. A., Petrila, J., & Mehra, S. (2005) Evaluating the efficiency and community safety goals of the Broward County Mental Health Court. *Behavioral Sciences & the Law*, *23*(2), 227–243.

Clear, T.R., & Frost, N.A. (2014). *The punishment imperative: The rise and failure of mass incarceration in America*. New York: New York Press.

Council of State Governments Justice Center. (2009). *Mental health courts: A guide to research-informed policy and practice*. New York: Council of State Governments Justice Center.

Cohen-Charash, Y., & Spector, P. E. (2001). The role of justice in organizations: A metaanalysis. *Organizational Behavior and Human Decision Processes*, *86*, 278–321.

Crawford, C., Chiricos, T., & Kleck, G. (1998). Race, racial threat, and sentencing of habitual offenders. *Criminology*, *36*, 481–512.

Crutchfield, R. D., Skinner, M. L., Haggerty, K. P., McGlynn, A., & Catalano, R. F. (2009). Racial disparities in early criminal justice involvement. *Race and Social Problems*, *1*, 218–230.

Dannerbeck, A., Harris, G., Sundet, P., & Lloyd, K. (2006). Understanding and responding to racial differences in drug court outcomes. *Journal of Ethnicity in Substance Abuse*, *5*(2), 1–22.

DeVall, K. E., & Lanier, C. L. (2012). Successful completion: An examination of factors influencing drug court completion for white and non-white male participants. *Substance Use & Misuse*, *47*(10), 1106–1016.

Dollar, C. B., & Ray, B. (2015). The practice of reintegrative shaming in mental health court. *Criminal Justice Policy Review, Special Issue on Restorative Justice and Community Corrections*, *26*(1), 29–44.

Festinger, D. S., Marlowe, D. B., Lee, P. A., Kirby, K. C., Bovasso, G., & McLellan, A. T. (2002). Status hearing in drug court: When more is less and less is more. *Drug and Alcohol Dependence*, *68*(2), 151–157.

Gallagher, J. R. (2013). Drug court graduation rates: Implications for policy advocacy and future research. *Alcoholism Treatment Quarterly*, *31*(1), 241–253.

Goldkamp, J. S. (1999). When is a drug court not a drug court? In C. Terry (Ed.), *The early drug courts: Case studies in judicial innovation*. Beverly Hills: Sage Publications.

Goldkamp, J. S., & Irons-Guynn. C. (2000). *Emerging judicial strategies for the mentally ill in the criminal caseload: Mental health courts in Fort Lauderdale, Seattle, San Bernardino, and Anchorage*. NCJ 182504. U.S. Department of Justice, Office of Justice Programs.

Goldkamp, J. S. White, M. D., & Robinson, J. B. (2001). Do drug courts work? Getting inside the drug court black box. *Journal of Drug Issues*, *31*(1), 27–72.

Gottfredson, D., & Exum, L. (2002). The Baltimore City Drug Treatment Court: One-year results from a randomized study. *Journal of Research on Crime and Delinquency*, *39*, 337–356.

Gottfredson, D. C., Kearley, B. W., Najaka, S. S., & Rocha, C. M. (2007). How drug treatment courts work an analysis of mediators. *Journal of Research in Crime and Delinquency*, *44*, 3–35.

Government Accountability Office (GAO). (2005). *Adult drug courts: Evidence indicates recidivism and mixed results for other outcomes: Report to congressional committees*. Retreived from U.S.G.A.O Office Website www.gao.gov/new.items/d05219.pdf

Griffith, D. A., Harvey, M. G., & Lusch, R. F. (2006). Social exchange in supply chain relationships: The resulting benefits of procedural and distributive justice. *Journal of Operations Management*, *24*(2), 85–98.

Higgins, G. E., & Jordan, K. L. (2005). Race and gender: An examination of the models that explain evaluations of the court system for differences. *Criminal Justice Studies: A Critical Journal of Crime, Law and Society*, *18*(1), 81–97.

Higgins, G., Wolfe, S., Mahoney, M., & Walters, N. (2009). Race, ethnicity, and experience: Modeling the public's perceptions of justice, satisfaction, and attitude toward the court. *Journal of Ethnicity in Criminal Justice*, *7*(4), 293–310.

Hosmer, L. R. T., & Kiewitz, C. (2005). Organizational justice: A behavioral science concept with critical implications for business ethics and stakeholder theory. *Business Ethics Quarterly*, *15*, 67–91.

Howard, D. (2014). Race, neighborhood, and drug court graduation. *Justice Quarterly*, *33*(1), 159–184.

Huddleston, W., & Marlowe, D. B. (2011). *Painting the current Picture: A national report on drug courts and other problem-solving court programs in the United States*. Washington, D.C.: National Drug Court Institute.

Konovsky, M. A. (2000). Understanding procedural justice and its impact on business organizations. *Journal of Management*, *26*(3), 489–511.

Kopelovich, S., Yanos, P., Pratt, C., & Koerner, J. (2013). Procedural justice in mental health courts: Judicial practices, participant perceptions, and outcomes related to mental health recovery. *International Journal of Law and Psychiatry*, *36*, 113–120.

Lind, E. A., & Tyler, T. R. (1988). *The social psychology of procedural justice*. New York, NY: Plenum.

Lurigio, A. J., & Snowden, J. (2009). Putting therapeutic jurisprudence into practice: The growth, operations, and effectiveness of mental health court. *Justice System Journal*, *30*, 196–218.

Marlowe, D. B., Festinger, D. S., Dugosh, K. L., Lee, P. A., Benasutti, K. M. (2007) Adapting judicial supervision to the risk level of drug offenders: Discharge and six-month outcomes from a prospective matching study. *Drug and Alcohol Dependence*, *88S*, 4–13.

Marlowe, D. B., Festinger, D. S., Lee, P. A., Dugosh, K. L. & Benasutti, K. M. (2006). Matching judicial supervision to clients' risk status in drug court. *Crime & Delinquency*, *52*, 52–76.

Mauer, M. (1999). *The crisis of the young African American male and the criminal justice system*. Prepared by The Sentencing Project for the U.S. Commission on Civil Rights. Retrieved from http://history.jburroughs.org/msmith/af-am%20justice%20system.pdf

McIvor G. (2009). Therapeutic jurisprudence and procedural justice in Scottish drug courts. *Criminology and Criminal Justice*, *9*(1), 29–49.

McKean, J., & Warren-Gordon, K. (2011). Racial differences in graduation rates from adult drug treatment courts. *Journal of Ethnicity in Criminal Justice*, *9*, 41–55.

Miller, J. L., & Johnson, D. C. (2009). *Problem solving courts: A measure of justice*. Lanham, MD: Rowman & Littlefield.
Mitchell, O., Wilson, D. B., Eggers, A., & MacKenzie, D. L. (2012). Assessing the effectiveness of drug courts on recidivism: A meta-analytic review of traditional and non-traditional drug courts. *Journal of Criminal Justice*, *40*, 60–71.
Munetz, M. R., Ritter, C., Teller, J. L., & Bonfine, N. (2014). Mental health court and assisted outpatient treatment: perceived coercion, procedural justice, and program impact. *Psychiatric Services*, *65*(3), 352–358.
Nagin, D. S. (1998). Criminal deterrence research at the outset of the twenty-first century. *Crime and Justice*, *23*, 1–42.
National Association of Drug Court Professionals. 2013. *Adult drug court best practices standards: volume 1*. http://www.nadcp.org/sites/default/files/nadcp/AdultDrugCourtBestPracticeStandards.pdf.
Nolan, J. L. (2001). *Reinventing justice: The American drug court movement*. Princeton, NJ: Princeton University.
Nowakowski, J. M., & Conlon, D. E. (2005). Organizational justice: Looking back, looking forward. *International Journal of Conflict Management*, *16*(1), 4–29.
Petrila, J., Poythress, N., McGaha, A., & Boothroyd, R. (2001, Winter). Preliminary observations from an evaluation of the Broward County Florida Mental Health Court. *Court Review*, 14–22.
Podsakoff, P. M., & MacKenzie, S. B. (1997). Impact of organizational citizenship behavior on organizational performance: A review and suggestions for future research. *Human Performance*, *10*, 133–151.
Porter, R., Rempel, M., & Mansky, A. (2010). *What makes a court problem-solving: Universal performance indicators for problem-solving justice*. New York, NY: U.S. Department of Justice.
Poythress, N. G., Petrila, J., McGaha, A., & Boothroyd, R. A. (2002). Perceived coercion and procedural justice in the Broward mental health court. *International Journal of Law and Psychiatry*, *25*, 517–533.
Pratt, C., Yanos, P. T., Kopelovich, S. L., Koerner, J., & Alexander, M. J. (2013). Predictors of criminal justice outcomes among mental health courts participants: The role of perceived coercion and subjective mental health recovery. *International Journal of Forensic Mental Health*, *12*(2), 116–125.
Ray, B., & Dollar, C. B. (2013). Examining mental health court completion: A focal concerns perspective. *The Sociological Quarterly*, *54*(4), 647–699.
Ray, B., & Dollar, C. B. (2014). Exploring stigmatization and stigma management in mental health court: Assessing modified labeling theory in a new context. *Sociological Forum*, *29*(3), 720–735.
Ray, B., Dollar, C. B., & Thames, K. (2011). Mental health courts as reintegrative shaming. *International Journal of Law and Psychiatry*, *34*, 49–55.
Redlich, A., & Han, W. (2014). Examining the links between therapeutic jurisprudence and mental health court completion. *Law & Human Behavior*, *38*, 109–118.
Redlich, A. D., Steadman, H. J., Callahan, L., Robbins, P. C., Vessilinov, R., & Özdog˘ru, A. A. (2010). The use of mental health court appearances in supervision. *International Journal of Law and Psychiatry*, *33*, 272–277. Rossman, S., Roman, J. K., & Zweig, J. (2011). *The multisite adult drug court evaluation: The impact of drug courts*. Retrieved from https://jpo.wrlc.org/bitstream/handle/11204/2050/3477.pdf?sequence=1

Redlich, A. D., Steadman, H. J., Monahan, J., Petrila, J., & Griffin, P. A. (2005). The second generation of mental health courts. *Psychology, Public Policy, and Law*, *11*(4), 527–538.

Sarteschi, C. M., Vaughn, M. G., & Kim, K. (2011). Assessing the effectiveness of mental health courts: A quantitative review. *Journal of Criminal Justice*, *39*, 12–20.

Spiropoulos, G. V., Salisbury, E. J., & Van Voorhis, P. (2014). Moderators of correctional treatment success: An exploratory study of racial differences. *International Journal of Offender Therapy and Comparative Criminology*, *58*(7), 835–860.

Spohn, C., Gruhl, J., & Welch, S. (1981). The effect of race on sentencing: A re-examination of an unsettled question. *Law and Society Review*, *16*, 71–80.

Steadman, H. J., Redlich, A. D., Griffin, P. A., Petrila, J., & Monahan, J. (2005). From referral to disposition: Case processing in seven mental health courts. *Behavioral Sciences & the Law*, *23*(2), 215–226.

Steffensmeier, D., Ulmer, J. T., & Kramer, J. (1998). The interaction of race, gender, and age in criminal sentencing: The punishment cost of being young, black, and male. *Criminology*, *36*, 763–797.

Strong, S. M., Rantala, R. R., & Kyckelhahn, T. (2016). *Census of problem-solving courts, 2012*. U.S. Department of Justice, Office of Justice Programs. NCJ 249803. Retrieved from www.bjs.gov/content/pub/pdf/cpsc12.pdf

Sun, I. Y. & Wu, Y. (2006). Citizens' perceptions of the courts: the importance of race, gender, and recent experience. *Journal of Criminal Justice*, *34*(5), 457–467.

Thibaut, J., & Walker, L. *Procedural justice: A psychological analysis*. Hillsdale, N.J.: Lawrence Erlbaum Associates.

Tyler, T. R. (1984). The role of perceived injustice in defendants' evaluations of tbeir courtroom experience. *Law Society Review*, *18*, 101–124.

Tyler, T. R. (2001). Public trust and confidence in legal authorities: What do majority and minority group members want from the law and legal institutions. *Behavioral Sciences & the Law*, *19*(2), 215–235.

Tyler, T. R. (2006). *Why people obey the law*. Princeton, NJ: Princeton University Press.

Tyler, T. R. (2009). Legitimacy and criminal justice: The benefits of self-regulation. *Ohio State Journal of Criminal Law*, *7*, 307–359.

Tyler, T. R., & Fagan, J. (2008). Legitimacy and cooperation: Why do people help the police fight crime in their communities? *Ohio State Journal of Criminal Law*, *6*, 231–275.

Tyler, T. R., & Huo, Y. J. (2002). *Trust in the law: Encouraging public cooperation with the police and the courts*. New York, NY: Russell Sage Foundation.

Tyler, T. R., Sherman, L., Strang, H., Barnes, G. C., & Woods, D. (2007) Reintegrative shaming, procedural justice, and recidivism: the engagement of offenders' psychological mechanisms in the Canberra rise drinking-and-driving experiments. *Law & Society Review*, *41*, 553–586.

van Dijke, M., DeCremer, D., Mayer, D. M., & Quaquebeke, N. V. (2012). When does procedural fairness promote organizational citizenship behavior? Integrating empowering leadership types in relational justice models. *Organizational Behavior and Human Decision Processes*, *117*(2), 235–248.

Wales, H. W., Hiday, V. A., & Ray, B. (2010). Procedural justice and the mental health court judge's role in reducing recidivism. *International Journal of Law & Psychiatry*, *33*(4), 265–271.

Watson, A., & Angell, B. (2007). Applying procedural justice theory to law enforcement's response to persons with mental illness. *Psychiatric Services*, *58*(6), 787–797.

Wexler, D. B., & Winick, B. J. (1991). *Essays in therapeutic jurisprudence*. Durham, NC: Carolina Academic Press.

Wilson, D. B., Michell, O., & MacKenzie, D. L. (2006). A systematic review of drug court effects on recidivism. *Journal of Experimental Criminology*, *4*, 459–487.

Winick, B. J., & Wexler, D. B. (2003). *Judging in a therapeutic key: Therapeutic jurisprudence and the courts*. Durham: Carolina Academic Press.Zapata-Phelan, C. P., Colquitt, J. A., Scott, B. A., & Livingston, B. (2009). Procedural justice, interactional justice, and task performance: The mediating role of intrinsic motivation. *Organizational Behavior and Human Decision Processes*, *108*, 93–105.

6 Investigating Compliance at the Macro Level

The Case of U.S. Interstate River Compacts

Tanya Heikkila and Edella Schlager

Introduction

This chapter contributes to the compliance discussion by examining a macro-level context where multiple levels of institutions and organizations interact. It considers how the complexity of this context challenges and influences how actors work to maintain compliance. In doing so, this chapter directly applies insights on the connections between the compliance context and compliance behaviors, as described in the compliance framework in Chapter 1. It also offers lessons for the framework by looking at the feedback of compliance outcomes on the compliance context. We examine these issues by studying interstate river allocation agreements (aka compacts) in the western United States.

Interstate compacts are an important governance tool in a federalist system of government. Compacts allow states to craft arrangements matched to particular settings and issues. States devise compacts to address regional scale problems that are highly salient to citizens and state officials. While states take the lead in developing and administering compacts, the federal government, either through its legislative or judicial powers, approves compacts to ensure that federal interests are not violated or that the U.S. Constitution is not undermined. In a federal system, compacts provide subnational governments a critical tool for addressing regional problems and opportunities.

In the United States, states have entered into interstate river compacts to resolve persistent conflicts among water users, provide stable and predictable institutional settings to encourage investment in water infrastructure, protect the needs of downstream users, and foster equitable sharing of water flowing across state lines. Interstate compacts assist states in meeting these goals by setting the rules that govern the amount of water, timing, location, and source of water that is shared. Thus, in this setting, compliance involves those actions taken by states, or by water users within a state, that meet the water allocation rules and requirements set out in interstate compacts.

To help ensure compliance, many compacts have commissions or compact administrations that serve as fora for states to discuss disagreements, problems, and conflicts. However, commissions do not have direct authority to regulate and take enforcement actions against individual water users within states. Instead, individual states maintain this authority, meaning that states must work together and rely on one another to ensure that water allocation rules are followed. Due in part to the multi-level interdependence among compact commissions, states, and water users, interstate compact compliance can be challenging (Schlager & Heikkila, 2009; Schlager, Heikkila, & Case, 2012). Therefore, the goal of this chapter is to examine how the compliance context of compacts drives compliance among states and to explore how the strategies actors use to maintain compliance feed back into the compliance context.

Compliance and noncompliance in the context of interstate river compacts is a particularly timely topic of study. Virtually every interstate river in the western United States is governed by a compact, meaning that cities from Denver to Los Angeles, and Phoenix to El Paso, as well as states' agricultural sectors and industries use compact-governed water. The oldest compact is nearing 100 years, and the youngest is almost 50 years old. From their origins until now, water has become increasingly scarce because of rising urban and agricultural demands, environmental needs, and more recently, climate change impacts. Increasing water scarcity has placed substantial pressure on compact administration and maintaining compliance. Compliance challenges spark conflicts among states. For example, when an upstream state fails to deliver required supplies downstream, noncompliance may negatively affect farmers that rely on water for production, or impair available supplies for municipal and environmental needs. Compliance challenges also spark conflicts within states. For instance, if states need to impose strict regulations on their water users to ensure that they comply with interstate compacts, then water users may resist these efforts. Encouraging and supporting compact compliance is not just about realizing rule following behavior, it is about protecting states' economies and ecosystems, and it provides a window into observing and explaining the dynamics of intergovernmental relations within a federal system.

The following section examines the dynamics of compliance among states and describes how this book's compliance framework applies to this macro setting. We then present an overview of the methods employed in this chapter for understanding the factors associated with compliance challenges. After exploring these factors, we look at the strategies and mechanisms to address compliance challenges including capacity building, enhancing rule compatibility, and enhancing monitoring and enforcement. In doing so, we also illustrate how conflict resolution processes play a role in incentivizing or compelling these strategies. Through this analysis, we uncover insights on the dynamic nature of compliance decisions. This view of compliance further highlights the interdependencies of actors across multiple scales and their long-term interdependencies.

Challenges of Compliance in an Interstate Setting

Regional, or transboundary, problems and opportunities require multiple jurisdictions to agree upon institutional arrangements that support cooperation to resolve collective problems and achieve desired outcomes. However, collective action problems often emerge in these settings because of differences between an actor's interests and goals and collective interests and goals (Ostrom, Gardner, & Walker, 1994). As federalism scholars point out, resolving collective action problems among governments requires finding a workable balance between self-governance and shared governance (Elazar, 1987; Skalaban, 1993; Weissert & Hill, 1994; Bednar, 2009). U.S. states, for instance, exercise substantial (but not exclusive) authority over water within their boundaries. Yet, to realize benefits that no single government can provide, such as large-scale water storage and distribution infrastructure or stable water rights in a transboundary river, states have to agree to limit their authority or to take costly actions that they would otherwise choose not to do. As Miller (2011, p. 487) notes, "there are times when a political actor can benefit by denying himself or herself, early in a political interaction, the option of choosing self-serving actions later on."

Bednar (2009) argues that the dynamic tension between self-rule and shared rule is ever-present among governments in federal systems, and consequently, compliance issues are ever-present. State officials may find it politically difficult to devise and adopt strict water regulations to make water available to out of state water users, thus, shifting the burden of water scarcity to another state in contradiction of water-sharing agreements (Weissert & Hill, 1994). Or, state water officials may be reluctant to actively administer existing water regulations, especially if that means limiting water diversions to allow water to flow to downstream users, thus shirking their duty to actively enforce (Derthick, 1974). Or, a federal agency may manage a reservoir to meet goals not shared by states or in ways that states perceive violate or encroach on their authority. Burden shifting, shirking, and encroachment, according to Bednar (2009), raise different types of compliance issues, and if a federal system is to be robust, the violating actor must be brought back into compliance in a way that allows for a re-balancing of self-rule and shared rule, or to better respond to changing values and goals. Given these broader challenges, some interstate river compacts experience persistent compliance issues (Schlager & Heikkila, 2011; Schlager et al., 2012).

The factors that shape compliance in the case of interstate river compacts fit squarely with several of the key factors identified in this book's compliance framework. These include the *broad compliance context*, especially the biophysical characteristics of river basins and broader system of rules. For example, the location of a state on a river conditions compliance issues (Schlager & Heikkila, 2011; Schlager et al., 2012). First, in an upstream state, water users are likely to be reluctant to limit their water use, especially during times of scarcity, to benefit water users in another state. Yet, without local water users' compliance, states cannot meet their compact water delivery requirements. Local water users' willingness to comply, however, is complicated by states' water laws. Although states entered into interstate compacts, initially they did not incorporate compact water rules into state water laws. Consequently, states allocated water rights exceeding the amount of water they were entitled to under the water compact. In addition, states entered into many compacts prior to widespread groundwater pumping and did not anticipate the effects of groundwater pumping on surface water flows. Most states, until very recently, have not regulated groundwater pumping. Both of these factors, combined with growing numbers of water users and uses, led to upstream states falling out of compliance with their compact water delivery commitments even though their water users were in compliance with state water laws (Schlager et al., 2012). In other words, the broader system of rules can be incompatible with the design of specific compact rules. Consequently, to achieve compliance with compacts, upstream states may need to revise their water laws, or strictly limit water diversions, which can result in active opposition from water users.

In addition to rule-design, other key aspects of the *specific compliance context* described in this book's framework, especially capacity and monitoring, are important in understanding compliance. For example, for downstream states, water "administration" (e.g., monitoring of uses and strict enforcement of water rights) by agencies in upstream states is largely a black box. Downstream states may not be privy to water consumption data or be aware of the quality of water rights enforcement in upstream states. If water deliveries do not meet compact requirements, downstream states cannot determine whether that is because of hydrologic conditions, lax water rights enforcement, or poorly designed water laws in the upstream state. When states do not have well-established water-monitoring capacity that links local water use, or when states lack clear lines of communication or cross-scale linkages in administrative staff between compact commissions and state water agencies, compliance may be challenged (Heikkila, Schlager, & Davis, 2011).

This complex set of conditions driving compliance problems also means that a complex of strategies (or compliance behaviors, as noted in this book's framework) are needed to bring states back into compliance when compacts are violated. For example, Bednar (2009) argues that federal systems require diverse and redundant mechanisms to identify and address acts of noncompliance. These overlapping mechanisms, ranging from courts to shared decision-making venues, to civic engagement and social movements, among others, provide opportunities to address compliance issues and adapt the intergovernmental arrangements to changing circumstances. As an example, our prior research (Schlager & Heikkila, 2009) has found that when compliance problems for interstate water compacts are relatively minor, or do not require costly actions to resolve, then states often negotiate or address compliance issues through commissions. However, when compliance issues are much more serious, and conflicts arise over the reason for noncompliance or appropriate solutions to achieve compliance, states require more formal or compulsory venues, such as the U.S. Supreme Court, to reach agreement (Schlager & Heikkila, 2009).

In sum, gaining and maintaining compliance among interstate river compacts is likely to involve a combination of intra-state and interstate cooperation, coordination, and conflict resolution. These compliance behaviors create outcomes (via problem solving and conflict resolution) that then change and reshape the compliance context. Such adaptation is not quick or simple. As Derthick (1974, p. 192) argues in studying horizontal federalism: "Regional action proceeds within a narrow sphere or at a slow pace." Therefore, this chapter aims to understand the dynamic nature of compliance in this complex, multi-level setting, as informed by the framework in Chapter 1.

Methods and Results

The data for this analysis come from historical records of 11 interstate river compacts in the western United States dealing with water allocation issues, which were part of a larger study on western water governance. These 11 compacts are the state agreements in the West that their members and Congress ratify, and that compact commissions or state water officials actively administer. They include the Arkansas, Bear, Big Blue, Costilla Creek, La Plata, Pecos, Republican, Rio Grande, Snake, South Platte, Upper Niobrara, and Yellowstone. Member states include Colorado, Idaho, Kansas, Montana, Nebraska, New Mexico, Texas, Utah, and Wyoming.[1]

States have been party to these compacts in some cases for nearly 100 years. Compacts offer a context where we can easily identify compliance issues through written records. These include court cases, the media, water agency reports, and the minutes of the annual meetings of compact commissions that monitor the basins. We collected data for compliance issues of the compacts studied through document coding of interstate compact meeting minutes, news media reports, and court cases. To collect these data, we used a standardized code form that allowed us to identify the number and type of compliance problems for each compact we studied over the lifetime of the compact. We defined compliance problems as a violation or dispute over compact water allocation rules. We reviewed all documents related to the compacts to identify when compliance problems have arisen, the issues associated with the compliance problems, and how the problem was resolved. We also coded the interstate compact documents and the rules that determine how compacts are administered, how they allocate water, and how they monitor and enforce compacts. Finally, we collected data on the biophysical context (e.g., types of water governed, streamflow conditions) and the state water institutions (e.g., water laws, water agencies) of the compact member states. This chapter describes these data according to the features of the compliance decision context, as outlined in this book's framework, which vary across the compacts. These include the broader biophysical context, evidence of capacity to administer the compact from the design of the compacts and state water administration, rule compatibility with the biophysical system and with states, and monitoring and enforcement of the compact rules. In our analysis, we also describe the strategies and mechanisms for resolving disputes over compliance, and how states and compact commissions adapt their capacity, rule compatibility, and monitoring or enforcement to support compliance.

Results

Factors Associated With Compliance Problems

Among the interstate compacts we have studied in the western United States, six have experienced compliance issues. Table 6.1 summarizes the compliance problems associated with each of the compacts. In line with the expectations from the literature review, we identified notable patterns when compliance problems arise, which we summarize below according to the factors identified in this book's framework. While we discuss each factor in order, they clearly interact and we will point that out along the way.

Table 6.1 Western Interstate Water Compact Compliance Problems

Compact (Year) and Member States	*Compliance Problems*
Arkansas (1949); CO, KS	1. Proposed reservoir may violate water allocation rule (1963–1963). 2. Groundwater pumping violates water allocation rule (1985–1995).
Bear (1958, 1980); UT, WY, ID	No major compliance issues, but the compact commission identified potential challenges to compliance over the years and took several actions to improve compact administration in support of compliance.
Big Blue (1971); NE, KS	None
Costilla Creek (1946); CO, NM	1. Water users break headgates (1952–1953). 2. Lax administration of water allocation rule (1997–2002).
La Plata (1922); CO, NM	Colorado water users claim compact water allocation rule violates their state-granted water rights (1928).
Pecos (1949); NM, TX	NM fails to deliver water to TX (1974–1987).
Republican (1943); CO, NE, KS	1. Groundwater pumping upstream, especially in NE, violates water allocation rule (1985–2002). 2. 2002 Settlement Agreement not enforced by upstream states (2010–2016).
Rio Grande (1938); CO, NM, TX	1. Upstream states fail to deliver (1951–1957). 2. Upstream states fail to deliver (1966–1985). 3. NM groundwater diversions deplete flows to TX (2013–present).
Snake (1950); WY, ID	None
South Platte (1923); CO, NE	None
Upper Niobrara (1963); WY, NE	None
Yellowstone (1951); WY, MT	Wyoming fails to provide adequate flows to MT (2007–2011).

* Upstream state is listed first followed by downstream states. With two compacts, Bear and Costilla Creek, the states are both upstream and downstream because of the rivers crossing state boundaries multiple times.

Broader Context: The biophysical setting plays a critical role in compliance problems. The most notable biophysical factors are the geography, the hydrology, and the variable climate of river basins. First, while often taken for granted, the geography of basins establishes the foundation for conflict among states. Upstream versus downstream is at the heart of many compliance issues. It sets up a zero-sum game around water allocation. The water allocated to one state is not available to the other state(s). All rivers included in this study, but for two, set up clear upstream–downstream dynamics. The two rivers that cross back and forth over state boundaries present a different dynamic. In such settings, a state and its water users are both upstream and downstream, moderating the zero-sum dynamic.

Second, a number of the rivers have hydrologically connected groundwater aquifers. What this means is that surface water and groundwater interact. Groundwater aquifers feed or support river flows and, conversely, river flows percolate underground and replenish groundwater aquifers. While we understand hydrologic connections better today, they were poorly understood at the time that states developed their water laws and when many of the interstate river compacts were devised and adopted. This resulted in two developments that present compliance challenges. States' surface water laws did not account for groundwater and for the effects of groundwater pumping on surface water flows. Likewise, compacts' water allocation rules also failed to account for groundwater. Later, as the technology for groundwater pumping developed and water users adopted these technologies, the effects of groundwater pumping on surface water flows quickly emerged. Surface water users claimed that their water rights were being infringed on and downstream states claimed that groundwater pumping in upstream states deprived them of water they were due under compact rules. To this day, states are struggling to manage hydrologically connected surface and groundwater sources effectively. In fact, all of the interstate river compacts that have appeared before the U.S. Supreme Court, but for two, have faced this vexing issue.

Third, climate variability refers to droughts of record. The western United States regularly experiences drought. Water users and state officials are accustomed to dealing with drought. For example, both western water rights systems and water storage infrastructure are adaptations to drought. However, especially severe types of drought raise compliance challenges. In the midst of droughts of record, upstream states find it physically challenging to shepherd modest amounts of water across state lines. Riverbeds are "leaky," evaporation rates are high, and, thus, significant amounts of water are "lost" before arriving at a state line.

Whether these biophysical characteristics make conflict and rule violations more likely depends on the organizational and institutional settings of interstate river compacts. Topics we turn to next.

Capacity: Capacity in this context refers to the human and organizational resources available to states and water users that make it possible to comply with interstate compacts. In examining the capacity of interstate compacts, we find that most compacts, through their rules, establish the authority among states to create some organizational capacity to administer compacts and support compliance. The compacts may authorize states to create administrative bodies or commissions, to devise rules and regulations to help administer and enforce the compacts, to hire employees, create specialized advisory or technical committees, collaborate with outside groups, have diverse representation, and to establish conflict resolution procedures. However, there is variance in the degree to which compact members invest in these capacity features.

Largely, in the cases that have not developed significant organizational capacity (La Plata, Snake, Upper Niobrara) compliance has not been an issue. In part, this may be because interstate water management concerns in these basins have not yet been serious enough to warrant the states' attention to these compacts, or because supplies have been adequate to meet demands or facilitate compliance (Schlager & Heikkila, 2009). On the other hand, compacts that have faced compliance issues either started with reasonable levels of organizational capacity, or have invested in capacity building. For instance, the types of organizational capacity we identified among compacts that have dealt with compliance issues range from creating new committees, hiring new staff, engaging in new collaboration with other organizations, or conducting research. Although some variance exists across the compacts in terms of organizational capacity, lack of capacity does not necessarily mean that compliance problems will emerge. At the same time, having high levels of capacity may not guarantee compliance will not be a problem. At a minimum, however, we have seen that when compliance issues arise, the compact administrations and states may need to invest in building new forms of capacity to help support compliance. These capacity-building efforts are discussed in more detail below.

Rule [In]Compatibility: The level of compatibility among the rules governing the different types of actors who must comply with compacts can play an important role in compliance. Compatibility issues can occur both within the compact rules or between compact rules and state rules, or between state rules and water user rules. Beginning with compact rules, incompatibility often reflects a mismatch between the water allocation rules and the biophysical system. The water allocation rule may be based on faulty hydrologic modeling, as was the case in the Pecos, or the boundaries of the compact may not conform to state boundaries, as is the case in the Rio Grande. In the Rio Grande, New Mexico's surface water delivery obligations end at the Elephant Butte Reservoir, just over 100 miles north of the state line with Texas. The remaining portion of New Mexico is considered to be part of Texas for compact purposes. In both instances, the downstream state, Texas, has filed Supreme Court cases against the upstream state, New Mexico, to clarify water delivery requirements.

Another type of rule incompatibility occurs between compact rules and state water laws. States largely did not incorporate compact commitments into their surface water laws and administration. Consequently, as state water administrators allocated surface water rights, they ignored compact requirements, allocating rights in water that would largely be unavailable if compact rules were followed. The same dynamic played out in relation to groundwater, as states have not actively or effectively regulated groundwater pumping, leading to negative impacts on surface water flows. In both cases, upstream states have experienced conflicts with water users as they attempt to align state water laws with compact water allocation rules.

Monitoring and Enforcement: Compliance issues also are shaped by the ability of states to monitor and enforce rules. What is monitored and how is particularly important. Initially, at the compact level, states only monitored surface water flows, especially across state boundaries. With the widespread emergence of groundwater pumping, and conflicts occurring at upstream states have failed to abide by water allocation rules, compact commissions have invested in modeling river systems, including surface water and groundwater interactions. More sophisticated modeling at the compact level is supported by states that have also invested in monitoring. States record surface water diversions by water users and they have begun to monitor wells by requiring well owners to install water meters.

Monitoring of water uses at the compact level and state level affects the capacity of states and compact commissions to enforce rules and bring rule violators back into compliance. To enforce the rules, information is needed about rule-following behavior. Without such information, conflict among parties to compacts is likely. The Yellowstone River Compact provides an illustration. Montana, the downstream state, claimed that Wyoming, the upstream state, was out of compliance with the compact's water allocation rule around 2007. However, the compact commission had not invested in monitoring beyond measuring state boundary flows. Montana knew that flows appeared to be declining, but did not know why. Without more information, combined with a reluctance on the part of Wyoming to invest in additional monitoring, Montana decided to file suit before the Supreme Court. In this case, lack of clear agreement on monitoring at the commission level inhibited enforcement resulting in a dispute over the question of compliance.

These factors—broader context, capacity, rule compatibility, and monitoring and enforcement—interact in ways that condition compliance behaviors. If these factors align, compliance appears effortless, however, if even one of these factors contradicts another, compliance can appear impossible to achieve, as we discuss next.

Strategies and Mechanisms to Address Noncompliance

When compact compliance issues arise, invariably it is the downstream state claiming that the upstream state is failing to follow the water allocation rules and is thus under delivering water. Compliance issues are typically sparked by biophysical events that expose the weaknesses and incompatibilities of rules. The responses, summarized in Table 6.2, often take the form of revising or enforcing existing rules, adopting new water laws, and investing in administrative capacity as well as more intensive and extensive monitoring. In this

Table 6.2 Addressing Compliance Problems

Compact	*Conflict Resolution Venue*	*Compliance Problem (Years)*	*Strategies or Mechanisms to Bring States Into Compliance*
Costilla Creek	Commission	Water theft	***Capacity building***: Commission hires water master
Costilla Creek	Commission	Lax enforcement	***Rule compatibility***: Commission revises operations manual of water master
Arkansas	Commission	Proposed reservoir	***Enforcement***: Colorado drops reservoir proposal
Arkansas	U.S. Supreme Court	Groundwater pumping depletes surface flows; state rule incompatibility; lax water administration	***Rule Compatibility; Capacity Building, and Monitoring/ Enforcement***: Colorado regulates pumping; monitors pumping, replacement water, new local water governance/ taxing authority; Colorado required to pay financial penalty to Kansas; states develop hydrologic model for water accounting purposes
Pecos	U.S. Supreme Court	Lax enforcement; state and compact rule incompatibility	***Monitoring/Enforcement; Rule Compatibility and Capacity Building***: Supreme Court appoints a river master to monitor compliance and river master uses agreed upon hydrologic model for accounting purposes; New Mexico required to pay financial penalty to Texas; New Mexico adjudicates water rights claims among Pecos water users and develops agreement among irrigation districts to prevent a call on the river, and purchases, leases water, and develops well field as part of a water portfolio to meet compact requirements
Republican	U.S. Supreme Court	Groundwater pumping depletes surface flows and state rule incompatibility	***Rule Compatibility, Capacity Building, and Monitoring/ Enforcement***: Nebraska adopts major water laws allowing for stricter regulation of groundwater, and taxing powers to pay for water purchases and leases; Nebraska develops hydrologic model that allows it to forecast water deliveries to Kansas; Colorado irrigators create

Compact	*Conflict Resolution Venue*	*Compliance Problem (Years)*	*Strategies or Mechanisms to Bring States Into Compliance*
			a special district to pay for water infrastructure and water purchases; Supreme Court enforces state agreements; Colorado passes new measurement rules for groundwater; compact commission and states come to final agreement on management strategies to enhance flexibility in meeting compliance
Rio Grande	Commission/ U.S. Supreme Court	Lax water enforcement; state and compact rule incompatibility	***Rule Compatibility***: Colorado adopts groundwater regulations; changes operations of reservoirs; Colorado actively enforces surface water rights, with compact as most senior water user; Texas files lawsuit in 2013, Supreme Court agrees to accept case in 2014, special master rules in 2017 that groundwater pumping in New Mexico violates the compact water allocation rules
Yellowstone	U.S. Supreme Court	Lax water enforcement	***Enforcement***: Wyoming must replace flows owed Montana

section, we examine compliance behaviors, exhibited through conflicts and their resolution, by taking a deep dive into the five compacts that the U.S. Supreme Court has addressed; two of these compacts have been before the Supreme Court twice. We begin with four compliance conflicts that although sparked by biophysical issues, involved state water officials not exercising their existing authorities to align water users' activities with compact water allocation rules—or lax enforcement of the compact. We then turn to a case in which rule incompatibility between compact water allocation rules and state water laws was severe, requiring a substantial transformation of state water laws. Finally, we examine a compact in which states disagree over what compliance means rather on how compliance should be achieved.

Addressing Lax Enforcement: The Rio Grande Compact Supreme Court cases and the more recent Yellowstone Compact Supreme Court case are examples of state water officials failing to actively administer or enforce state water rights and therefore comply with compact water commitments. The Rio Grande Basin experienced a drought of record in the mid- to late 1950s. The Rio Grande Compact allows Colorado and New Mexico to under and over deliver water within specified limits. Both states under delivered water during the drought, but New Mexico remained within the requirements established by the compact, and worked to reduce its water debt. Colorado did not. In the early 1960s, New Mexico and Texas filed a Supreme Court lawsuit against Colorado. In the "shadow of the court," the three states negotiated an agreement where Colorado would pay down its water debt. After several years in which Colorado abided by the agreement, New Mexico and Texas had the lawsuit dismissed. More recently, a similar situation emerged in the Yellowstone. After the downstream state (Montana) complained that the upstream state had been out of compliance for several years, Montana sued Wyoming, taking the compliance question to the Supreme Court. While the resulting mechanism was relatively straightforward—more active enforcement of water rights in Wyoming—it did require the force of a Supreme Court case to make it happen. Currently, the Rio Grande Compact is before the Supreme Court. Texas filed suit in 2013 claiming that groundwater pumping in the 100-mile stretch of the river above the Texas state line is affecting surface water flows and depriving it of the water it is owed under the compact. New Mexico state water administrators and water users have recognized groundwater pumping as problematic in this region. For instance, the New Mexico state engineer put in place well regulations, such as well meters and a moratorium on additional wells in the late 1990s, however, placing a moratorium on wells without strictly regulating pumping from existing wells is insufficient to limit impacts. The Supreme Court will likely decide in favor of Texas's claim, which will prompt New Mexico to develop new policies and regulations to realize compliance.

The fourth example is more complicated and demonstrates how water users can exercise their political clout to constrain state water administration. In the 1960s, Colorado granted the state water engineer the authority to devise rules and regulations to manage groundwater pumping after farmers and irrigation districts complained about declining surface water flows. The state engineer had the authority to regulate groundwater pumping, but found it difficult to exercise that authority in the Arkansas River Basin, where farmers who relied heavily on groundwater formed well associations and actively and successfully resisted strict regulations. In 1985, Kansas filed a Supreme Court lawsuit against Colorado arguing that groundwater pumping was depleting surface flows, depriving Kansas water users of their water. Resolving the groundwater issue required Colorado to adopt various accounting and monitoring requirements, that feed into a complex model and manual that the Court mandated be used for administering the compact. Colorado's state engineer was directly ordered to use his authority to enforce new monitoring rules. These include mandatory well metering starting in 1994, which must be re-verified at intervals of no less than four years. Colorado is required to collect groundwater pumping data on a monthly basis.

Basin-centered arrangements have been developed that also foster capacity. Colorado water users in the Arkansas River Valley created a conservancy district with taxing powers. The revenues are used to purchase or lease Arkansas River water rights that would otherwise be sold to water users in other river basins, thus keeping the water in basin to meet basin and interstate water demands (Lower Arkansas Valley Water Conservancy District, 2018). In addition, in 2008 when the compliance issues were finally settled, the Court awarded damages to Kansas of close to $35 million for undelivered water for past compliance violations (U.S. Department of Justice, 2008).

Addressing State Rule Incompatibility: Unlike Colorado, in which state law granted the authority to regulate groundwater pumping to the state water engineer, in Nebraska, until relatively recently, the state water agency had no legal authority to regulate groundwater pumping. In the 1990s Kansas, the downstream state in the Republican River Compact, began raising concerns over the impacts of groundwater pumping on surface water flows. As the Nebraska commissioner to the Republican Compact Commission noted, the state had no authority to address the issue. Nebraska water law did not recognize the hydrologic connection between surface and groundwater. In addition, the administration of each type of water occurred through different agencies with no overlap in authorities. The state issued and administered surface water rights but local natural resources districts, governed by elected boards, possessed the exclusive authority to regulate groundwater.

Kansas filed a Supreme Court lawsuit in 2000 against the two upstream states—Nebraska and Colorado. After the Supreme Court ruled in 2002 that the compact included groundwater, the upstream states made various strides toward compliance, particularly in Nebraska. For instance, since the Nebraska Department of Natural Resources Director lacked authority to regulate groundwater, the state had to invest in stricter groundwater regulation. This required both legislative changes that acknowledged a hydrologic connection between ground and surface water and promoting more integrated planning of surface and groundwater by local Natural Resource Districts (NRDs). Despite these efforts, implementation and funding was slow and Kansas continued to view Nebraska as noncompliant with the compact.

Although the states attempted non-binding arbitration between 2007 and 2009, Kansas filed suit again in 2010. In 2011, the Court appointed a special master to begin the process of enforcing the 2002 agreement between the states. Nebraska continued to invest in legislative and financing efforts to ensure more integration of groundwater and surface water management. The state also approved resources to allow the local NRDs to purchase water that would be placed in the river to address impacts from pumping and move some irrigated lands out of production. Also, while the Supreme Court case was under review, the commission and states began to negotiate solutions to the enduring compliance challenges, looking for ways to bring more flexibility into the water management approaches states could take to comply (e.g., allowing Nebraska to adjust when it supplies water for compact compliance purposes). After the Supreme Court case was settled in 2015 with Kansas receiving $5.5 million in damages from Nebraska for compact violations, the three states came to a final settlement via the compact commission on the new water management strategies for compliance in 2016.

Compact and State Rule Incompatibility: Resolving compliance issues, as illustrated earlier, is difficult, but when states disagree over what compliance means, the efforts to resolve such differences become even harder. The Pecos River Compact between New Mexico and Texas exemplifies this problem. Differences between the states over the meaning and administration of the compact's water allocation rule emerged a few short years after the compact was adopted in 1949. The water allocation rule required that New Mexico provide water to Texas equivalent to the "1947 condition." The 1947 condition is represented by a hydrological model based on historic river flows and flooding events. To determine the amount of water that New Mexico must deliver to Texas in any given year, data on river flows and flooding were used to solve the model.

Beginning in the 1950s, Texas began to question whether the model appropriately represented river flows. Furthermore, groundwater pumping increased in New Mexico. Nevertheless, both states continued to attempt to make the 1947 condition model work by improving data collection. Also, New Mexico began removing non-native stream-side vegetation in an effort to increase river flows, assuming that the vegetation consumed large volumes of water.

In the early 1970s, as the officials who negotiated and administered the compact retired, the new state officials, especially those representing Texas, turned to the U.S. Supreme Court to resolve the disagreement over the water allocation rule. After 14 years of arguing over the water allocation rule, in 1988, the Court imposed a settlement that allowed Texas to develop a workable hydrologic model that established the annual amount of water New Mexico was to deliver. It also imposed an independent third party, known as a river master, to monitor New Mexico's compliance. If New Mexico fell out of compliance, the river master was authorized to take over water administration in the New Mexico portion of the Pecos and ensure that the appropriate amount of water was delivered to Texas (Titus, 2003). The decision sparked a spate of legislative and regulatory activity in New Mexico, aimed at more strictly regulating groundwater, adjudicating surface water rights, and establishing a state program whereby the New Mexico State Engineer purchased surface water rights and made the water available to meet the compact water allocation requirements.

These cases illustrate that as water scarcity increases, compact commissions and states respond and attempt to realize and ensure long-term compliance. Once groundwater pumping becomes pronounced, however, downstream states often turn to the U.S. Supreme Court as upstream states rarely have the political will or capacity to strictly regulate an easily accessible source of water that is immune to drought.

Discussion and Conclusion

Within a multi-level setting, compliance at the macro scale—i.e., an interstate agreement—involves multiple types of actors across scales. In our research on interstate water compacts, these actors include compact commissions, states, and water users. The compliance outcomes in this setting can be complicated by the *broad compliance context* (e.g., under drought conditions and groundwater-surface water interactions) and by the *compliance situation context*, as identified in this book's framework. In terms of the compliance situation context, we find compliance challenges and disagreements often arise when actors at one level lack *capacity* for compliance, or if *the design of rules* at one level are *incompatible* another level, or if *monitoring* is inadequate (especially downstream), which are three key features of the framework. Yet, as our research has shown, the compliance behaviors of states and compact commissions have included substantial investments over time in trying to maintain or restore compliance in basins that face compliance problems. This may require passing laws and regulations that provide actors with the authority to regulate and enforce compact rules. It may also involve establishing strategies or rules to allow more flexible water uses. Investments in capacity, especially monitoring of both river systems and water users, support these strategies. At the same time, knowledgeable and authoritative conflict resolution mechanisms are needed when actors disagree on the fundamental reasons for noncompliance or appropriate solutions, but low-cost mechanisms in the macro context can be elusive. That is, states may have to resort to an adverse decision by the Supreme Court to motivate more strict water administration and regulation in upstream states. As indicated in the framework in Chapter 1, these outcomes produce feedback effects (e.g., building capacity and monitoring). An important contribution of this research to the framework is the lesson that access to a formalized conflict resolution venue when capacity building efforts fail or fundamental disagreements ensue, may be important in other macro-level or multi-level settings.

Of course, the interstate water context may present unique circumstances that incentivize actors to invest in compliance-enhancing strategies. For example, in the interstate water context, states and water users are motivated to engage ongoing attempts to enhance capacity, rule compatibility, and monitoring/enforcement to provide predictability and stability in the governance of and access to a highly salient resource. The productivity of large infrastructure projects and the economies and industries of states and cities depend on maintaining compliance and managing conflict. Over the long term, this continued investment in governance may position states and water users to better respond to impending challenges, in particular, climate change. As precipitation patterns change and as droughts and floods become more intense, states and water users will have to confront changing water allocation rules to better match them with new hydrologic patterns. Decades of experience in responding to multi-level compliance challenges may provide them with capacity to respond in ways that encourage problem solving and discourage conflict and divisiveness. The extent to which this prior experience will be successful in sustaining compliance under changing climatic contexts is an area ripe for future research.

Note

1 Other western U.S. compacts include the Klamath and Belle Fourche, which have not been actively administered. The Colorado River Compact is also excluded from this analysis as distinct from the other active compacts in that the federal government plays a central role in its administration. It is also an outlier in terms of the number of states involved and institutional complexity of the compact. We also exclude compacts in the eastern United States because the legal and institutional structure for water allocation differs markedly from the western context.

References

Bednar, J. (2009). *The robust federation: Principles of design*. New York, NY: Cambridge University Press.

Derthick, M. (1974). *Between state and nation: Regional organizations of the United States*. Washington, DC: The Brookings Institution.

Elazar, D. J. (1987). *Exploring federalism*. Tuscaloosa. Alabama: University of Alabama Press.

Heikkila, T., Schlager, E., & Davis, M. W. (2011). The role of cross-scale institutional linkages in common pool resource management: Assessing interstate river compacts. *Policy Studies Journal*, *39*(1), 121–145.

Lower Arkansas Valley Water Conservancy District. (2018). History. http://www.lavwcd.org/history.html [accessed April 26, 2018].http://www.lavwcd.com/our-story.html.

Miller, G. J. (2011). Credible commitment. In B. Bertrand, D. Berg-Schlosser, & L. Morlino (Eds.), *International encyclopedia of political science* (pp. 487–489). Thousand Oaks, CA: Sage Publications.

Ostrom, E., Gardner, R., & Walker, J. (1994). *Rules, games, and common-pool resources*. Ann Arbor, MI: University of Michigan Press.

Schlager, E., & Heikkila, T. (2009). Resolving water conflicts: A comparative analysis of interstate river compacts. *Policy Studies Journal*, *37*, 367–392.

Schlager, E., & Heikkila, T. (2011). Left high and dry? Climate change, common-pool resource theory, and the adaptability of western water compacts. *Public Administration Review*, *71*(3), 461–470.

Schlager, E., Heikkila, T., &Case, C. (2012). The costs of compliance with interstate agreements: Lessons from water compacts in the western United States. *Publius: The Journal of Federalism*, *42*(3), 494–515.

Skalaban, A. (1993). Policy cooperation among the states: The case of interstate banking reform. *American Journal of Political Science*, 415–428.

Titus, F. 2003. Lessons from the Pecos River. In P. Johnson, L. Lewis, G. Price, & F. Titus (Eds.), *Waters of the lower Pecos River New Mexico* (pp. 3–8). Albuquerque, NM: New Mexico Bureau of Geology and Mineral Resources.

U.S. Department of Justice. (2008, January). *Fifth and Final Report Volume II Proposed Judgement and Decree—No 105*. http://water.state.co.us/DWRIPub/Documents/KSvsCO105_5thReportV2_Alittleworth_20071010.pdf.

Weissert, C. S., & Hill, J. S. (1994). Low-level radioactive waste compacts: Lessons learned from theory and practice. *Publius: The Journal of Federalism*, *24*(4), 27–43.

7 Police Noncompliance

Why Law Enforcers May Deviate From Laws, Rules, and Reform Mandates

Stuart Henry, Joshua Chanin, Megan Welsh, and Dana Nurge

Introduction

In this chapter, we examine the various contexts that influence compliance/noncompliance by police officers subject to macro-level behavioral directives. At issue are the relationships between societal, organizational, community, individual, and situational factors that affect compliance with federally driven police reform efforts. More specifically, we review organizational and individual compliance with directives associated with the U.S. Department of Justice's "pattern or practice" initiative, a program designed to identify and remedy systemic violations of civil rights.

As indicated at the outset of this book, a variety of contextual factors affect the extent to which individual institutional agents, in our case police officers, comply with behavioral directives. We are particularly interested in what leads individual officers, in collaboration with fellow officers, to translate compliance in-form directives at the micro level into norms of compliance in-practice, in the process establishing something less than full implementation of the formal directive. For example, officers can decide to fudge, minimize, or compromise the compliance in-form mandates to a version of compliance in-practice. We examine whether any patterns of law enforcement behavior facilitate this shift from in-form to in-practice. To do so we explore the set of societal, organizational, individual, and situational contexts that are reflected in the discourse and dialogue among officers as part of their shared police subculture. The discourse itself becomes a narrative justifying less than full compliance. It is important, in other words, to consider the full range of formative contexts of compliance or noncompliance actions that are subsequently reflected in the outcome at various levels of compliance.

In the context of Ostrom's (1999) work on institutional studies, the compliance issues we focus on can be considered as an illustration of the relationship between formal and informal rules and how, in the introduction of new formal rules, such as Department of Justice mandates, informal rules can continue to persist in the form of in-practice norms that can undermine the intent of the formal rules to bring about changes in behavior. Indeed,

> in periods of transition, informal rules may prove especially tenacious and resistant to change, existing in parallel—or even direct contradiction—to

> formal rules. New rules and structures can be effectively incorporated into "the old ways," leaving customary patterns of behaviour intact—neutering or subverting the intended changes in values and/or power relationships.
>
> (Leach & Lowndes, 2007, p. 185)

This is because institutional change is "contingent and context dependent process, rather than something that can be imposed from the outside through formal mechanisms alone" (Leach & Lowndes, 2007, p. 199). This contingency is rooted in the "interdependent web of an institutional matrix" (North, 1990) that includes not only subcultural patterns and practices but differing rule sets and "players" or agents with different degrees of power and influence over how the rules are interpreted, adapted, develop, and evolve in different local and situational contexts (Lowndes, 2005, p. 293). In this sense

> rules . . . are not free-floating. They are "nested." They are "nested" or embedded within wider institutional frameworks that exist above, below and alongside . . . are shaped by rules that emanate from higher tiers of government . . . by "institutional templates" that circulate in the wider society and economy (media, business, education), and by locally specific cultures and conventions ("how things are done around here").
>
> (Lowndes, 2005, p. 294)

It is for this reason that we cannot assume that different rule sets will all move in the same direction or be reinforcing just because they come from the ostensibly more powerful top-down mandates because these will sometimes clash with bottom-up institutional influences and "interact in important ways to produce an uneven patterning of uniformity and diversity" of behavior and practice (Lowndes, 2005, p. 293).

We begin our examination with a look at the context of formal compliance mandates on police agencies. We then look at the effects of such reform on police practices, particularly on police practices of resistance to reform. The contextual factors affecting resistance to DOJ-led reform are examined, with a focus on those involving police use of neutralizations that justify or excuse noncompliant moral disengagement (Sykes & Matza, 1957; Matza, 1964). These patterns of neutralization and moral disengagement illustrate the nested nature of formative contexts of police resistance to pattern or practice reform referred to earlier.

Pattern or Practice Reform

Under the 1994 Violent Crime Control and Law Enforcement Act, any "pattern or practice of conduct by law enforcement officers . . . that deprives persons of rights, privileges, or immunities secured or protected by the Constitution or laws of the United States" (42 U.S.C. Sec. 14141) is unlawful. This law is enforced by the U.S. Department of Justice (DOJ), which is charged with correcting past abuse and deterring future misconduct by police agencies. To date, enforcement has occurred most frequently over excessive use of force and from racial profiling (Chanin, 2017). DOJ enforcement typically involves a civil suit brought against a police department found in violation of provisions of the Act. In response, police departments negotiate an agreement of pattern or practice reform rather than fight the DOJ in court (Childress, 2015; Rushin, 2014). So, at this first level of compliance action, the conditions of reform are not a clear behavioral directive, so much as a negotiated space to make change. Importantly, this process demonstrates that the standards of compliance are themselves potentially negotiable.

Most such settlement negotiations have resulted in a legally binding document outlining specific organizational and managerial reforms designed to bring the offending jurisdiction into constitutional compliance. These consent decrees, typically involve five broad mandates:

> (1) strengthen incident reporting and chain of command oversight; (2) develop an internal database designed to track and manage officer behavior, often referred to as an early intervention system; (3) enhance officer training; (4) simplify and clarify the citizen complaint process; and (5) strengthen the jurisdiction's external citizen complaint investigative process.
>
> (Chanin & Sheats, 2017, p. 3)

Pattern or practice reforms also establish detailed terms of organizational compliance, including specific timelines for implementation and funding for independent oversight.

Consent decree implementation is a time-consuming, onerous process, though incentives exist to promote organizational compliance. The faster a department can demonstrate the necessary reforms; the faster DOJ oversight is terminated. The incentives for individual officers are not so clear, particularly because the intent of pattern or practice reforms is to drive major changes to the way street-level officers do their jobs.

In fact, police officers in several affected jurisdictions have criticized such changes to their daily work, arguing that (1) the additional paperwork and record keeping takes time away from policing; (2) accountability of officers creates a fear of reprimand, which increases job-related stress; (3) morale is thereby undermined; and (4) police are forced to act less aggressively, which can lead some officers to avoid situations potentially leading to scrutiny and reprimand (Bernstein, 2012; Stone, Foglesong, & Cole, 2009). Such "avoidant police behavior" forms a category of noncompliant deviance from norms and expectations of reform policy that is a focus of this chapter.

Although some evidence suggests that pattern or practice reforms "minimize unwanted police misconduct and generate desirable policy outcomes, particularly during the period of Department of Justice oversight" (Chanin, 2015, p. 163), there are limits to the sustainability of these reforms after the period of oversight. Partly these limits can be explained as levels of noncompliance to reform directives. Indeed, like other bureaucratic actors, police may express opposition to unfavorable policy changes by acting in ways that are inconsistent with established rules, norms, and community expectations (Brehm & Gates, 1999). Some individual officers may refuse to perform at their best as a way of expressing their dissatisfaction or disagreement with the policy change (e.g., Prendergast, 2001, 2002; Shi, 2009). Such in-practice compliance is a degree of underperformance that arguably makes communities less safe than if the officers were complying in-form.

Police Deviance and Noncompliance Regarding Pattern or Practice Reform Requirements

A pattern of reduced police activity involving passive, reactive policing is called "depolicing," a form of "dissent shirking" that appears in many organizations when an employee opposes and actively resists a policy (Brehm & Gates, 1999, p. 30). In the case of police work, theory suggests that increases in officer oversight may lead to dissent shirking (Brehm & Gates, 1999) and that such behavior is a natural response to changes in an officer's perceived value to the community and society (Shi, 2009). Such police resistance can arguably reduce public safety since it involves less proactive policing, less aggressive interventions, and fewer arrests.

Qualitative and anecdotal evidence indicates that police officers subject to pattern or practice reforms are willing to engage in less proactive policing in response to disputes over working conditions (Osher, 2010; Stone et al., 2009; Sutton, 2015), and public criticism (Oliver, 2015; Wolfe & Nix, 2016; Kaste, 2015; Turner, 2015). The key question is: How does this set of feelings, sentiments, and accounts translate into police behavior, and what form does the behavior take? Does officer rhetoric about less proactive policing manifest as lower arrests or in some other form of deviance from rules and policy?

As many pattern or practice reforms are designed to address racial disparities in officer use of force and/or traffic enforcement, officers have also articulated concerns over being labeled racist because of seemingly excessively targeting persons of minority race or ethnicity (Black or Hispanic) over Caucasians or Asians (Byron, 2012; Leo, 2001; MacDonald, 2016). Affected officers have also expressed feelings of anger and alienation because of the perception that the community, the public, and various ethnic minorities within the community mistrust or resent law enforcement (e.g., Fuocco, 1997; Harvey, 2015; Howlett, 2001). These accounts have led some to argue that accountability-driven reform (compliance in-form) "may have backfired, by reducing the incentives for officers to do their primary job, namely, confronting and arresting criminals" (Prendergast, 2001, pp. 20–21; Oliver, 2015), and that the consent decree process makes officers "less active on the street" and hurts department morale, leading to widespread depolicing (Davis, Ortiz, Henderson, Miller, & Massie, 2002, p. 51; Davis, Henderson, & Ortiz, 2005; Bernstein, 2012; Stone et al., 2009).

Empirical support for these claims is less robust, however (Chanin & Sheats, 2017; Rushin & Edwards, 2016). Some scholars have suggested that depolicing may be time-limited—an initial emotionally driven response reverts to similar levels or even stronger policing over time (Stone et al., 2009, p. 30). Part of the explanation for this reversion may be that police value the safety of their city over individual motivations that drive resistance to complying with pattern or practice reform, and as officers are recruited they are less affected by the preexisting practices that led to reform (Chanin, 2011). The result is that new officers are more likely to comply in-form rather than in-practice, such that in-form compliance expands over time.

To provide more empirical evidence on the extent and durability of police resistance to compliance, Chanin and Sheats (2017) conducted an analysis of FBI Uniform Crime Report data on misdemeanor arrest rates for ten police departments that faced formal investigation between 1994 and 2008. This research sought to explore whether (1) the potential for declining officer morale following criticism or scandal and (2) reform specifically designed to reduce officer noncompliance with norms, law, and policy through increased oversight and accountability accounted for depolicing as measured by arrest, particularly discretionary arrest in misdemeanor cases. Consistent with the other findings, these data show "that neither DOJ investigation, the release of investigative findings, nor a jurisdiction's agreement to submit to DOJ-led reform, was causally related to statistically significant declines in arrest rates" (Chanin & Sheats, 2017, p. 14).

While there are several possible explanations for these results, a challenge is that anecdotal evidence, qualitative evidence, and media reports have consistently claimed that depolicing, which is noncompliance with societal norms about policing, is an effect of reform. This could be argued to be a displacement effect, suggesting that compliance with one set of behavioral norms produces the counteractive effect of noncompliance with another set of macro-level norms. However, the effect of resistance may be not so much less policing but alternative ways to continue the very behaviors reforms were supposed to curb, such as excessive use of force and racial profiling. In other words, noncompliance to the original behavioral directive for reform may be brought about as in-practice rather than in-form compliance.

A more nuanced explanation for the contradictory findings might be that officers operate within a wider framework of responses shaped by broader contextual, organizational, and situational factors, which impact the informal ways they engage policing practice. Instead of making cost/benefit calculations or responding emotionally to changes with which they disagree, they might exercise creative expression by following formal policy (in-form compliance) but not following rules to the letter (in-practice compliance). As Chanin and Sheats (2017) note,

> This systematic deviation from rules and policy in the form of practice and process deviance might be a strategic but safer way, given DOJ oversight

> and reform process implementation, to both share and express dissent. Thus, dissent shirking might be manifest as dissent deviance.
>
> (Chanin & Sheats, 2017, p. 17)

These factors also animate concerns officers have expressed in response to compliance with other similar, though non-pattern or practice-related behavioral directives. Preliminary analysis of survey (n = 350) and interview (n = 52) data from a recent study of traffic enforcement patterns in San Diego showed that both internal and external criticism affected how officers perceived their roles and performed key tasks associated with their jobs (Chanin, Welsh, Nurge, & Henry, 2017).

In the section that follows, these San Diego data are analyzed to illustrate the relationship between broad and specific formative contexts. For example, the proliferation of new technologies to capture officer-citizen encounters (broad organizational context) can be influenced by individual officer perceptions of risk, peer expectation, and other division-level cultural imperatives (specific situational contexts). These data, along with other qualitative observations, are analyzed in the context of broad societal, organizational, and situational contexts in which officer action is embedded. Here the different formative contexts can be envisaged as nested, having both distal and proximate impacts on officer behavior, particularly their tendency to comply with policy and practice reform or resist reform through deviant or noncompliant actions, and this can occur both individually and collectively.

Broader Contexts Impacting Police Officer Behavior

As indicated, there are several broad contexts within U.S. culture that shape attitudes and actions surrounding the police—a reality that affects both "pattern or practice" and non-"pattern or practice" jurisdictions. One such context is the discourse on race, racial bias, and the history of law enforcement use of force on ethnic and racial minorities (Geller & Toch, 1996; Kappeler, Sluder, & Alpert, 1998). A 2016 Center for Policing Equity Report examined 19,000 use-of-force incidents in 12 jurisdictions from 2010 to 2015, and found that race-based disparities in use of force were consistent across "what law enforcement officers call the use-of-force continuum—from relatively mild physical force, through baton strikes, canine bites, pepper spray, Tasers and gunshots" (Williams, 2016), with Black citizens experiencing a mean use of force score, a metric of frequency and severity, approximately 3.8 times higher than that of Whites (Goff, Lloyd, Geller, Raphael, & Glaser, 2016, p. 25).

This discourse has been magnified in recent years because of technological advancements in mobile phones and cameras and the proliferation of instant publishing through social media. Cell phone video footage taken by suspects, onlookers, and passersby of police arrest incidents, particularly those resulting in police use of force, are now made public through social media and network news programs at the time of the incident. Our interviews reveal that police officers complain that this footage provides merely fragmentary moments in the context of longer processes, which excludes important details not witnessed by the observer (Chanin et al., 2017).

Similarly, the proliferation of police body-worn cameras, while also designed to provide a comprehensive record of the encounter (at least from the point that the officer turns it on), may reveal the officer in violation of rules or approved policy or practice. As many of these encounters occur within the fraught context of police–minority community relations, body-worn camera footage may increase the likelihood that police actions will be subject to public, organizational, and legal scrutiny. This can range from internal and external review to FBI and U.S. attorney inquiry, and, in the most extreme cases, a DOJ pattern or practice investigation.

These charges have been accentuated through a series of high-profile cases in which Black males have been killed by police officers during or following a vehicle stop or attempted arrest. Federal authorities began investigating the police department in Ferguson, Missouri, in response to the shooting death of Michael Brown in the summer of 2014 (Byers, 2014). Freddie Gray's death while in the custody of the Baltimore, Maryland, Police Department prompted a similar investigation (Mosendz, 2015). In each case, and several other similar tragedies, a close look at department practices revealed evidence of a more systematic, organizational dysfunction, ultimately resulting in the introduction of a pattern or practice reform effort (Chanin, 2017).

Technology and use of cameras by the public and police is sensitized by the expectation of an incident of bias being witnessed and published on social media. Thus, while these actions by individuals in groups could be said to be situational and organizational actions, the broader context for these actions is the technological development that enabled them to be affordable, pervasive, and simple to use. The availability of social media then allows the incidents to become part of a popular culture of transparency previously unavailable. The combination of these societal-level technological and cultural changes provides a context for increased police scrutiny by the public that empowers those previously structurally powerless and produces political forces with far-reaching effects. Overall, this analysis demonstrates one of the themes of this book: the importance of community attributes in the broader compliance context. It highlights that communities can be narrow or large (or at different scales), with each having a formative impact.

Community Context Impacting Police Officer Behavior

At the local community or neighborhood level, the wider impact of police excessive use of force and profiling that is part of the national public discourse translates into local reaction by political groups and other activists. Partly the result of media attention to high-profile deaths by police, and partly a result of political movements and activist struggles from groups like Black Lives Matter, police are increasingly feeling that a subsection, if not all the public in their communities, distrusts, avoids, rejects, and/or misunderstands them.

Our interviews with San Diego Police Department officers revealed that they believe that racial disparities in the use of force, traffic stops, and other police actions are exaggerated by media, which magnifies and distorts police behavior, concentrating on negative incidents. For officers, such sensationalism fuels community hostility and negatively frames police–citizen encounters, making a negative outcome more likely. This view suggests that racial disparities in police-citizen encounters are purely a media-driven phenomenon magnifying the actions of a small minority of rogue, racist officers whose actions are not representative of the department, and yet are used to negatively impact police–community relations.

Some officers interviewed believe that this media attention produces a negative discourse about police, which in turn feeds national movements such as Black Lives Matter. The views of protesters—many of whom are demonstrating elsewhere against actions taken by other police departments—empower and inflame "police haters" in local neighborhoods, in the process creating negative feelings among otherwise supportive residents. Moreover, officers informed us that they believe the media's distorted coverage of police affects the local community in general. As a result, some residents, particularly in communities of color, avoid contact with police and resist acknowledging them in daily encounters for the good work they do. Overall, these officers believe that the media's wider effect impacts local communities, and results in local police activity being misunderstood and misjudged.

Officers report that this can have two effects at the local community level. First, it can result in depolicing and other enforcement-avoidant police behavior, driven by an increased fear of official sanctions. Second, it can produce provocation by suspects to bait police officers into overreacting, so these incidents can then be videoed and published. Thus, the broader societal–organizational context changes the dynamics of the local interaction of police–public encounters in ways that would not be possible without these wider contextual effects.

Situational Context Impacting Police Officer Behavior

The relationship between these wider level forces and local level contexts can impact police patterns of activity in compliant and noncompliant responses to pattern or practice reform. Together, existing police attitudes about rules and individual psychological factors can lead police officers to develop a resentment that they are being subject to criticism for what they perceive is inaccurate and misleading information. This may result in an accumulation of process defense strategies resulting in potentially deviant noncompliant behavior on the part of individual officers. A particularly salient development is when the broader societal and situational contexts serve to neutralize an individual officer's sense that they may be engaged in harmful behavior. Indeed, officers in the recent study of traffic stops in San Diego indicated that in a variety of ways they were not profiling ethnic minorities but were responding to specific violations. They argued that auto stops reflected (1) driver behavior (commission or omission); (2) driving behavior-moving violations; (3) vehicle maintenance-vehicle noncompliance: equipment faulty/failure, vehicle noncompliant, tinted windows; (4) vehicle/driver noncompliance with licensing (driver license, vehicle license, insurance in violation).

We also found that among officers we interviewed, some saw a relationship between crime and the auto stop. Either this was the result of things or people being out of place, or inconsistent with expectations such as (1) the driver appears in a geographical area or context that is inconsistent with the officer's expectation; (2) stop-related racial disparities reflect racial disparities in criminal behavior; and (3) criminal behavior involves cars as part of the crime modus operandi, bringing them into the realm of auto stops, and leading to the view that auto stops were an effective crime detection/prevention technique.

Officers also noted that the attitude and demeanor of the driver toward police can produce police negative outcomes. This is because in the wider socio-political climate discussed earlier, police are more sensitized to citizen behavior that is noncompliant, disrespectful, evasive, or hostile. According to officers, these behaviors are more likely to result in formal action: (1) citation, (2) search, (3) arrest, and/or (4) use of force. Attitudes and demeanor that are compliant, respectful, and polite are more likely to result in the issuance of a verbal warning, or even an information/learning opportunity for the driver with the police as their guardian/teacher.

Finally, our interviews reveal an important micro-process practice that is consistent with previous research on policing. Police use typologies/stereotypes of media, public, criminals, and themselves that result in people subject to auto stops being classified into one of these categories, and the actions taken are dependent on the category into which they are placed. This micro-process practice is part of what sociologists of deviance refer to as "the theory of office" but is simply a process of stereotypical classification or labeling.

Police Stereotypes of the Public, Suspects, Journalists, and Themselves

The theory of office explains how agencies' personnel who are faced with dealing with deviance organize their handling and processing of those deviants. Agencies, in this case police agencies, identify, process, and manage those they suspect of rule violation to "provide a sense of order and meaning to controllers" (Pfuhl & Henry, 1993, p. 132). The resulting order solves organizational problems in routinized and standard ways, promoting smooth and efficient agency operation while protecting the agency from criticism by outside observers. Included in the process are stereotypes (which are standard categories overlaid with stereotypical meaning) based on selected and sometimes exaggerated characteristics (Hawkins & Tiedeman, 1975). Police officers are socialized from the recruitment stage to use methods of processing that are not only consistent with the law but also with specific agency practice and informal processes they learn "on the job."

Early research on police use of stereotypes showed that officers construct common sense understandings about the public, the media, and citizens: "If an encounter with a citizen can be normalized, the officer can be relatively confident of the general nature of the interaction and ultimate resolution of the problem" (Lundman, 1980, p. 20). Two main stereotypes police officers use to classify the suspect members of the public are: the asshole and the suspicious person (other categories are subclassified identified as the creep, big mouth, clown, scumbag, shit head, and fool). "Assholes" are likely to be dealt with harshly. In contrast, at the time of this early research, people classified as "suspicious" were likely to be treated professionally, provided they displayed the appropriate respectful, deferential demeanor. In either case, the use of this strategy helped normalize and routinize the way that officers dealt with people (van Maanen, 1978).

However, in our study in 2016, some 40 years later, the officers we interviewed had two categories for community members, but a third category for likely suspects, and two categories for themselves. Community members were described as either (1) sheep or (2) political activists. Most community members are viewed as generally hard-working citizens who just want to get on with their lives but are vulnerable to the media and political influence. They are described as sheep. A small minority are "politicos," "police haters" who whip up the community to be hypersensitive to negative police behavior. In contrast, those outside the community who are "likely suspects" are classified as (3) criminals. Officers described this third group variously as "wolves" preying on the "sheep" and used stereotypical labels to dehumanize them as gangsters, pimps, or drug dealers. As a result, if suspects were classified into this third category, they might be more likely to be treated unprofessionally and forcibly.

Interestingly, we also found that police classified their own officers into one of two kinds: (4) sheepdogs or (5) bad apples. Most police are described as good cops—"sheepdogs" who are "guardians" protecting the "sheep" from the wolves.[1] An exceptional minority of police officers are seen by fellow police as bigots, dumb cops, or racist bad apples, who need to be fired, as they feed the negative media and counteract the good work done by the majority of officers.

As indicated earlier, the police also had strong stereotypes of the media and of journalists, who they distrusted even more than researchers. We frequently heard from police that the media are only interested in a dramatic story that hits the headlines and is typically negative toward police, except when a major disaster occurred, and police are first responders, which is the only time police get praise/recognition. These negatively reported incidents are made to seem much worse when journalists identify patterns of police brutality and link them to other events such as those in Ferguson, Baltimore, and elsewhere.

It should be noted that police use of stereotyping is an in-practice compliance process; it is not part of the in-form operations of police. This opens the possibility for noncompliant practices in dealing with those negatively stereotyped as criminals, while also overlooking those misclassified as sheep, who might be dangerously predatory. Importantly, as we shall see in the next section, each of these levels of influence can also serve to justify police actions that are noncompliant with the provisions of pattern or practice reform, and also potentially in violation of macro-level policy and law protecting citizen rights. This happens through a second micro process called moral neutralization, which renders such violations non-moral issues to those adopting neutralizing narratives.

Moral Neutralization as a Precursor to Police Noncompliance

Moral neutralization explains how attitudes toward rules learned through social interaction in situational contexts can render what ostensibly is a rule or law, or in our case, reforms designed to remedy systemic police misconduct, not morally binding on police. Three approaches to neutralization offer insight that is particularly applicable to why organizations experience noncompliance to their rules and norms.

Human Action, Human Agency, and Police Agency

People act purposefully and in a self-regulating way, based partly on experience but also on the situational context, such that "human action, being socially situated, is the product of a dynamic interplay of personal and situational influences" (Bandura, 2001, p. 154). Humans act on the world they experience rather than just reacting to regulation by others; people are self-regulators of their own motivation and the activities they pursue. "Persons are neither autonomous agents, nor simply mechanical conveyers of animating environmental influences" (Bandura, 2001, p. 156), but they develop because of the interactions that they have with their experiences and observations. Cognitive, emotional, and biological factors interact with "behavioral patterns" and "environmental events, to influence each other, such that changes in one result in changes in the other" (Bandura, 2001, pp. 156–157).

This approach to human behavior and action recognizes not only that persons and situations affect each other but also that the behavior they produce can feedback and interact with other persons and situations. Thus, behavior is "an interacting determinant rather than a detached by-product" of social interaction with others and one's environment (Bandura, 2001, p. 157). People "function as contributors to their own motivation, behavior, and development within a network of reciprocally interacting influences" (Bandura, 2001, p. 169). They think about likely courses of action and select or discard them before enacting them. In their behavioral choices people are not only guided by expectations, but also have the capacity for self-direction and, importantly, for self-regulation (Bandura, 1999b, 2001). People are selectively attentive in monitoring aspects of their own behavior, and whether they perform an action will depend on how they judge it against personal guidelines and standards, by reference to the behavior of others, and in relation to values and a sense of personal adequacy.

This agentic view of human behavior, developed by Albert Bandura, has major implications for compliance theory. It suggests that compliance does not follow from external behavioral directives; rather, directives are processed to become self-governing, self-generated rules, such that in-form compliance will always result in in-practice compliance. Considering the issue of police compliance with pattern or practice reform from an "agentic perspective," as Bandura calls it, police officers do not simply follow the new policy but, rather, interpret it in the context of their wider contextual, organizational, and local experiences as applied to situations, as well as to their own personal guidelines and standards. This includes the climate of police–community relations and wider issues about race and policing, as well as their own experience of such relations.

If reform mandates (and the Constitution) prohibit targeting certain ethnic/racial minorities, yet officer experience and information about crime incidence suggests that certain groups are more likely to violate laws, then officers' interpretation of the reform will likely adapt the law to informal practices that continue to target those most suspected. However, they will do so not because of citizens' race/ethnicity, but because of certain cues or codes that stand for race: they are responding to "calls for service," they are "policing some geographic areas rather than others," they are sensitive to perceived threats to their view of order, and they have expectations for police–citizen encounters that may not recognize cultural variations in what counts as respect, disrespect, and threat. Thus, who gets stopped for traffic violations may depend on these proxy cues/codes rather than on an explicit targeting of race/ethnic minorities. However, rather than this being a fixed patterned response, it is an emergent interactive agency, changing and building as new experiences are added to situations and contexts, themselves shaped by broader influences.

Neutralizing the Moral Bind of Behavioral Directives

Words and phrases that excuse or justify one's actions are not simply post-facto rationalizations occurring to relieve the noncompliant of culpability for actions but words and phrases that could serve as "vocabularies of motive" (Mills, 1940; Cressey, 1970). They can inhibit someone from engaging in deviance from rules and norms by showing the potential rule breaker that using such excuses or justifications after an untoward act might be rejected by someone in authority or with regulatory oversight, who is charged with investigating the behavior. In this sense, they can be self-regulatory mechanisms. Alternatively, excuses and justifications could be projected as acceptable by future questioners, allowing the potential offender a sense of "freedom" from compliance under certain situations or circumstances.

This notion of the liberating effect of excuses and justifications called "techniques of neutralization" on the potential for noncompliance in the face of behavioral directives can free people from the moral bind of norms, rules, and laws, in effect sending them on a "moral holiday" (Sykes & Matza, 1957, p. 667; Matza, 1964). The central idea behind neutralization is that "the excuses and justifications that deviants use to rationalize their behaviors might themselves be implicated in the etiology of deviant behavior" (Maruna & Copes, 2004, p. 2). The idea that motivating words and phrases can render a social actor, in this case police officers who are subject to pattern or practice reform, morally free to avoid compliance with rules and norms, doesn't need a specific deviant police subculture to teach officers such thoughts. Mainstream culture has an underbelly of "subterranean values" which coexist with conventional values. By learning and being socialized into conventional values and norms, people are simultaneously socialized into the negation of those values, through knowing their exceptions and situations of non-applicability (Matza & Sykes, 1961). This means that people can claim exemptions in the belief that under certain mitigating circumstances, they are not bound by the law, policy directives, or recommended practice. This "loosening" of control, or release from moral convention, occurs through neutralization. Neutralization comprises words and phrases that excuse or justify lawbreaking or noncompliant behavior, such as claiming an action was "self-defense," or that "it was necessary under the circumstances," or "that it was taken to avoid a greater harm." Neutralization can be "unwitting," something that occurs to an actor that results from the unintended duplication, distortion, or extension of customary beliefs relating to when and under what circumstances exceptions are allowed. Neutralization, then, frees the actor from the moral bind of law or the imperative to follow policy compliance directives, so that he or she may now choose whether or not to abide by them.

Excuses and justifications that provide a moral release have been classified into several "techniques of neutralization" (Sykes & Matza, 1957). These, along with others, have been found in research on police when accounting for their questionable behavior. Following, three of the most salient techniques are summarized and applied to police practices that potentially provide officers with moral freedom from perceived culpability for noncompliance and even deviance.

1. Denial of responsibility (i.e., behavior is beyond individual control, e.g., "It's not my fault," "I don't make the laws; I just enforce them"). Officers might also claim to have no other choice; either because of fellow officer peer pressure, or unethical supervision: "just following orders" (Fitch, 2011). This implies that a police officer committing a deviant act defines him/herself as lacking responsibility for his/her actions since the act is carried out as part of a police officer's duty (Gottschalk, 2012). A variant of this denial of responsibility is to claim diffusion of responsibility: that the officer is only part of an overall process (Fitch, 2011; Bandura, 2001).

2. Denial of victim (or blaming the victim). This is the claim that the victim's previous actions made the action justified/deserved (e.g., "They had it coming to them"). The "victim" is socially constructed as a deserving and legitimate target, while the deviant actor becomes a "moral avenger" (Pfuhl & Henry, 1993). This can be claimed by police for those whom they classify as gangsters or criminals. Because there is no legitimate victim, there is no misconduct; the victim invited suffering because they broke the law (Fitch, 2011). This in effect attributes blame to the victim, justifying one's own behavior as a rational response or even compelled by forcible provocation (Bandura, 1999b).
3. Metaphor of the ledger (Klockars, 1974). This technique is used when police claim that their inappropriate behavior is acceptable because most of their time is spent doing police service characterized by integrity and accountability (Gottschalk, 2012). For example, "I've done more good than bad in my life," "occasionally we may be a little too forceful, but most of the time we are protecting the public against predators who are out to hurt them." In other words, the noncompliant behavior is one instance in a series of otherwise good behavior.

Moral disengagement, the use of psychological maneuvers or mechanisms for disengaging moral control, is often interwoven into neutralizing behavior: "Investing harmful conduct with high moral purpose not only eliminates self-censure, but it engages self-approval in the service of destructive exploits as well. What was once morally condemnable becomes a source of self-pride" (Bandura, 2001, p. 178). One of the most pernicious forms of moral disengagement comes in the form of "dehumanization." This process "strips people of human qualities. Once dehumanized, they are no longer viewed as persons with feelings, hopes and concerns but as subhuman objects" (Bandura, 2001, p. 179, 1999a). Dehumanization of the suspect occurs in police–citizen encounters when officers stereotype suspects using words or categories that are less than human, such as "dirt bag" or "scum" or "gangsters," or for that matter, "wolves," making them easier to victimize.

Conclusion

It is clear from the preceding discussion that compliance with behavioral directives is a complex, interactive process. Police compliance with the terms of pattern or practice reform agreements is affected by a range of nested contexts or semi-autonomous social orders that combine with individual, situational officer experiences and cognitive processes to produce, at best, a patchwork of compliance and noncompliance. The forms in which noncompliance actions are manifest may be less politically driven as implied by the concept of "dissent deviance," and more situationally emergent variables, depending on the confluence of proximate and distal factors that become part of the ongoing response to reform, current events, and discourse on key themes such as race.

While it is clearly an empirical question to establish patterns of conformity and compliance, it is also important to acknowledge that recognition of police officers as active human agents means that what emerges as compliance in-practice can develop and change because of the surrounding contexts and local interpretation. To date, the implementation of pattern or practice reform directives has largely been driven by DOJ staff in consultation with independent monitors and police leadership. This top-down process has seldom included the voices of street-level officers and other relevant agency staff (Chanin, 2017). This oversight, indicative of the view that organizational reform is a one-sized-fits-all endeavor, insulated from various internal and external contexts, has contributed to implementation delays (Chanin, 2011; 2014), and threatened the sustainability of change (Chanin, 2015).

In other words, compliance in-form seems a variable but unreachable goal in the presence of moral neutralization discourses and other strains of dissent that can explain, and even motivate a person to not comply with norms, rules and laws. Such narratives may be countered by alternatives that permeate the discourse of police subcultures by deconstructing stereotypes and identifying the harmful consequences of their actions. These strategies serve to counter opposition to organizational change to the extent that they are authentic and informed by lived experiences, which suggests that elected officials, DOJ staff, and agency leaders would be served by incorporating officer perspectives into the design and implementation of reform.

Note

1 This analogy stems from the account given by Dave Grossman "on sheep, wolves and sheepdogs" in Grossman and Christensen (2004). What is interesting is that some police officers have incorporated this role of sheepdog with which they identify, and which serves to legitimate their behavior and sometimes justify their excessive use of force in combating the "wolves."

References

Bandura, A. (1999a). Moral disengagement in the perpetration of inhumanities. *Personality and Social Psychology Review, 3*(3), 193–209.

Bandura, A. (1999b). Social cognitive theory of personality. In D. Cervone, A. Bandura, & Y. Shoda (Eds.), *The coherence of personality: Social-cognitive bases of consistency, variability, and organization* (pp. 185–225). New York, NY: The Guilford Press.

Bandura, A. (2001). Social cognitive theory of personality. In L. A. Pervin & O. P. John (Eds.), *Handbook of personality: Theory and research* (2nd ed., pp. 154–196). New York, NY: The Guilford Press.

Bernstein, M. (2012, November 23). Portland police union leader says officers are reluctant to use force and are getting injured because of DOJ agreement. *The Oregonian*. Retrieved April 9, 2016, from www.oregonlive.com/portland/index.ssf/2012/11/portland_police_president_says.html

Brehm, J., & Gates, S. (1999). *Working, shirking, and sabotage: Bureaucratic response to a democratic public*. Ann Arbor, MI: University of Michigan Press.

Byers, C. (2014, November 15). Crime up after Ferguson and more police needed, top St. Louis area chiefs say. *St. Louis Post-Dispatch*. Retrieved April 9, 2016, from www.stltoday.com/news/local/crime-and-courts/crime-up-after-ferguson-and-more-police-needed-top-st/article_04d9f99f-9a9a-51be-a231–1707a57b50d6.html

Byron, L. (2012, August 3). Are Seattle police officers holding back? *KING 5 News*. Retrieved April 9, 2016, from www.king5.com/story/news/local/seattle/2014/08/03/13146738/

Chanin, J. (2011). *Negotiated justice? The legal, administrative, and policy implications of "pattern or practice" police misconduct reform* (Ph.D. Dissertation), American University, Washington, DC.

Chanin, J. (2014). On the implementation of pattern or practice police misconduct reform. *Criminology, Criminal Justice, Law & Society*, *15*(3), 38–56.

Chanin, J. (2015). Examining the sustainability of pattern or practice police misconduct reform. *Police Quarterly*, *18*, 163–192.

Chanin, J. (2017). The early stages of pattern or practice police misconduct reform: An examination of the DOJ's investigation and negotiation processes. *Police Quarterly, Special Issue: Consent Decrees*, *20*(3) 250–274.

Chanin, J., & Sheats, B. (2017). De-policing as dissent shirking: Examining the effects of pattern or practice misconduct reform on police behavior. *Criminal Justice Review*, 1–22. https://doi.org/10.1177/0734016817704696.

Chanin, J., Welsh, M. B., Nurge, D., & Henry, S. (2017). *Report to city of San Diego on police auto-stop analysis*. San Diego: San Diego State University.

Childress, S. (2015, December 14). Policing the police: Inside 20 years of federal police probes. *PBS Frontline*. Retrieved May 18, 2016, from www.pbs.org/wgbh/frontline/article/inside-20-years-of-federal-police-probes/

Cressey, D. R. (1970). The respectable criminal. In J. Short (Eds.), *Modern criminals* (pp. 105–116). New York, NY: Transaction Publishers and Aldine.

Davis, R. C., Henderson, N. J., & Ortiz, C. W. (2005). *Can federal intervention bring lasting improvement in local policing? The Pittsburgh consent decree*. New York: Vera Institute of Justice.

Davis, R. C., Ortiz, C. W., Henderson, N. J., Miller, J., & Massie, M. K. (2002). *Turning necessity into virtue: Pittsburgh's experience with a federal consent decree*. New York: Vera Institute of Justice.

Fitch, B. D. (2011, October). Focus on ethics: Rethinking ethics in law enforcement. *FBI Law Enforcement Bulletin*. Retrieved June 10, 2016, from https://leb.fbi.gov/2011/october/focus-on-ethics-rethinking-ethics-in-law-enforcement

Fuocco, M. A. (1997, March 5). Police recoil: Union chief says no "extra step" if court approves city-justice pact. *Pittsburgh Post-Gazette*, A1.

Geller, W. A., & Toch, H. (1996). *Police violence: Understanding and controlling police abuse of force*. New Haven, CT: Yale University Press.

Goff, P. A., Lloyd, T., Geller, A., Raphael, S., & Glaser, J. (2016). *The science of justice: Race, arrests, and use of force*. New York, NY: John Jay College of Criminal Justice, Center for Policing Equity.

Gottschalk, P. (2012). Police criminality and neutralization: An empirical study of court cases. *Police Practice and Research*, *13*(6), 501–512.

Grossman, D., & Christensen, L. (2004). *On combat: The psychology and physiology of deadly conflict in war and in peace*. Millstadt, IL: WSG Research Publications. Retrieved January 29, 2018, from www.killology.com/sheep-wolves-and-sheepdogs

Harvey, W. L. (2015, July 27). De-policing and reality for police professionals. *Officer.com*. Retrieved from www.officer.com/article/12089778/de-policing-and-reality-for-police-professionals

Hawkins, R., & Tiedeman, G. (1975). *The creation of deviance: Interpersonal and organizational determinants*. Columbus, OH: Charles E. Merrill.

Howlett, D. (2001, August 8). "De-policing" a response to community's criticism. *USA Today*, p. 4A. Retrieved April 9, 2016, from http://usatoday30.usatoday.com/news/nation/2001/08/08/cincy-sidebar.htm

Kappeler, V. E., Sluder, R. D., & Alpert, G. P. (1998). *Forces of deviance: Understanding the dark side of policing (Vol. 2)*. Prospect Heights, IL: Waveland Press.

Kaste, M. (2015, January 8). When morale dips, some cops walk the beat—but do the minimum. *NPR News*. Retrieved April 9, 2016, from www.npr.org/2015/01/08/375914022/when-morale-dips-some-cops-walk-the-beat-but-do-the-minimum

Klockars, C. (1974). *The professional fence*. New York, NY: Free Press.

Leach, S., & Lowndes, V. (2007). Of roles and rules: Analysing the changing relationship between political leaders and chief executives in local government. *Public Policy and Administration*, *22*(2), 183–200.

Leo, J. (2001, July 30). Cincinnati cops out. *U.S. News & World Report*, *131*, 10.Lowndes, V. (2005). Something old, something new, something borrowed . . . How institutions change (and stay the same) in local governance. *Policy Studies*, *26*(3/4), 291–309.

Lundman, R. J. (1980). *Police and policing: An introduction*. New York, NY: Holt, Rinehart and Winston.

MacDonald, H. (2016, July 19). Op-ed: Obama is responsible for fanning the flames of racial discord. *Dallas Morning News*. Retrieved September 6, 2017, from www.dallasnews.com/opinion/commentary/2016/07/19/heather-mac-donald-obama-responsible-fanning-flames-racial-discord

Maruna, S., & Copes, H. (2004). Excuses, excuses: What have we learned from five decades of neutralization research? In *Crime and Justice* (pp. 1–100). Chicago, IL: University of Chicago Press.

Matza, D. (1964). *Delinquency and drift*. New York, NY: John Wiley.

Matza, D., & Sykes, G. (1961). Juvenile delinquency and subterranean values. *American Sociological Review*, *26*, 712–719.

Mills, C. W. (1940). Situated actions and vocabularies of motive. *American Sociological Review*, *5*, 904–913.

Mosendz, P. (2015, May 28). Baltimore police union blames crime surge on officers' fear of arrest post-Freddie Gray. *Newsweek*. Retrieved April 9, 2016, from www.newsweek.com/baltimore-police-union-blame-rise-crime-officers-fear-arrest-post-freddie-gray-336942

North, D. (1990). *Institutions, institutional change and economic performance*. Cambridge: Cambridge University Press.

Oliver, W. M. (2015). Depolicing: Rhetoric or reality? *Criminal Justice Policy Review*. Published online before print. Retrieved May 18, 2016, from http://doi.org/10.1177/0887403415586790

Osher, C. N. (2010, October 21). Cops deny a slowdown. *The Denver Post*, p. A-01.

Ostrom, E. (1999). Institutional rational choice: An assessment of the institutional analysis and development framework. In P. Sabatier (Ed.), *Theories of the policy process* (pp. 35–72). Boulder, CO: Westview Press.

Pfuhl, E. H., & Henry, S. (1993). *The deviance process* (3rd ed.). New York, NY: Aldine de Gruyter.

Prendergast, C. (2001). *Selection and oversight in the public sector, with the Los Angeles Police Department as an example*. NBER Working Paper No. 8664. Retrieved April 9, 2016, from www.nber.org/papers/w8664

Prendergast, C. (2002). *The response of the Los Angeles police department to increased oversight*. Public services productivity: Papers presented at a seminar held in HM Treasury on 13 June 2002, pp. 19–22. Retrieved April 9, 2016, from www.nber.org/papers/w8664

Rushin, S. (2014). Federal enforcement of police reform. *Fordham Law Review*, *82*, 3189–3247.

Rushin, S., & Edwards, G. (2016). De-policing. *Cornell Law Review*, *110*, 721–782.

Shi, L. (2009). The limit of oversight in policing: Evidence from the 2001 Cincinnati riot. *The Journal of Public Economics*, *93*, 99–113.

Stone, C., Foglesong, T., & Cole, C. M. (2009). *Policing Los Angeles under a consent decree: The dynamics of change at the LAPD*. Harvard Kennedy School Program in Criminal Justice Policy and Management. Retrieved April 9, 2016, from www.hks.harvard.edu/criminaljustice/publications/Harvard_LAPD_Report.pdf

Sutton, R. (2015, May 5). Op-ed: The dangers of de-policing—will cops just stand down? *The New York Post*. Retrieved April 9, 2016, from http://nypost.com/2015/05/05/the-dangers-of-de-policing-will-cops-just-stand-down/

Sykes, G., & Matza, D. (1957). Techniques of neutralization: A theory of delinquency. *American Sociological Review*, *22*, 664–670.

Turner, D. (2015, May 11). Is a "police slowdown" behind recent spike in Baltimore crime? *ABC2 Baltimore*. Retrieved April 9, 2016, from www.abc2news.com/news/in-focus/is-a-police-slowdown-behind-recent-spike-in-baltimore-crime

van Maanen, J. (1978). The asshole. In P. K. Manning & J. van Mannen (Eds.), *Policing: A view from the street* (pp. 221–238). Santa Monica, CA: The Goodyear Publishing Company.

Violent Crime Control and Law Enforcement Act of 1994, Pub. L. 103-322, 42 U.S.C ch. 136.

Williams, T. (2016, July 7). Study supports suspicion that police are more likely to use force on Blacks. *New York Times*. Retrieved from July 27, 2017, from www.nytimes.com/2016/07/08/us/study-supports-suspicion-that-police-use-of-force-is-more-likely-for-blacks.html

Wolfe, S. E., & Nix, J. (2016). The alleged Ferguson effect and police willingness to engage in community partnership. *Law and Human Behavior*, *40*, 1–10.

8 Humanistic Rational Choice and Compliance Motivation in Complex Societal Dilemmas

Daniel A. DeCaro[1]

Introduction

Cooperation—working together to solve difficult problems—and compliance—following rules, norms—are essential to society. All institutions (i.e., rule systems) and major societal endeavors require cooperation and compliance to function (Ostrom, 1998). Therefore it is important to understand the factors associated with robust cooperation/compliance.

Governance systems are supposed to encourage cooperation/compliance (Ostrom, 1998). However, the psychological processes involved in fundamental aspects of governance (e.g., enforcement, participatory democracy) are poorly understood. This shortcoming in our understanding of motivation and decision making in human governance contributes to ineffective governance systems, which undermine cooperation/compliance (DeCaro, Arnold, Frimpong-Boamah, & Garmestani, 2017).

In this chapter, I address several fundamental questions about cooperation and compliance in complex societal dilemmas illustrated in this book. These dilemmas deal with rulemaking, regulations and incentives, and participatory democracy across a range of scales and settings. To address this complexity, I apply Humanistic Rational Choice Theory (HRCT), a synthesis of perspectives on human behavior (DeCaro, under review). HRCT provides a comprehensive model of the individual decision maker. This model explains when and why individuals comply in complex governance situations. Hence, HRCT is a behavioral theory for the Compliance Situation Context discussed in this book's conceptual framework (Figure 1.1, Chapter 1). I conclude the chapter with future research and preliminary principles for policymakers and practitioners.

Humanistic Rational Choice Theory

There are many theories of compliance motivation and decision making (see Parks, Joireman, & Van Lange, 2013 for review). Humanistic Rational Choice Theory (HRCT) (DeCaro, under review) synthesizes perspectives from multiple disciplines to explain several fundamental questions about cooperation/

compliance, which have eluded prior theories (Poteete, Janssen, & Ostrom, 2010). For example, when and why do self-interested stakeholders (e.g., individuals, organizations) comply voluntarily, even when it is personally costly; self-govern; and collaborate to solve competitive dilemmas? Why do regulatory systems, incentives, and participatory decision making sometimes backfire?

Contrary to popular theory, the case studies in this book illustrate that decision makers engage in *extra-role compliance behaviors* that exceed minimal requirements. For example, hotel firms enroll in voluntary conservation programs (Curley and Swann, Chapter 4, this volume), and drug offenders enroll in rehabilitative courts (Ray & Brooks Dollar, Chapter 5, this volume), which place significant constraints on their personal freedom and subject them to additional regulations. These actors (e.g., aquaculture farmers) often care about the moral impacts of their behavior (Siddiki, Chapter 2, this volume). They also take costly steps to maintain long-term cooperative relationships, for example, hiring compliance auditors, or imposing self-regulations or more stringent rules (Heikkila & Schlager, Chapter 6, this volume). Other times, they may only partially comply, or find subtle ways to circumvent their moral responsibility (Henry et al., Chapter 7, this volume). HRCT accounts for these puzzling behaviors by rethinking basic assumptions about rationality (i.e., self-interest) and motivation.

Rationality and Self-Interest

Cooperation and compliance typically occur in one of two broad societal dilemmas (Parks et al., 2013). In resource dilemmas, stakeholders must share limited resources (e.g., groundwater), and the basic challenge is collective restraint and resource sustainability. In public good dilemmas, stakeholders must contribute resources (e.g., taxes, effort) to generate a collective benefit (e.g., water infrastructure) without selfishly free-riding.

Traditional Rational Choice Theory assumes that decision makers are narrowly self-interested, caring exclusively about personal costs and benefits (Hardin, 1968). Strong, centralized authorities, with the power to monitor and enforce behavior, must coerce stakeholders to cooperate and comply to resolve societal dilemmas (deterrence model of compliance) (Bowles, 2008). Hence, people are externally motivated and voluntary behavior is highly unlikely.

Though partly correct, this perspective is overgeneralized (Miller, 1999; Ostrom, 2010). People do cooperate and engage in extra-role compliance (e.g., voluntary compliance, self-regulation). Bounded rationality recognizes these aspects of human nature (e.g., Ostrom, 1998, 2010). However, the underlying motivations are unclear, creating a significant gap in scholarly understanding of essential human behaviors (Poteete et al., 2010).

HRTC (DeCaro, under review) resolves this gap by recognizing that individuals are inherently agentic and *humanistically self-interested*. People strive to solve problems that affect their lives (Bandura, 2001), and they care about broader fundamental needs, such as procedural justice (i.e., fair decision processes), distributive justice (i.e., equity in costs/benefits), competence, and belonging (Ryan & Deci, 2017a; Tyler, 2006). These needs shape self-interest (i.e., self-determination), giving rise to both selfishness and intrinsic motivation, altruism, and voluntary cooperation (e.g., DeCaro et al., 2015; Fehr & Fischbacher, 2004).

Thus, whereas Traditional Rational Choice Theory assumes people are trapped in non-cooperative social dilemmas, and must be forced to comply, HRCT assumes people are motivated by their fundamental needs and humanistic self-interest, to solve important societal dilemmas, and want to comply with governance systems that satisfy their fundamental needs. I describe this relationship next and outline its implications for the case studies later.

Fundamental Needs, Legitimacy, and Intrinsic Motivation

HRCT examines the involvement of several core psychological processes to account for complex patterns of motivation, cooperation, and compliance (Figure 8.1). HRCT proposes that the factors that promote cooperation and compliance do so by affecting fundamental needs (and perceptions of legitimacy), which then determines the level and type of motivation and important group cognitions such as trust (motivational subsystem). These motivational processes unfold within the person's subjective construal of the situation (mental model), coloring the types of governance systems they perceive as legitimate and, therefore, motivating. I explain these elements of HRCT next, beginning with the motivational subsystem.

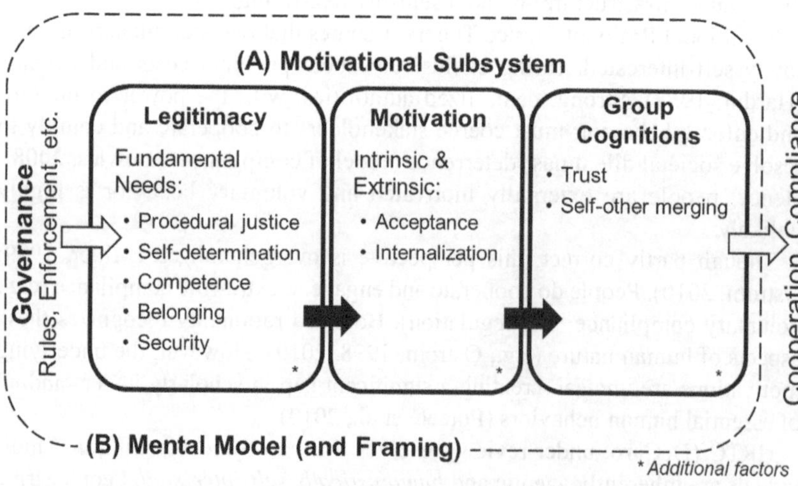

Figure 8.1 Social-Psychological Processes Involved in Humanistic Rational Choice

Legitimacy

Legitimacy of governance processes and authorities is essential to good governance, helping build trust, smooth conflicts, and encourage cooperation and compliance (Tyler, 2006). As illustrated in Figure 8.1, when governance systems (e.g., rules, enforcement mechanisms) are perceived as legitimate, intrinsic motivation (e.g., rule acceptance) and group cognitions such as trust tend to improve, facilitating cooperation/compliance. Governance systems tend to be perceived as legitimate when they satisfy stakeholders' fundamental social-psychological needs, as described next.

Fundamental Needs

The basic relationship among legitimacy, fundamental needs, and motivation have been described in social psychology (Ryan & Deci, 2017a; Tyler, 2006). DeCaro has further developed these principles to address complex governance systems and societal dilemmas (e.g., DeCaro et al., 2015, 2017; DeCaro, under review).

Fundamental social-psychological needs refer to aspects of social life that fundamentally drive human behavior and are essential for well-being (Deci & Ryan, 2000). Fundamental needs addressed in HRCT parallel fundamental dimensions of governance. *Procedural justice* refers to fair decision-making procedures that support self-expression and decision influence (Tyler, 2006). *Self-determination* refers to pursuing goals in ways that align with one's core values and sense of agency (Ryan & Deci, 2006). *Security* refers to safety, predictability, and orderliness in social interactions and governance systems. Security supports long-term planning and commitment: people cope poorly when rule systems are unpredictable/erratic, and they do not want to be taken advantage of by rule breakers or defectors (Hobbes, 1651/1909). Finally, people need a sense of *belonging* within social groups and *competence* at solving problems in their lives (Bandura, 2001).

According to HRCT, these needs energize self-interest and exist alongside basic material and economics needs, driving motivation. As described next, HRCT assumes people look to governance systems to fulfill their fundamental needs, asking themselves: Is this system procedurally fair? Does it support my self-determination, competence, and belonging? Does it provide my material (economic) needs and security, and address my important goals? If not, individuals are unlikely to be motivated to cooperate or comply.

Intrinsic and Extrinsic Motivation

Governance systems affect people's intrinsic and extrinsic motivations. Individuals are typically more cooperative/compliant when they (1) wholeheartedly endorse the activities they are asked to do (internalized motivation) (Deci & Ryan, 2000) and (2) accept the institutions (rule systems, norms) they operate within (Tyler, 2006).

Self-Determination Theory (Deci & Ryan, 2000) distinguishes between several types of intrinsic and extrinsic motivations, with differing degrees of internalization. For example, highly *integrated* compliance motivations include belief in the inherent importance of the rule and moral right or responsibility. *Introjected* motivations include guilt and self-pressure. *External* motivations include negative social pressure (e.g., shaming), rewards/punishments (incentives), and surveillance. Individuals who are primarily internally motivated (e.g., high integration) often exhibit greater voluntary cooperation/compliance (e.g., DeCaro et al., 2015).

In contrast, individuals motivated primarily for external reasons, such as monetary reward or punishment, may not persist without continued external reinforcement (Bowles, 2008). Externally motivated individuals may also engage in deviant or avoidant behaviors, seeking to undermine governance systems they do not accept (Castro & Mouro, 2011). This behavior is more likely when governance systems harm people's fundamental needs with inadequate participatory democracy or oppressive use of regulatory systems (DeCaro et al., 2017). People often try to restore their needs through various means (DeCaro, under review): e.g., defiance (Miron & Brehm, 2006), reform (McComas, Stedman, & Hart, 2011), and self-governance (Ostrom, 1998).

Thus, when governance systems support fundamental needs, they will tend to be perceived as legitimate, increasing individual acceptance and internalization (intrinsic motivation) and encouraging robust cooperation/compliance (Figure 8.1). Group cognitions, such as trust, also contribute to compliance motivation.

Group Cognitions

Trust and self-other merging are two fundamentally important group cognitions. When individuals trust one another or relevant authorities, they tend be more cooperative/compliant, and more tolerant of risk and uncertainty (Tyler, 2006). Tolerance is important because cooperation/compliance is risky in societal dilemmas: cooperators frequently have to contribute valuable resources (e.g., time, effort, materials, goods), and rule breakers could take advantage of these contributions (Ostrom, 1998). Trust is especially important during periods of crisis, conflict, or change (e.g., Leach & Sabatier, 2005; Tyler & Degoey, 1995).

Self-other merging refers to thinking of oneself as part of an important, liked group ("we") instead of as an independent agent ("I"). Self-other merging is beneficial for that group, increasing their trust, institutional acceptance, and internalization. Merging also causes individual and group self-interest to align (collective interest), further facilitating cooperation/compliance (De Cremer & Tyler, 2005). As described later, there are important downsides to self-other merging: shared identity improves cooperation within groups ("in-group favoritism") but also increases prejudice towards others ("out-group bias"), which contributes to other kinds of noncompliance (e.g., racial profiling and discriminatory law enforcement: Henry et al., Chapter 7, this volume).

Trust and self-other merging are influenced by governance. Effective participatory decision making and enforcement can establish legitimacy, engendering trust and encouraging self-other merging (Tyler, 1990, 2006). This effect can be both indirect, as depicted in in Figure 8.1, and direct, such as when legitimacy directly influences feelings of trust.

DeCaro et al. (2015) demonstrated the indirect relationship of legitimacy and trust/self-other merging by examining the effects of voting and enforcement in a resource dilemma experiment. Some groups voted on conservation rules to manage the resource and could use economic fines to enforce them (voted-enforce condition). Other groups had the rules assigned to them (imposed-enforce). Groups in the voted-enforce condition complied best, and continued to comply voluntarily, even after enforcement was removed. In the imposed-enforce condition, groups complied poorly, and this worsened—an 18% drop in compliance—after enforcement ceased. These results are consistent with HRCT. Individuals in the voted-enforce condition reported higher levels of procedural justice and self-determination (from voting) and higher security (from enforcement); higher rule acceptance and internalization (specifically, integrated motivation), and self-other merging. These perceptions predicted their voluntary cooperation. Participatory decision making legitimized both the rules and their enforcement, satisfying fundamental needs and empowering group members to trust one another and reach their shared goals. Enforcement had opposite effects in the imposed-enforce condition: The imposed rules and their enforcement were perceived as illegitimate and oppressive, undermining intrinsic motivation and hindering trust and self-other merging.

As this example illustrates, motivational processes occur within a broader context. This context is shaped by factors such as history, environment, culture and socialization, politics, and economy, as described in this book's main conceptual framework (Figure 1.1, Chapter 1). Each person's understanding of this context, and their place within it, constitutes their *mental model* of the compliance situation. This mental model shapes their perceptions, motivations, and decisions, generating complex social interactions (Ostrom, 2005). HRTC examines the relationship between stakeholders' mental models and their perceptions, to account for a wider range of societal dilemmas and more complex forms of cooperation/compliance. Specifically, people's mental models of the situation color their perception of governance systems, altering the perceived legitimacy and acceptability of those systems, among other consequences (Mental Model, Figure 8.1).

Mental Models

Mental models can consist of lay beliefs about complex system dynamics (e.g., ecological and social systems) and more circumscribed aspects of a system (e.g., a group's behavior) (Doyle & Ford, 1998). Mental models develop from personal experience and socialization. In HRCT, mental models are important, because they contain socialized beliefs and direct attention towards specific aspects of a compliance situation, coloring how information is interpreted, which determines the types of governance systems and compliance behaviors particular individuals deem advantageous or appropriate. This moderating effect of mental models on motivations and perceptions is depicted in Figure 8.1 as a dotted box, implying that all decisions take place within stakeholders' construal of the compliance situation. HRCT addresses three aspects of this process: (1) cognitive biases, (2) identity and norms of contextually appropriate behavior, and (3) framing and group bias.

Cognitive Biases

Decision makers use mental models to understand complex problems. Inaccurate mental models contribute to faulty decisions (Kahneman, 2003) and inadequate policy design, hindering cooperation/compliance (see DeCaro et al., 2017 for review). For example, if individuals intrinsically want to comply with energy conservation rules, but misunderstand the costs/benefits associated with energy saving options, then they may not comply effectively (Attari, DeKay, Davidson, & De Bruin, 2010). In other instances, faulty mental models decrease intrinsic motivation. For example, in 2014, conservative U.S. politicians erroneously equated localized weather patterns with climate and interpreted a blizzard as evidence against "global warming," undermining public support for climate change policies (e.g., Moskowitz, 2014). Faulty mental models can also create conflict and impede coordination, such as when liberals and conservatives fight over their incommensurate beliefs about climate change (Weber & Stern, 2011), or river basin managers fail to reconcile their competing definitions of the problem (Vreudenhil et al., 2010).

Contextualized Norms of Appropriate Behavior

Mental models also influence cooperation/compliance by conveying norms of contextually appropriate behavior. According to the Logic of Appropriateness (LOA) theory (Weber, Kopelman, & Messick, 2004), each person in a societal dilemma asks themselves (consciously or non-consciously), "What does a person like me (identity) do (norms of appropriate behavior) in a situation like this (mental model)?" (see also, Cárdenas & Ostrom, 2004). After categorizing the situation and one's role, appropriate behaviors (norms) come to mind. This LOA may either encourage or discourage compliance, depending on the context.

For example, because of widely held parental norms, parents typically feel morally obligated to get their children on time after daycare. Gneezy and Rustichini (2000) describe how these norms (internalized motivations) were undermined when a daycare introduced a monetary penalty for tardiness. After the penalty was introduced, parents apparently re-conceptualized the situation as an economic transaction (mental model) in which tardiness was no longer a moral taboo but a purchasable luxury service (LOA). Thus, individuals became externally motivated for a previously internalized norm, and voluntary compliance (timeliness) decreased.

This is just one example of how mental models shape motivations and perceptions. For instance, mental models (e.g., cultural beliefs) also influence the perceived legitimacy and appropriateness of participatory democracy (DeCaro & Stokes, 2013), as discussed later. In the next section, I discuss how the popular portrayal (i.e., "framing") of compliance issues by particular groups in society influences behavior.

Framing and Group Bias

Framing refers to the way a topic is portrayed to call to mind a particular mental model. Frames suggest a particular definition of the situation, thereby affecting motivation and decisions (Figure 8.1). For example, political conservatives in the United States ideologically dislike taxes (mental model). Thus, when Hardisty, Johnson, and Weber (2010) framed the same environmental policy as either a carbon "tax" (negative frame) or a carbon "offset" (neutral frame), conservatives rejected the "tax" but accepted the "offset"; liberals were not affected by the frame.

As the previous example illustrates, different stakeholder groups often have different mental models, containing different attitudes and beliefs. Interest groups and ideological figureheads (e.g., politicians) can therefore use frames strategically to manipulate public acceptance and control cooperation/compliance (Benford & Snow, 2000). For example, Gallup polls show that since the 1980s, support for environmental policies has decreased sharply among conservatives, differing from liberals and scientists. This pattern of political polarization corresponds with lobbying by powerful oil/gas corporations and conservative leaders (Farrell, 2016), who have successfully framed environmental policies as detrimental to the economy and personal freedom (e.g., "war on coal") (Weber & Stern, 2011), threatening two sacred values in conservatives' mental models. Meanwhile, liberals frame these issues in terms of social equity and environmental sustainability (Feinberg & Willer, 2015). These mindsets have not been properly reconciled in popular discourse, and societal cooperation has suffered (Merry, 2017).

Framing can also be used to dodge moral responsibility or justify noncompliance, especially to other, like-minded people (i.e., in-groups) (Bandura, 1999). In this chapter, I address two case studies described later. The key actors are authority figures—police officers (Chapter 7) and court administrators (Chapter 5)—responsible for implementing laws. These authorities used cultural stereotypes—widely held frames—to justify (i.e., neutralize) their discriminatory treatment of particular groups based on race, class, and gender. In doing so, they turned the LOA on its head, essentially asking themselves, "What does a person like me (identity/role) do to this type of person (assigned identity), in a situation like this (mental model)?" Stereotypes were then used to justify deviant noncompliance with criminal justice law (e.g., equal treatment).

Inequitable treatment of certain groups generally follows a pattern: negative stereotyping and framing, moral disengagement, mistreatment and noncompliance (Bandura, 1999). In the case of police officers (Chapter 7, this volume), they framed most members of a particular community as criminals unworthy of standard ethical protections (mental model), and then behaved discriminatively (LOA). HRCT predicts that such moral disengagement is more likely when individuals are extrinsically motivated, such as when they feel coerced.

Speaking more broadly, any significant issue of cooperation/compliance in society (e.g., policing, healthcare, environmental policy) will be debated by interest groups seeking influence. The winning narrative(s)—or frames—shape subsequent policies (in-form) and their implementation (in-practice), determining when, why, and to what individuals comply (Castro & Mouro, 2011). For example, the issue of police brutality is a hotly debated topic in current U.S. culture, which is having tangible impacts on law, norms, and cooperation/compliance. Hence, frames at macro, meso, and micro levels interact to shape mental models. HRCT examines the contents of mental models to understand how those narratives shape behavior.

Other Factors

Many other factors, such as other motivations (e.g., social value orientation), group-level processes, societal processes (e.g., economics, politics), and specific governance mechanisms, modify these core social-psychological processes (e.g., Parks et al., 2013). Such factors are denoted by asterisks in Figure 8.1 and should be considered when examining behavior in any particular situation (DeCaro, under review).

Next, I use HRCT to analyze the case studies in this book. These cases illustrate fundamental principles of human behavior regarding three foundational aspects of governance—participatory democracy, regulatory systems, and incentives—across multiple compliance domains and scales.

Case Studies

This book's case studies illustrate several important themes in cooperation and compliance (Poteete et al., 2010). First, when and why do seemingly self-interested stakeholders voluntarily cooperate and engage in costly extra-role compliance behaviors? Second, when do regulatory systems, incentives, and participatory decision-making processes promote cooperation/compliance, versus backfire? Third, do otherwise competitive stakeholders caught in a cooperative dilemma self-organize long-term coordinated solutions to improve compliance?

Voluntary Cooperation and Compliance

HRCT recognizes that extra-role compliance such as voluntary cooperation typically arises from wholehearted acceptance and internalization (principle 1). This principle is illustrated by Siddiki's case study of aquaculture management (Chapter 3, this volume). Aquaculture producers' main reasons for obeying official rules—and unofficial community guidelines (norms)—was personal guilt and fear of social disapproval (reputation), not monetary sanctions. Producers also said the rules and norms regulating their industry were inherently important (acceptance, internalized motivation) to protect public health and produce quality products, which they intrinsically valued.

Overall, these motivations contain some extrinsic elements but are relatively intrinsic (Ryan & Ryan, 2017b). Furthermore, maintaining a positive reputation is essential to group cohesion and community building (i.e., trust, self-other merging, and belonging) (De Cremer & Tyler, 2005), which is essential for sustained cooperation (Milinski, Semmann, & Krambeck, 2002).

HRCT also recognizes the complexity of humanistic self-interest, being energized by multiple motivations, which include economic and strategic gain. However, unlike traditional rational choice theory, narrow self-interest is tempered by other needs (principle 2). For example, in Curley and Swann's (Chapter 4, this volume) analysis of voluntarily conservation programs, anticipated economic benefits were important. Homeowners with a stronger economic interest (i.e., higher property values) were more likely to enroll in a more stringent loan program, with binding penalties for noncompliance. For hotel companies, the potential to prevent more stringent regulations by external authorities was important. This decision to place greater regulations on oneself makes sense within agents' broader needs. Homeowners and companies do potentially gain economically from energy savings; companies additionally may gain positive reputation (brand) effects by acting environmentally responsible. Moreover, a company's desire to prevent future regulations suggests they are also acting to protect their self-determination, security (e.g., predictability), and competence (e.g., effective business management).

However, HRCT directs us to dig deeper into motivations. Day-to-day compliance with voluntary conservation programs is another issue, beyond enrollment. As Curley and Swann (Chapter 4, this volume) acknowledge, voluntary enrollers often fail to take real action or maintain quality compliance. Companies and government agencies routinely enroll in sustainability initiatives without contributing substantively to policy or behavioral change (Lubell, 2004). Homeowners often undo energy-saving devices and behaviors shortly after enrolling. This suboptimal compliance is less likely when individuals wholeheartedly endorse conservation goals and feel that the conservation programs support their broader social–psychological needs (e.g., Aitken, Pelletier, & Baxter, 2016; Clark, Kotchen, & Moore, 2003; Webb, Soutar, Mazzarol, & Saldaris, 2013). I discuss the role governance systems play in supporting fundamental needs and encouraging robust, internally motivated compliance next.

Regulatory Systems, Incentives, and Participatory Decision Making

Governance systems are a primary source of need satisfaction in society, because the rule systems we operate within affect nearly every aspect of our everyday lives (Ryan & Deci, 2017a). In an idealized world, regulations, incentives, and participatory (e.g., shared and inclusive) decision-making procedures would be designed to properly satisfy fundamental needs (e.g., security, self-determination, fairness), creating a sense of legitimacy and acceptance, which can support optimal motivation, well-being, and societal cooperation/compliance (DeCaro, under review). In reality, governance systems produce mixed outcomes.

Governance systems are complex, and many factors undoubtedly determine observed outcomes (Ostrom, 2005). By analyzing the psychological effects of governance systems in different contexts, potential mechanisms may be revealed and better solutions found (DeCaro, under review). It is also important to understand how stakeholders conceptualize a situation (mental model), because perceptions of governance systems are personally subjective and socially constructed (i.e., influenced by framing). Mental models and corresponding logics of appropriateness (i.e., norms), influence which types of governance systems different stakeholders perceive as legitimate and accepted (principle 3).

HRCT predicts that legitimacy of participatory decision-making procedures, such as a majority vote, depends on cultural context, among other factors (DeCaro et al., 2013). Participatory processes can be empowering in one context and oppressive in another. For example, recall that in DeCaro et al.'s (2015) resource dilemma experiment, participants' perceived enforcement as legitimate and empowering (mental model) when rules were decided by a vote and, therefore, complied voluntarily (LOA). The opposite occurred when rules were imposed. The study was conducted in a Western democratic culture, using anonymous strangers randomly assigned to groups (i.e., a situation with low prior trust). In this context, strangers needed a legitimate governance system (voting) and enforcement (economic sanctions) to help them make decisions fairly and protect their agreements, so they could build trust and learn to cooperate.

Vollan (2008) conducted a similar experiment in South Africa, comparing villagers with high levels of trust and long-term cooperation (Namibia) to those with lower levels (Namaqualand). Groups with low prior trust cooperated (and complied) best with voting and enforcement, and worst with positive incentives (monetary rewards) for cooperation. Groups with high prior trust cooperated best with positive incentives. Vollan did not measure motivations and perceptions, but surmised that voting and enforcement improved cooperation among low trust groups, because it was perceived as empowering (as confirmed by DeCaro et al., 2015), and decreased cooperation among high trust groups, because it disrupted their typical way of doing things (i.e., mental model, norms) and was therefore perceived as oppressive.

Generally speaking, governance conditions must be logically appropriate, matching contextual and cultural mental models, to be considered legitimate (DeCaro et al., 2013). For example, communities sharing a solar power system in Santa Maria del Loreto, Cuba, felt that it was legitimate for the mayor to decide energy governance rules himself, because they trusted his past decisions, and he was a knowledgeable electrician (Jenny, Fuentes, & Mosler, 2006). Individuals in Western cultures defer decision control to experts, too (e.g., doctors, elected officials). In collectivistic societies (e.g., China), inclusive (i.e., collective) self-determination is generally emphasized over individualistic self-determination: cultural norms imply that it is legitimate for trust leaders within one's in-group (e.g., mother, elder, boss) to make important decisions on one's behalf (Rudy, Sheldon, Awong, & Tan, 2007).

Thus, mental models determine how governance systems are perceived, helping to explain why similar governance mechanisms yield different results in different situations, and why different individuals respond to the same governance systems differently. According to HRCT, what ultimately matters is whether actors feel coerced and oppressed, or empowered.

This principle is illustrated by two of the case studies in this book. Both cases examined the U.S. criminal justice system. In the first study (Ray and Brooks Dollar, Chapter 5), the main actors are defendants enrolled in problem-solving courts and the court officials. Problem-solving courts are special courts to rehabilitate offenders with drug or mental health issues. The primary question is what motivates defendants to comply with court rehabilitation, and what motivates court officials to fairly administer the law. The second study (Henry et al., Chapter 7) examined police compliance with federally mandated reform, to correct racist police brutality.

Defendants generally comply with law when criminal justice agents and justice systems are legitimate, satisfying needs for procedurally justice and self-determination (Tyler, 1990, 2006). For example, Ray and Brooks Dollar (Chapter 5) found that compliance in problem-solving courts increased as defendants' perceptions of procedural justice increased over a three-month period. Wild, Yuan, Rush, and Urbanoski (2016) similarly found that compliance increases when defendants do not feel coerced into rehabilitation and are internally motivated (e.g., believe rehabilitation is important).

However, the key factors that determine when individuals perceive rehabilitative courts as procedurally just are poorly understood (Shaffer, 2011). HRCT may help inform this question. In particular, in Wild et al.'s (2016) study, 33% of defendants who voluntarily enrolled in rehabilitation said they felt coerced into it and therefore did not comply well. An additional 33% who were actually court ordered to enroll said they felt autonomous. What explains this subjectivity in perceptions of self-determination?

DeCaro et al.'s (2015) investigation of voting and enforcement may provide some insight. When rules were imposed, approximately 50% of the individuals in each group said they believed the rule would be effective; these individuals felt less coerced and accepted the rule. They intrinsically wanted that particular rule anyway and endorsed it. In situations where individuals voted, another effect occurred. The losing voters felt the rule would be ineffective, felt coerced, and did not comply well, until enforcement was present (midway through the experiment). Later the losing voters internalized the rule and complied voluntarily (end of experiment). Thus, individuals' initial impressions (mental models) of governance situations matter, and governance processes that occur after that point continue to shape perceptions and motivation. A similar principle may be at play in problem-solving courts: A meta-analytic review determined that compliance was influenced by differences in the defendants, administrators, and program implementation (Shaffer, 2011). Thus, to fully understand how problem-solving courts function, defendants' mental models need to be assessed, in addition to motivations and perceptions.

Espinosa's case study of adolescent drug use (Chapter 3, this volume) may be informative. By interviewing drug users, Espinosa clarifies beliefs that inform their mental models. Some interviewees mentioned using marijuana to cope with their problems, physical and mental health issues, and to socialize. They said they would curtail their drug use if there were healthier, legal alternatives that still met their needs. Furthermore, they would be willing to comply with rehabilitative programs, if the rules were fair (procedural justice) and the penalties for noncompliance were reasonable (legitimate enforcement). However, drug users are also influenced by their parents' attitudes towards drug use, peers' attitudes, and whether one feels capable of resisting temptation (i.e., self-efficacy, perceived control) (Kam et al., 2009). Furthermore, drugs impair motivation, memory, planning, and decision making, so drug users do not always behave consistently with their attitudes; they also have conflicting goals. Hence, drug users are unique in terms of their needs (Morse et al., 2014), rational choice (Reyna & Farley, 2006), and mental models.

The way court officials conceptualize different drug users is another important factor. Specifically, Ray and Brooks Dollar (Chapter 5) found evidence that court officials perceive similar violations differently, based on the defendants' race and gender. During progress evaluations, violations by White female defendants were treated less harshly than violations by White males, and especially Black females. Black defendants were more likely to be flagged as noncompliant and removed from the program. Court officials justified (neutralized) their discriminatory decisions by appealing to cultural norms. For example, when a White female defendant (identity) failed to appear at a routine court evaluation, allowances were made based on gender-specific stereotypes, or frames (e.g., family care); meanwhile, a White male (identity) with the same violation was terminated from the program. Thus, perceived gender and race (identity) brought to mind stereotypes (mental models) that colored how administrators treated particular groups (LOA)—causing those administrators to behave discriminatively under the law. Unequal treatment under the law is a form of deviant noncompliance by civil servants, and is, therefore, particularly detrimental to societal cooperation because it erodes legitimacy and trust (Tyler, 1990, 2006).

Henry et al.'s (Chapter 7, this volume) case study of racial profiling provides a deeper look at this phenomenon. The issue of racial profiling and police brutality against Blacks is a hotly debated topic in current U.S. politics, and historically (Nelson, 2016). Some police departments in the United States have been federally mandated to reform after widely politicized brutality. Henry et al. interviewed police officers undergoing reform. Generally speaking, compliance was low: police officers continued to engage in subtle discriminatory behavior (e.g., profiling), brutality, and selective reduction in policing (i.e., depolicing) in predominantly Black communities. Police officers used neutralization techniques (e.g., diffusion of responsibility) and popular stereotypes (frames) within their departments (meso level) and broader society (macro level) to justify their behavior.

Rather than speak directly in racial terms, police officers said they were dealing with criminal communities (mental model, stereotype) (denial of victim), in which greater force is appropriate (norm). More generally, police sorted people into three categories: sheep, political activists, and criminals (e.g., wolves). The "wolves" prey on the "sheep." In this narrative (frame, mental model), the officers' primary duty is to protect the sheep and capture the wolves. If anyone behaved belligerently, or "unusually," they would be categorized as a wolf and treated differently. The characteristics of a wolf correspond to racial and socioeconomic stereotypes. Hence, Black individuals in particular communities receive the brunt of police brutality. This scenario is also an example of in-group favoritism and out-group bias: Police officers mentioned they felt loyalty to their department and its (prejudiced) norms, which sometimes conflicted with official law.

It is important to understand why police officers may resist reform. Police officer's moral disengagement probably stems from multiple sources: deep-seated beliefs (mental models), group bias (in-group favoritism), cognitive limitations (people use simple heuristics, such as category-based judgments, to cope with complex decisions in stressful environments), and feelings of coercion and unfairness in the reform process itself. Officers complained that mandated reforms are overly punitive (excessive monitoring, penalties), based on inaccurate information, and excessively undermine police autonomy (Henry et al., Chapter 7, this volume). These complaints imply that police officers' fundamental needs are not being adequately satisfied. If it is important to satisfy defendants' fundamental needs (e.g., procedural justice, self-determination) during rehabilitation in problem-solving courts (Ray and Brooks Dollar, Chapter 5), then it is also important to satisfy police officers' needs during reform. Otherwise they will be extrinsically motivated and will not internalize the reforms (Gillet, Huart, Colombat, & Fouquereau, 2013).

Low levels of trust between officers and communities is making policing efforts more difficult and dangerous in Henry et al.'s (Chapter 7, this volume) case study. According to HRCT, an effective remedy may be community partnership and mutual reconciliation, with shared decision making and joint monitoring and enforcement (e.g., Groenewald & Peake, 2004; Ostrom &

Whitaker, 1974). Shared governance has the greatest potential to satisfy everyone's fundamental needs, establish legitimacy, and build trust, supporting a long-term cooperative relationship. Principles of long-term cooperation, self-organization, and shared governance are discussed next.

Long-Term Cooperation, Self-Organization, and Shared Governance

Whereas traditional rational choice theory emphasizes narrow self-interest and compliance, HRCT emphasizes long-term cooperative relationships. Specifically, traditional rational choice theory tends to seek immediate cooperation/compliance, forced by strict monitoring and enforcement (Hobbes, 1651/1909). Broader forms of cooperation/compliance (e.g., self-organization, shared governance) and preparatory behaviors (e.g., capacity building) are deemphasized (Ostrom, 1998, 2010). The potential long-term detrimental side effects of regulatory systems are also overlooked (Bowles, 2008). In contrast, HRCT focuses on the ways governance mechanisms, such as regulations, may be used to safely support long-term cooperation and extra-role compliance, helping competitive stakeholders learn to trust one another and devise their own solutions to shared problems (e.g., DeCaro et al., 2015).

Many of the cases in this book illustrate the importance of long-term cooperative relationships. For example, aquaculture producers recognize that to sustain their businesses they must maintain a positive reputation and constructive relationship with regulators, by proactively monitoring production quality (Siddiki, Chapter 2). Police departments must maintain a constructive relationship with the communities they serve to ensure everyone's safety (Henry et al., Chapter 7), and court officials and defendants in problem-solving courts must maintain a similar relationship to ensure fair treatment and effective rehabilitation (Ray and Brooks Dollar, Chapter 5).

According to HRCT, long-term cooperative relationships thrive when governance systems help stakeholders reach mutually agreed upon solutions that adequately address their shared (i.e., interdependent) fundamental needs (Principle 4). This principle implies that using regulatory systems merely to force compliance is not optimal, because this generally only satisfies one party and could backfire. Second, rules and regulations must be legitimized, e.g., using culturally appropriate participatory decision making and/or shared enforcement (DeCaro et al., 2015, 2017). Ostrom's (2000, 2010) seminal work on shared governance (i.e., self-governance) demonstrated that effective regulatory systems often include educational, co-managerial, rehabilitative, and participatory decision-making components designed to maintain positive, long-term relationships.

Consider Heikkila and Schlager's (Chapter 6) case study of compliance in 11 western U.S. interstate river compacts (i.e., water sharing agreements). It is essential for states involved in compacts to maintain amicable long-term relationships to avoid costly protracted conflicts and catastrophic failure of water resources, especially during scarcity (e.g., record-breaking droughts). According to Heikkila and Schlager, "states have entered into interstate river compacts to resolve persistent conflicts among water users, provide stable and predictable institutional settings to encourage investment in water infrastructure, protect the needs of downstream users, and foster equitable sharing of water flowing across states." Some phases of these interactions are more amicable and mutually satisfying than others, and the compacts differ considerably. However, the strategies compact stakeholders use to comply with their agreements (e.g., information sharing, shared decision making, legislative concessions) generally suggest that they value long-term cooperation and care about more than narrow self-interest (e.g., equity, procedural justice).

The compacts examined differ in the quality of their relationships: some are more antagonistic than others. It would be informative to investigate when and why key decision makers decide to pursue narrow compliance versus a long-term cooperative relationship. For example, in the Costilla Creek Compact, partner states (Colorado, New Mexico) have taken a relatively voluntary proactive approach to cooperation/compliance. A water master was hired by a shared decision-making body (commission) to oversee water monitoring, communication, and coordination, and to address previous disputes over lax regulation and compliance. Similarly, in the Bear Compact (Idaho, New Mexico, Wyoming), a commission-level water master facilitates coordination among the water masters in each state, and the partners meet annually, with funding and technical support for their joint operations (cf. Heikkila, Schlager, & Davis, 2011). These arrangements emerged after initial conflict, but were managed well; states pursued self-regulation (self-governance), designed for long-term cooperation.

Other compacts, involving some of the same states, have continued conflict (Heikkila and Schlager, Chapter 6). In these compacts, regulatory activities appear more coercive, used primarily for punishment to achieve narrow compliance. For example, Kansas lies at the middle of sustained conflict with Colorado and Nebraska in the Republican Compact (Colorado, Kansas, Nebraska). Colorado and Nebraska have taken costly steps to satisfy water demands in the agreement with Kansas, forced by lawsuits (Schlager & Heikkila, 2011). Recently (i.e., 2016), the three states in the Republican Compact negotiated a compromise solution, giving the upstream states (e.g., Nebraska) more flexibility to meet downstream demands. Prior to this point a commission-level water master was hired in 2011 to oversee compliance. However, these compromises came about only after a series of Supreme Court lawsuits, spanning 2000–2015. Thus, proactive self-governance seems weak in the Republican agreement, as the federal government (e.g., Supreme Court) is frequently called upon to arbitrate disagreements and enforce compliance.

What factors drive these relationships? Some preliminary observations may be helpful. First, in effective partnerships, stakeholders often stand to gain some mutual, roughly equal economic or strategic benefit (Milman, Bunclark, Conway, & Adger, 2013). However, Colorado and Nebraska are upstream to

Kansas in the Republican Compact, so they bear greater costs to generate benefits primarily for Kansas (Schlager et al., 2012).

Second, if HRCT's assumptions are correct, then legitimacy and trust are probably very low in the Republican Compact after years of escalating disputes. Fundamental needs for procedural justice and security are probably not satisfied well by unfair decision-making procedures and oppressive regulatory actions (e.g., lawsuits). For example, Colorado has been forced to make painful, publicly unpopular concessions (e.g., draining a reservoir). When compact members resolve conflicts voluntarily they typically share the costs more equally (Schlager et al., 2012). These more voluntary conflict resolution steps typically involve mechanisms that may better satisfy fundamental needs (e.g., shared decision making, communication, mediation, self-regulation). Hence, these arrangements may be perceived as more legitimate, potentially increasing acceptance and compliance (e.g., Leach & Sabatier, 2005).

Third, state decision makers' mental models of the dilemma and how the dilemma is portrayed in public discourse (framing) are also important (cf. Castro & Mouro, 2011). States that are able to sustain constructive cooperative relationships may have similar, or compatible, goals and challenges; they may also share similar conceptualizations of the situation or shared norms that help them find mutually satisfactory solutions (Leach & Sabatier, 2005; Milman et al., 2013). These aspects of HRCT and complex governance need additional attention in future research.

Conclusion and Future Directions

Scholars and practitioners (e.g., policymakers) wonder about the motivations and cognitions that drive cooperation and compliance. For example, why do individuals and organizations voluntarily comply, self-regulate, and volunteer for regulatory systems that monitor their compliance and punish deviance. Why do competitive stakeholders collaborate (i.e., self-govern) to jointly solve difficult problems? Why do participatory decision making, regulatory systems, and incentives backfire? HRCT argues that these behaviors depend on people's goals and their contextual construal of the situation (their mental models), and how well governance systems satisfy fundamental needs, creating a sense of legitimacy and acceptance. Hence, they cooperate/comply best when their needs and goals are satisfied, and governance mechanisms like regulations backfire, in part, when they undermine these, or adversely affect intrinsic motivations.

HRCT fits into the conceptual framework of this book (Figure 1.1, Chapter 1) by providing a model of the individual decision maker. This model is contextualized by the broader compliance context. Future research is needed to understand precisely how contextual factors at multiple scales translate into individuals' motivations and decisions (e.g., DeCaro et al., 2017). First, future research needs to investigate different actors' standpoints (mental models) and subjective experiences (e.g., need satisfaction), and try to determine how these translate into complex social interactions (e.g., framing, cooperation).

For example, DeCaro and Stokes (2013) outlined general guidelines to assess context-specific psychological effects of participatory decision-making systems. These methods have been used to diagnose participatory systems worldwide (e.g., Druschke & Hychka, 2015; Turner et al., 2014). These studies could be extended to determine how frames and mental models contributed (e.g., Castro & Batel, 2008).

Second, my application of HRCT to each case study represents testable hypotheses for future research. For example, in Henry et al.'s case study of police reform (Chapter 7, this volume), I suggested that police officers are more likely to use moral disengagement (e.g., blaming the victim) to justify their own deviance when they feel coerced or perceive reform as illegitimate. Moral disengagement and extrinsic motivation may actually go hand-in-hand. Individuals who are extrinsically motivated often attribute their behavior to a-moral factors, such as economics, fear of punishment, or disinterest (Deci & Ryan, 2000). For example, recall that parents who once felt morally obligated to pick up their children on time from daycare stopped doing so after monetary penalties were introduced, reframing the situation as an economic transaction, or purchasable service (Gneezy & Rustichini, 2000). The potential relationship between extrinsic motivation and moral disengagement has not received much attention, but could greatly enhance rational choice theory and influential theories of motivation, such as Self-Determination Theory. For instance, it would be informative to study the relationship between moral disengagement, framing, and internalized motivation in each of compliance domains featured in this book.

The motivational theoretical precursors to HRTC (e.g., Self-Determination Theory) have been successfully applied to multiple behavioral domains (e.g., work, healthcare, law) and cultures (Ryan & Deci, 2017a; Tyler, 2006). HRCT integrates these motivational theories with rational choice theory (e.g., Hardin, 1968; Ostrom, 1998), increasing their explanatory power and addressing more complex questions about human behavior.

Note

1 Daniel A. DeCaro, Social Decision Making and Sustainability Lab, Department of Urban and Public Affairs, Department of Psychological and Brain Sciences, University of Louisville, 426 W. Bloom St, Louisville, KY 40208. Contact: daniel.decaro@louisville.edu

This chapter is based upon work supported by the National Science Foundation under Grant No. 1658608. Any opinions, findings, and conclusions or recommendations expressed in this material are those of the author(s) and do not necessarily reflect the views of the National Science Foundation.

References

Aitken, N. M., Pelletier, L. G., & Baxter, D. E. (2016). Doing the difficult stuff: Influence of self-determined motivation toward the environment on transportation proenvironmental behavior. *Ecopsychology*, *8*(2), 153–162.

Attari, S. Z., DeKay, M. L., Davidson, C. I., & De Bruin, W. B. (2010). Public perceptions of energy consumption and savings. *Proceedings of the National Academy of Sciences, 107*(37), 16054–16059.

Bandura, A. (1999). Moral disengagement in the perpetration of inhumanities. *Personality and Social Psychology Review, 3*(3), 193–209.

Bandura, A. (2001). Social cognitive theory: An agentic perspective. *Annual Review of Psychology, 52*(1), 1–26.

Benford, R. D., & Snow, D. A. (2000). Framing processes and social movements: An overview and assessment. *Annual Review of Sociology, 26*, 611–639.

Bowles, S. (2008). Policies designed for self-interested citizens may undermine "the moral sentiments": Evidence from economic experiments. *Science, 320*, 1605–1609.

Cárdenas, J. C., & Ostrom, E. (2004). What do people bring into the game? Experiments in the field about cooperation in the commons. *Agricultural Systems, 82*(3), 307–326.

Castro, P., & Batel, S. (2008). Social representation, change and resistance: On the difficulties of generalizing new norms. *Culture and Psychology, 14*(4), 475–497.

Castro, P., & Mouro, C. (2011). Psycho-social processes in dealing with legal innovation in the community: Insights from biodiversity conservation. *American Journal of Community Psychology, 47*(3–4), 362–373.

Clark, C. F., Kotchen, M. J., & Moore, M. R. (2003). Internal and external influences on pro-environmental behavior: Participation in a green electricity program. *Journal of Environmental Psychology, 23*(3), 237–246.

De Cremer, D., & Tyler, T. R. (2005). Managing group behavior: The interplay between procedural justice, sense of self, and cooperation. *Advances in Experimental Social Psychology, 37*, 151–218.

DeCaro, D. A., Arnold, C. A. (T.), Frimpong-Boamah, E., & Garmestani, A. S. (2017). Understanding and applying principles of social cognition and decision making in adaptive environmental governance. *Ecology and Society, 22*(1), 33. Retrieved from https://doi.org/10.5751/ES-09154-220133

DeCaro, D. A., Janssen, M. A., & Lee, A. (2015). Synergistic effects of voting and enforcement on internalized motivation to cooperate in a resource dilemma. *Judgment and Decision Making, 10*(6), 511–537.

DeCaro, D. A. (under review). Humanistic rational choice: Understanding the fundamental motivations that drive self-organization and cooperation in commons dilemmas. In B. Hudson, J. Rosenbloom, & D. Cole (Eds.), *Routledge handbook of the study of the commons*. Routledge International Handbooks.DeCaro, D. A., & Stokes, M. (2013). Public participation and institutional fit: A social—psychological perspective. *Ecology and Society, 18*(4), 40. Retrieved from http://dx.doi.org/10.5751/ES-05837-180440

Deci, E. L., & Ryan, R. M. (2000). The "what" and "why" of goal pursuits: Human needs and the self-determination of behavior. *Psychological Inquiry, 11*, 227–268.

Doyle, J. K., & Ford, D. N. (1998). Mental models concepts for system dynamics research. *System Dynamics Review, 14*(1), 3–29.

Druschke, C. G., & Hychka, K. C. (2015). Manager perspectives on communication and public engagement in ecological restoration project success. *Ecology and Society, 20*(1), 58. Retrieved from http://dx.doi.org/10.5751/ES-07451-200158

Farrell, J. (2016). Corporate funding and ideological polarization about climate change. *Proceedings of the National Academy of Sciences, 113*(1), 92–97.

Fehr, E., & Fischbacher, U. (2004). Social norms and human cooperation. *Trends in Cognitive Sciences*, *8*(4), 185–190.

Feinberg, M., & Willer, R. (2015). From gulf to bridge: When do moral arguments facilitate political influence? *Personality and Social Psychology Bulletin*, *41*(12), 1665–1681.

Gillet, N., Huart, I., Colombat, P., & Fouquereau, E. (2013). Perceived organizational support, motivation, and engagement among police officers. *Professional Psychology: Research and Practice*, *44*(1), 46.

Gneezy, U., & Rustichini, A. (2000). A fine is a price. *Journal of Legal Studies*, *29*, 1–17.

Groenewald, H., & Peake, G. (2004). *Police reform through community-based policing: Philosophy and guidelines for implementation.* New York, NY: International Peace Academy, Saferworld. Retrieved from www.ipinst.org/2004/09/police-reform-through-community-based-policing-philosophy-and-guidelines-for-implementation

Hardin, G. (1968). Tragedy of the commons. *Science*, *162*(13), 1243–1248.

Hardisty, D. J., Johnson, E. J., & Weber, E. U. (2010). A dirty word or a dirty world? Attribute framing, political affiliation, and query theory. *Psychological Science*, *21*(1), 86–92.

Heikkila, T., Schlager, E., & Davis, M. W. (2011). The role of cross-scale institutional linkages in common pool resource management: Assessing interstate river compacts. *Policy Studies Journal*, *39*(1), 121–145.

Hobbes, T. (1651/1909). *Leviathan.* Oxford: Clarendon Press.

Jenny, A., Fuentes, F. H., & Mosler, H-J. (2006). Psychological factors determining individual compliance with rules for common pool resource management: The case of a Cuban community sharing a solar energy system. *Human Ecology*, *35*(2), 239–250.

Kahneman, D. (2003). A perspective on judgment and choice: Mapping bounded rationality. *American Psychologist*, *58*(9), 697–720.

Kam, J. A., Matsunaga, M., Hecht, M. L., & Ndiaye, K. (2009). Extending the theory of planned behavior to predict alcohol, tobacco, and marijuana use among youth of Mexican heritage. *Prevention Science*, *10*(1), 41–53.

Leach, W. D., & Sabatier, P. A. (2005). To trust an adversary: Integrating rational and psychological models of collaborative policymaking. *American Political Science Review*, *99*(4), 491–503.

Lubell, M. (2004). Collaborative environmental institutions: All talk and no action? *Journal of Policy Analysis and Management*, *23*(3), 549–573.

McComas, K. A., Stedman, R., & Hart, P. S. (2011). Community support for campus approaches to sustainable energy use: The role of "town–gown" relationships. *Energy Policy*, *39*, 2310–2318.

Merry, M. K. (2017). Creating political will through framing: Strategies for environmental communication. *Sustain*, *37*, 25–29.

Milinski, M., Semmann, D., & Krambeck, H-J. (2002). Reputation helps solve the "tragedy of the commons." *Nature*, *415*(24), 424–426.

Miller, D. T. (1999). The norm of self-interest. *American Psychologist*, *54*(12), 1053–1060.

Milman, A., Bunclark, L., Conway, D., & Adger, W. N. (2013). Assessment of institutional capacity to adapt to climate change in transboundary river basins. *Climatic Change*, *121*(4), 755–770.

Miron, A. M., & Brehm, J. W. (2006). Reactance theory—40 years later. *Zeitschrift Für Sozialpsychologie*, *37*, 9–18.

Morse, D. S., Cerulli, C., Bedell, P., Wilson, J., Thomas, K., . . . Williams, G. C. (2014). Meeting health and psychological needs of women in drug treatment court. *Journal of Substance Abuse Treatment*, *46*(2), 150–157.

Moskowitz, P. (2014). Cold weather snap fuels misinformation over climate change. *Aljeezera America*. Retrieved from http://america.aljazeera.com/articles/2014/1/5/cold-weathersnapbringsconfusionoverclimatechange.html

Nelson, A. (2016). The longue durée of Black Lives Matter. *American Journal of Public Health*, *106*(10), 1734–1737.

Ostrom, E. (1998). A behavioral approach to the rational choice theory of collective action. *American Political Science Review*, *91*, 1–22.

Ostrom, E. (2000). Crowding out citizenship. *Scandinavian Political Studies*, *23*(1), 3–16.

Ostrom, E. (2005). *Understanding institutional diversity*. Princeton, NJ: Princeton University Press.

Ostrom, E. (2010). Beyond markets and states: Polycentric governance of complex economic systems. *American Economic Review*, *100*, 1–33.

Ostrom, E., & Whitaker, G. P. (1974). Community control and governmental responsiveness: The case of police in black neighborhoods. In W. D. Hawley & D. Rogers (Eds.), *Improving the quality of urban management* (pp. 303–334). Beverly Hills: Sage Publications.

Parks, C., Joireman, J., & Van Lange, P. (2013). Cooperation, trust, and antagonism: How public goods are promoted. *Psychological Science in the Public Interest*, *14*(3), 119–165.

Poteete, A. R., Janssen, M. A., & Ostrom, E. (Eds.). (2010). Pushing the frontiers of the theory of collective action and the commons. In *Working together: Collective action, the commons, and multiple methods in practice* (pp. 215–247). Princeton, NJ: Princeton University Press.

Reyna, V. F., & Farley, F. (2006). Risk and rationality in adolescent decision making: Implications for theory, practice, and public policy. *Psychological Science in the Public Interest*, *7*(1), 1–44.

Rudy, D., Sheldon, K. M., Awong, T., & Tan, H. H. (2007). Autonomy, culture, and well-being: The benefits of inclusive autonomy. *Journal of Research in Personality*, *41*, 983–1007.

Ryan, R., & Deci, E. L. (2006). Self-regulation and the problem of human autonomy: Does psychology need choice, self-determination, and will? *Journal of Personality*, *74*(6), 1557–1586.

Ryan, R. M., & Deci, E. L. (2017a). Economic and political systems. In R. M. Ryan & E. L. Deci (Eds.), *Self-determination theory: Basic psychological needs in motivation, development, and wellness* (pp. 591–615). New York, NY: The Guilford Press.

Ryan, R. M., & Deci, E. L. (2017b). *Goal contents theory: Aspirations, life goals, and their varied consequences* (pp. 272–292). New York, NY: The Guilford Press.

Schlager, E., & Heikkila, T. (2011). Left high and dry? Climate change, common-pool resource theory, and the adaptability of western water compacts. *Public Administration Review*, *71*(3), 461–470.

Schlager, E., Heikkila, T., & Case, C. (2012). The costs of compliance with interstate agreements: Lessons from water compacts in the western United States. *Publius: The Journal of Federalism*, *42*(3), 494–515.

Shaffer, D. K. (2011). Looking inside the black box of drug courts: A meta-analytic review. *Justice Quarterly*, *28*(3), 493–521.

Turner, R. A., Fitzsimmons, C., Forster, J., Mahon, R., Peterson, A., & Stead, S. M. (2014). Measuring good governance for complex ecosystems: Perceptions of coral reef-dependent communities in the Caribbean. *Global Environmental Change*, *29*, 105–117.

Tyler, T. R. (1990). *Why people obey the law*. New Haven, CT: Yale University Press.

Tyler, T. R. (2006). Psychological perspectives on legitimacy and legitimization. *Annual Reviews of Psychology*, *57*, 375–400.

Tyler, T. R., & Degoey, P. (1995). Collective restraint in social dilemmas: Procedural justice and social identification effects on support for authorities. *Journal of Personality and Social Psychology*, *69*(3), 482–497.

Vollan, B. (2008). Socio-ecological explanations for crowding out effects from economic field experiments in southern Africa. *Ecological Economics*, *67*, 560–573.

Vreudenhil, H., Slinger, J., Kater, E., & Thissen, W. (2010). The influence of scale preferences on the design of a water innovation: A case in Dutch river management. *Environmental Management*, *46*(1), 29–43.

Webb, D., Soutar, G. N., Mazzarol, T., & Saldaris, P. (2013). Self-determination theory and consumer behavioural change: Evidence from a household energy-saving behaviour study. *Journal of Environmental Psychology*, *35*, 59–66.

Weber, E. U., & Stern, P. C. (2011). Public understanding of climate change in the United States. *American Psychologist*, *66*(4), 315–328.

Weber, J. M., Kopelman, S., & Messick, D. M. (2004). A conceptual review of decision making in social dilemmas: Applying a logic of appropriateness. *Personality and Social Psychology Review*, *8*(3), 281–307.

Wild, T. C., Yuan, Y., Rush, B. R., & Urbanoski, K. A. (2016). Client engagement in legally-mandated addiction treatment: A prospective study using self-determination theory. *Journal of Substance Abuse Treatment*, *69*, 35–43.

9 Conclusion

Tanya Heikkila, Salvador Espinosa, and Saba Siddiki

This book addresses the perennially important topic of compliance, or the conformance (or non-conformance) with the directives that people collectively devise to guide human behavior. These behavioral directives include the rules, norms, and strategies embodied in public policies (e.g., laws, regulations, executive orders). They can also include those rules, norms, and strategies widely recognized as legitimate but not codified in formal writing, such as those reflected in social practices. Behavioral directives serve a variety of functions. They give order to social interaction or compel behavior toward the attainment of social or organizational goals. They also signal which behaviors and goals are favored by those who create them. Ultimately, without compliance, our behavioral directives cannot enable the attainment of social goals. For this reason, the study of compliance has captivated scholars from across the social sciences for decades. This book presents research on a variety of salient public compliance topics by scholars from various social science backgrounds who have a shared interest in understanding what motivates compliance at the individual, group, and/or systemic levels.

The book opens with a framework that offers guidance on the types of factors to consider when assessing compliance, drawing on scholarship from public policy, social psychology, sociology, criminology, and related disciplines. The framework posits a constellation of factors emanating from or relating to individuals, the broader biophysical and social environments in which they are embedded, and features of the directives against which their compliance is assessed. Also presented within the framework are different levels of compliance behavior (i.e., micro, meso, and macro). According to the compliance framework, at the micro level, the analyst is interested in compliance/noncompliance by individuals. At the meso level, the focus is on compliance/noncompliance decisions by a group or by individuals in a group that collectively determine group compliance. At the macro level, compliance is assessed from an aggregate, or systemic, perspective. Assessments situated at this level focus on compliance/noncompliance, for example, by communities or groups of organizations.

The empirical research featured in this book illustrates how compliance manifests, and can be formally studied, at the different levels identified in the compliance framework. Several of the empirical chapters examine compliance at the micro, or individual, level, including the chapters by Siddiki and Espinosa, while Curley and Swann, and Ray and Brooks Dollar explore both micro and meso levels.

Siddiki focuses on what motivates compliance with U.S. aquaculture regulations and finds that feelings of guilt and shame, and fear of social disapproval, together, are more influential in shaping decisions to comply with aquaculture regulations by farmers and regulatory personnel than is a fear of monetary sanctions.

Espinosa's research is premised on the position that policy success ultimately depends on how well policy designers understand the connections among a policy, the attitudes of the individuals whose actions one is trying to influence, and the objectives that policy designers are trying to achieve. Through his research, Espinosa argues that in order to facilitate the link between policy design and policy outcomes, one must identify the factors that are most relevant in policy targets' decision making, how policy targets perceive the consequences of different policy decisions, and the circumstances under which policy targets would be willing to alter their behavior in accordance with policy design.

Curley and Swann assess what motivates individuals to voluntarily comply with residential energy programs and find, in their context, that individuals are heavily influenced by material rewards. In their research, Curley and Swann also conduct a meso-level analysis of compliance behavior, studying what motivates businesses to comply with green lodging programs. They find in their meso-level analysis, that peer effects are a more dominant compliance motivator than material incentives.

Ray and Brooks Dollar also examine compliance at both the micro and meso levels in their analysis by looking at compliance among particular types of criminal offenders (e.g., drug offenses, juvenile delinquency) who go through sentencing within problem-solving courts. They find that the perceptions of procedural justice in these processes—or perceptions that the process is fair—motivates individuals in the courts to comply with the law or mandates of the court. They also discuss how problem-solving courts are bound by the macro-level context of the criminal justice system. This research can provide important insights not only into how we understand these multi-level compliance questions, but also provide practical insights on how to hold offenders accountable for criminal behaviors while simultaneously offering incentives that encourage pro-social behaviors.

Both, Heikkila and Schlager and Henry et al. address compliance at higher levels. Heikkila and Schlager examine the challenges of compliance and noncompliance at the macro level in the context of interstate river allocation (i.e., river compacts). Within this context, they assess the conditions under which compliance problems arise in interstate compact settings, particularly as they relate to the specific compliance context identified in this book's framework. These include actors' capacity to encourage rule-following behavior, the compatibility of rules governing water allocation, and monitoring and enforcement mechanisms. Heikkila and Schlager's findings further provide insights on how compliance outcomes feedback into the compliance context, as illustrated by the strategies that actors use to maintain or restore compliance when compliance is challenged.

Henry et al. focus on what leads individual officers, in collaboration with fellow officers, to translate in-form directives at the micro level into norms of compliance in practice, and in the process, establish less than full compliance with in-form directives. In their research, they link an array of societal, organizational, individual, and situational factors to the discourse among officers in their police subculture and argue that this discourse itself becomes a narrative justifying noncompliance.

Finally, the chapter by Daniel DeCaro articulates a model of individual decision making—the Humanistic Rational Choice Theory—that integrates many of the insights presented throughout the empirical chapters. As illustrated in the empirical chapters, a key premise of Humanistic Rational Choice Theory is that decision making is motivated by an array of fundamental needs (e.g., security, belonging, fair decision procedures, self-determination) that shape and constrain self-interest, compliance, and cooperation. Relatedly, compliance motivation depends on an individual's subjective understanding of the compliance situation (i.e., one's mental model) and how well the governance system (i.e., rules, decision procedures, regulatory systems) satisfy an individual's fundamental needs, within that subjective context.

The decision-making theory that DeCaro presents, along with the empirical studies of compliance featured throughout this book, highlight core elements mentioned in the first chapter and remind us about the importance of addressing questions about compliance with an interdisciplinary and multi-level perspective. These elements include:

1. Compliance can be studied at multiple scales: micro (i.e., individual), meso (i.e., group), or macro (i.e., systems), and that these scales interrelate.
2. Compliance can take different forms: mandated compliance, voluntary compliance, self-regulation, collaboration, and cooperation.
3. Individuals are simultaneously governed by multiple sets of in-form and in-use directives that are specific to the compliance context, but which also stem from broader biophysical and social contexts. As a result, the various directives are sometimes the same, and other times, different.
4. The study of compliance can be approached descriptively, diagnostically, or normatively. Descriptive assessments of compliance examine patterns in compliance outcomes. Diagnostic studies of compliance seek to identify the factors or mechanisms that explain observed patterns in

compliance outcomes. Normative studies of compliance speak to the implications of patterns of compliance in relation to broader goals of governance.

5. Compliance is influenced by a variety of interrelated individual and contextual factors.

Framework Application and Development

We developed the framework for the introductory chapter of this book based on compliance literature from diverse fields of study. Additionally, many of the ideas for the key factors and the multiple levels of decision making, as represented in the framework, emerged through the chapter authors' discussion in a two-day workshop that preceded the writing of the book. The framework provided a useful tool to give us a common language for communicating the complexity of compliance, especially given our varying academic backgrounds and substantive foci. It also helped provide a structured analytical platform for exploring our individual compliance cases. At the same time, to dive into some of the specific features of the framework that were most relevant in a given chapter, we needed guidance from theories or models that speak to our specific compliance questions.

What we learned from the application of the framework across all cases is that several factors are common for understanding compliance. For example, most of the chapters recognize common factors within the compliance situation context, such as monitoring/enforcement, capacity, rules, and individual psychological factors. Individual psychological factors were, not surprisingly, more of a focus in chapters with cases at the micro level (e.g., Siddiki, Espinosa, and Curley and Swann). Chapters that dealt with cases operating at meso and macro levels were more likely to bring in some of the broader contextual factors identified in the framework. The Ray and Brooks Dollar chapter on problem-solving courts was notable in highlighting how individual-level perceptions of the "procedural justice" of the system within which the individuals had to comply raised important questions about the broader compliance context. That is, the individual subjective opinions about this context can be particularly important.

Related to the individual psychological context, the DeCaro chapter also provides a way to extend the framework in new directions. It underscores the depth of individual-level cognitive processes that can shape compliance, which the framework itself does not fully capture. To build the framework, we can use the model presented by DeCaro to inform expectations, or theory building, about how aspects of the framework work together. Other chapters raised important questions about the model of the individual that could be integrated. For example, Espinosa's discussion of cognitive dissonance among marijuana users about perceived costs and benefits of marijuana use remind us that assessments or perceptions of costs and benefits may not necessarily be rational, yet people still seem to weigh perceived costs and benefits (even if they are skewed).

We also learned from the empirical chapters that several other elements of the framework can be developed in more depth. For example, Siddiki's chapter emphasized how the underlying types of perceived "costs" of sanctions matter—e.g., social disapproval being more important than monetary sanctions—for motivating compliance. Curley and Swann highlighted how motivations for "voluntary" compliance can fall into material, expressive, or solidary factors. These factors help identify some of the potentially important "attitudes about compliance" that are mentioned in the framework but were left underdeveloped in the introduction.

Another factor examined in the chapter on interstate compacts, which the framework does not identify, is the role of conflict resolution processes. The Heikkila and Schlager chapter highlighted how these processes influence and reshape the compliance context, and ultimately compliance behaviors. As recognized in the introduction, and by the DeCaro and Henry et al. chapters, people often contest the basic meaning of "compliance." When this occurs, we need processes, venues, or other mechanisms to settle disputes. In those processes, the basic rules or interpretation of the rules can change and these changes can then have new and unpredictable interactions with the broader compliance context. Or, the capacity of actors may change in relation to their ability to implement new rules. As such, compliance decisions and outcomes inevitably change. While the arrows we built into the figure representing the compliance framework acknowledge this dynamic process, we could pay closer attention to how particular types of compliance outcomes (e.g., contested compliance or inequitable costs of compliance imposed on particular actors) can result in conflict and then activate conflict resolution mechanisms that are part of the broader compliance context.

In The empirical chapters also provide some new ways of thinking about the variation in types of outcomes, as depicted on the right side of the framework, which are associated with the range of compliance and noncompliance behaviors. These may include different types of individual benefits (e.g., social approval or health benefits), individual costs (e.g., social shaming or physical harm), meso benefits (e.g., when firms participating voluntarily in environmental programs work together to reduce energy use), meso costs (e.g., the unraveling of a voluntary program), and macro benefits (e.g., sustained community resources or predictability of societal behaviors) and macro costs (e.g., unraveling of social contracts).

Expanding the framework comes with tradeoffs, of course. It could make the framework too complex to effectively apply or learn from the framework. (Imagine, for example, Figure 1.1 from Chapter 1 having even more boxes or sub-boxes, lines, and arrows. Ultimately, such a representation could become unwieldly). This complexity could be addressed with a nested approach, which would involve digging into specific pieces and pulling out key elements of the framework for closer examination. This nested approach could then be used build more explicit theories into the sub-processes. As a framework gets more sophisticated however, some level of training or familiarity with related theories is likely necessary for empirical diagnostics.

Future Research

The preceding discussion showcases how the compliance cases presented throughout this book confirm relationships posited within the compliance framework, and how the cases can inform future development of the compliance framework. Clearly, the most direct way to develop the compliance framework through future research is to apply it deliberately within a variety of compliance cases. Doing this would further understanding of the applicability of the proposed framework to compliance situations not included in this volume. This could help assess the extent to which its various components can be used to develop generalizable knowledge of the compliance phenomenon across disciplines, and encourage discussions about the interconnections across levels of analysis.

The development of the framework can also be informed by future research that offers deeper insight on certain elements of the framework; particularly if such research relies on models and theories that are compatible with the compliance framework and core assumptions upon which it is based. Especially valuable would be research that offers more nuanced explanation, building on the findings in this book, about how the variables included within the compliance framework relate when dealing with different forms of compliance. This research might, for example, examine the relative salience of different types of broad and situational context variables in affecting compliance with in-form versus in-use directives, in mandated versus voluntary compliance settings, or in mature versus relatively nascent compliance contexts. Additional research oriented at offering more precision in relating variables in different compliance settings could also further clarify what sets of factors tend to dominate when addressing compliance at different levels.

Future studies could also offer more guidance regarding interactions among framework variables across scales. This research could, for example, offer additional guidance on the forces that propel/inhibit the translation of micro-level, to meso-level, to macro-level compliance, i.e., the translation from individual-, to group-, to community-level compliance/noncompliance and the determinants of these interactions. One way to go about this research would be to assess how outcomes of compliance at one level influence the broad and situational contexts influencing compliance decisions at higher or lower levels. Drawing on findings from many of the cases in this book, additional research could be conducted on interactions among variables at a single level of analysis. The chapter authors offer many examples of factors that can moderate or mediate the influence of others in shaping compliance decision making.

Studies that identify how broad and situational context variables moderate psychological variables to shape compliance behavior would also be valuable.

It is important to emphasize here that just as the creation of the compliance framework was informed by scholarship spanning multiple social science disciplines, so too should its development. Building a robust compliance framework that applies across a wide range of compliance scenarios will require scholars to look across disciplinary boundaries for theoretical and analytical insight.

Policy Implications

We conclude with a reflection on the policy implications of the research presented in this book and a discussion of the ways in which our findings can inform policymaking.

An interdisciplinary approach to the study of compliance offers insights on how analysts can be more intentional in studying or monitoring compliance. Ultimately, this can help improve the design and effectiveness of behavioral directives embodied in rules or norms, or policy interventions. Clearly, compliance is not something that occurs automatically. It is the result of processes where an intricate network of individual, organizational, and contextual factors operate. Understanding what motivates compliance (or the lack of it) will depend upon our ability to identify the factors that are relevant in a particular situation and the causal interconnections among those factors. The chapters in this book provide readers with examples that illustrate the operation of these connections across policy domains. We have to start, however, by breaking down the complexity of these behavioral processes into manageable pieces. The empirical chapters in this volume did this first by focusing on a particular level of analysis. Focusing on a specific level of analysis hones in on the types of behaviors of interest (e.g., individual versus organizational versus social–governance systems). Doing so also drives more attention to particular factors in the framework that may be more salient. For instance, individual levels of analysis raise questions about the role of factors embedded in the psyche of individuals (e.g., feelings of shame or guilt, as explained in Siddiki's study on aquaculture, or the need to gain legitimacy among peers, as explained in the study on voluntary compliance by Curley and Swann). When moving up to organizations (meso) or cross-organizational (macro) settings, other factors come into play (e.g., the design of rules for procedural justice in problem-solving courts discussed by Ray and Brooks Dollar; monitoring and enforcement approaches by states in the interstate water compact setting discussed by Heikkila and Schlager; or the broader political or social norms for policing discussed by Henry et al.).

Having an adequate understanding of the interconnections among the factors that influence compliance decisions at different levels of analysis can help improve the quality of a behavioral intervention. The exploratory study reported by Espinosa, to cite an example, identifies individual-level factors with the potential to shape compliance decisions among marijuana users. Let us assume that the same analysis is conducted with a larger sample of consumers and their perceptions about a particular rule are similar. Regulators could use this knowledge to design behavioral interventions with a higher likelihood of success.

The scholars contributing to this book offer further insights about the determinants of compliance in various situations. In the search for more robust and plausible explanations of compliance phenomena, we need to take into account that factors shaping compliance decisions tend to operate in multi-level settings. Both the specific compliance context and the broader compliance context, as the various chapters confirm, play a central role in the decision-making process and need to be taken into account when designing mechanisms to promote compliance. For example, in the macro-level context explored by Heikkila and Schlager, the incompatibility of rules in the specific compliance context across levels of decision making created challenges for compliant behaviors for interstate water agreements. Understanding not only how the design of these rules matters, but also how the broader biophysical setting (e.g., drought conditions) can affect compliance, may help tailor rules in these agreements in a way that would foster greater compliance.

An additional lesson that can be useful when thinking about the issues discussed throughout the book has to do with the incentives for noncompliance that individuals and organizations sometimes face. As DeCaro cogently points out, motivations to comply, or not to comply, depend upon subjective constructs but also on factors reflecting the inherent features of a governance system. Features such as enforcement mechanisms or existing decision-making procedures can hinder the perceived trust and perceived legitimacy of the regulatory system. This, in turn, can affect the willingness of an individual or organization to cooperate and abide by the established regulations. This is something that scholars and practitioners need to take into account if the aim is to improve policy design and ensure that the gap between policy goals and resulting outcomes is reduced.

Final Remarks

The preceding discussion highlights that an improved understanding of compliance requires an interplay among the efforts of scholars and practitioners, as well as students. Scholars need to understand the practical challenges relating to compliance in different domains. Practitioners can enable this understanding by offering guidance to scholars on the gaps in knowledge that would benefit from evidence-based research. Students can play a critical role in translating theory as they move into practice. Ultimately, through these various activities and interactions, the endeavor is to improve the design of governance systems. This is not feasible without a deep understanding of compliance. This book serves as a tool to encourage inquiry and shape future studies of compliance.

Index

Page numbers in **bold** indicate tables; those in *italic* indicate *figures*.